Cover photograph by Francis Brunel
"A Mountain Range of Ladakh North of Kashmir"

SPIRITUAL ASPECTS OF THE HEALING ARTS

Compiled by Dora Kunz

Foreword by Dolores Krieger, Ph.D.,
R.N., author of *Therapeutic Touch*

The Theosophical Publishing House
Wheaton, Ill. U.S.A.
Madras, India / London, England

A Quest original. First edition 1985. Second printing, 1986.
All rights reserved. No part of this book may be repro-
duced in any manner without written permission except
for quotations embodied in critical articles or reviews.

For additional information write to:
The Theosophical Publishing House
306 West Geneva Road
Wheaton, Illinois 60189

A publication of the Theosophical Publishing House, a
department of the The Theosophical Society in America

Library of Congress Cataloging in Publication Data

Spiritual aspects of the healing arts.

  (A Quest book)
  "A Quest original."
  Includes bibliographies.
  1. Medicine and psychology—Addresses, essays,
lectures. 2. Holistic medicine—Addresses, essays, lec-
tures. I. Kunz, Dora, 1904-
R726.5.S65   1985   610   85-40410
ISBN 0-8356-0601-5

Printed in the United States of America

Pythagoras said that the most divine art was that of healing. And if the healing art is most divine, it must occupy itself with the soul as well as with the body: for no creature can be sound so long as the higher part in it is sickly.

Apollonius of Tyana

Acknowledgments

The articles in this volume appeared in *The American Theosophist*, several in the Spring, 1984, Special Issue, also titled *Spiritual Aspects of the Healing Arts*. The one exception is Dennis Chernin's piece, "Holistic Medicine," which was written for this book. Renée Weber's article, "Philosophical Foundations and Framework for Healing," is an excerpt from a longer one on the subject that was published in *Re-Vision*, Fall, 1979, and also appears as a chapter in Borelli and Heidt, eds. *Therapeutic Touch: A Book of Readings* (Springer Publications, 1981). Henryk Skolimowski's paper, "Wholeness, Hippocrates, and Ancient Philosophy," was presented at the Fourth Eco-Philosophy Conference on Wholeness and Ways of Being Whole, Dartington Hall, Devon, England, and also appears in his book *The Theatre of the Mind: Evolution in the Sensitive Cosmos* (Theosophical Publishing House, 1984). A revised and shorter version of Vern Haddick's piece, "Karma and Therapy," appeared in *The American Theosophist* in 1981. *The American Theosophist* has published portions of Dora Kunz's and Erik Peper's "Fields and Their Clinical Implication," and reprints of the entire text are available (see the last page of the article).

Contents

Foreword by Dolores Krieger, Ph.D., R.N.   ix

Contributing Authors   xi

Part I   Healing as a World View

          1 *The Future of Medicine*
            Larry Dossey, M.D.   3

          2 *Wholeness, Hippocrates, and Ancient
            Philosophy* Henryk Skolimowski, Ph.D.   14

          3 *Philosophical Foundations and Frame-
            works for Healing* Renée Weber, Ph.D.   21

Part II   Unseen Sources of Healing

          4 *Spiritual Aspects of the Healing Arts,*
            Bernard S. Siegel, M.D., Barbara Siegel   47

          5 *Many Doors to Healing*
            Otelia J. Bengtsson, M.D.   61

          6 *The Influence of the Unconscious on
            Healing* H. Tudor Edmunds, M.D.   68

          7 *Spiritual Awareness as a Healing Process*
            George L. Hogben, M.D.   82

          8 *The Spirit in Health and Disease*
            Laurence J. Bendit, M.D.   92

Part III   New Dimensions in Healing Practices

     9 *Holistic Medicine: Its Goals, Models,*
       Historical Roots Dennis Chernin, M.D.   101

   10 *The Healing Arts in Modern Health Care*
       Janet F. Quinn, Ph.D., R.N.   116

   11 *A Holistic Merger of Biofeedback and*
       Family Therapy
       Erik Peper, Ph.D., Casi Kushel, M.F.C.C. 125

   12 *Biofeedback and Transformation*
       Elmer Green, Ph.D., and Alyce Green   145

Part IV   Broader Perspectives on Healing the Psyche

   13 *Rediscovering Basic Wholeness*
       John Welwood, M.D.   165

   14 *Psychotherapy as Perceptual Training*
       Roger Walsh, M.D.   174

   15 *Karma and Therapy*
       Vern Haddick, Ph.D.   181

   16 *Finding the Message of Illness*
       Ira Progoff, Ph.D.   197

Part V   Human Fields and the Energies of Healing

   17 *Fields and their Clinical Implications*
       Dora Kunz and Erik Peper, Ph.D.
          Part I 213; Part II 224; Part III 232;
          Part IV 240; Part V 251

   18 *High-order Emergence of the Self during*
       Therapeutic Touch
       Dolores Krieger, Ph.D., R.N.   262

   19 *Therapeutic Touch as Meditation*
       Janet Macrae, Ph.D., R.N.   272

   20 *Compassion, Rootedness, and Detachment:*
       Their Role in Healing A conversation with
       Dora Kunz, conducted by Renée Weber   289

Foreword

DOLORES KRIEGER, PH.D., R.N.

Healing is a mystery that does not easily yield to the casually worded question. True healing elicits response from depths of the human condition that are not well understood in our time. Its enactment draws power from personal commitments that are foreign to our daily tacit acceptance of aggression and competition as a way of life. Rather, healing aligns with life-affirming forces such as compassion and humane support.

At the healer-healee interface a curious paradox undergirds the mystery: It is not that *a* the healer is healing *b* the healee but rather that both are expressions of a unified therapeutic interaction. In the process both are mutually healed, made whole and at-one. In a moment of clear vision we then may realize that as healers we have opted for nothing less than a self-to-self relationship. Therefore, we need no longer feel shy at the mention of such concepts as "the spiritual aspects of healing," for healing naturally encompasses the entire spectrum of the human condition, if we will but lend our full consciousness to it.

The questions we could ask of healing are manifold: What is healing? What are its delimitations? With what kinds of illnesses is it most effective? How can we recognize those who have high potential for healing others? Are there valid bases for determining the best coupling of healer and healee? Finally, one must wonder how an ability we understand so poorly can be so selective as to inhibit the growth of tissues in malignancies and yet stimulate the growth of tissues in wound healing.

We are left with the conclusion that, yes, healing is an enigma. However, if we will we can indeed plumb its depth to the extent that we are willing to know our selves on its own terms. Such is the quest upon which this book focuses. It is only you, the reader, who can attest to its resolution.

Contributing Authors

LAURENCE J. BENDIT, M.D., psychiatrist, lecturer, and author, was awarded degrees of M.A., M.D., and B.Chir. (Surgery) from Cambridge University, as well as other British medical diplomas, including that of specialist in psychological medicine. He has made a substantial contribution to the literature of psychology and theosophy. Among his best known works are *Self Knowledge: A Yoga for the West, The Mirror of Life and Death* and, with his late wife, Phoebe D. Bendit, *The Psychic Sense, This World and That,* and *The Transforming Mind* (Theosophical Publishing House).

OTELIA BENGTSSON, M.D., received both her A.B. and her M.D. from Cornell University. She interned and was later House Doctor at the New York Informary for Women and Children, the hospital founded in 1853 by pioneer women in medicine. She then became associated with several physicians in the treatment of allergy, and after a long career is now retired.

DENNIS K. CHERNIN, M.D., practices holistic medicine in Ann Arbor, Michigan. A graduate of the University of Michigan Medical School, he was a psychiatric resident at the University of Wisconsin. He is on the faculty at the Himalayan Institute of Yoga Science and Philosophy and has taught classes in homeopathy and meditation at the University of Michigan (extension), and he is currently finishing a Masters of Public Health there. Dr. Chernin is co-author of *Homeopathic Remedies.*

LARRY DOSSEY, M.D., practices internal medicine with the Dallas Diagnostic Association and is also actively engaged in clinical research. He is Chief of Staff, Medical City Dallas Hospital and an adjunct professor in the Department of Psychology, North Texas State University. He is author of *Space, Time, and Medicine* and *Beyond Illness* (Shambhala Publications, 1982 and 1984).

H. TUDOR EDMUNDS, M.D., took his degree in Medicine at Kings College Hospital in London, and later filled posts in a London Dental Hospital and a London Fever Hospital, following which he entered general practice, retiring in 1962. He served as Chairman of the Science Group of the Theosophical Research Center in London and has published articles in the Center's publication, *The Science Group Journal.*

ELMER GREEN, Ph.D., and ALYCE GREEN work in the Voluntary Controls Program at the Menninger Foundation, Topeka, Kansas, and are co-authors of *Beyond Biofeedback* (Dell, 1977). They have devoted years of inquiry into healing and meditation, and their pioneering scientific work has helped establish biofeedback as an important advance in medical science.

VERN HADDICK, Ph.D., is a writer and counselor-educator who lives in the San Francisco Bay Area. He holds graduate degrees from the University of California, Berkeley, and Columbia University and for many years has traveled extensively throughout North America and Europe.

GEORGE HOGBEN, M.D., is a Holistic Physician and Psychiatrist practicing in Rye, New York. He is a student of spirituality in medicine and healing and has lectured and organized symposia on this topic.

DOLORES KRIEGER, Ph.D., R.N. is Professor of Nursing at New York University. She has lectured and led workshops on Therapeutic Touch in the United States and other countries for over ten years. Her books include *Therapeutic Touch: How to Use Your Hands to Help or to Heal* (Prentice-Hall, 1979) and *Foundations for Holistic Health Nursing Practices: The Renaissance Nurse* (J.B. Lippincott, 1981).

DORA KUNZ has applied her clairvoyant abilities in medical contexts for many decades, working with physicians in paranormal diagnosis and in counseling patients. Neurologist Shafica Karagulla has written up some of her work with Kunz on epilepsy and other disorders in *Breakthrough to Creativity* (DeVorss, 1968) and in a new book to be published in 1986. Mrs. Kunz and Dolores Krieger, Professor of Nursing at New York University, developed Therapeutic Touch, an application of healing techniques designed especially for health professions and the settings in which they work. Since the early 1970s Kunz and Krieger have held annual healers' workshops for health professionals. Kunz also lectures and gives workshops on meditation and healing. President of the Theosophical Society in America since 1975, she is Chairman of its publishing house and Editor-in-Chief of its journal *The American Theosophist*.

CASI KUSHEL, M.S., M.F.C.C., is a family therapist in private practice in Berkeley, California. She is on the faculty at the California Graduate School of Marital and Family Therapy and St. Mary's College, Moraga. She was formerly associated staff at the University of California (San Francisco) Human Sexuality Program.

JANET MACRAE, Ph.D., R.N., is an adjunct professor in the Division of Nursing, New York University. She has practiced Therapeutic Touch for many years and has taught numerous workshops throughout the country.

ERIK PEPER, Ph.D., is past President of the Biofeedback Society of America and currently lectures in Interdisciplinary Sciences at San Francisco State University. He has a private autogenic biofeedback practice in Berkeley and is co-author of *Mind/Body Integration: Essential Readings in Biofeedback* (Plenum, 1979).

IRA PROGOFF, Ph.D., is the creator of the widely-used *Intensive Journal* method of individual development. Of his several books, *At a Journal Workshop* and *The Practice of Process Meditation* describe the main techniques and Journal exercises for using the *Intensive Journal* process in both its personal and spiritual aspects. His most recent book, *Life-Study*, describes how to carry out the *Intensive Journal*

exercises on behalf of individuals in history who are
personally significant to us, thus serving as *Journal Trustee*
for them. Dr. Progoff is director of the Dialogue House
National *Intensive Journal* Program. From time to time he
conducts workshops and retreats in various parts of the
country.

JANET QUINN, Ph.D., R.N., is Professor of Nursing, College of
Nursing, University of South Carolina. Some of her other
published articles have appeared in *Foundations for Holistic
Health Nursing Practices* (J.B. Lippincott, 1981) and *Therapeutic Touch* (Springer Publishing Company, 1981).

BERNARD SIEGEL, M.D., F.A.C.S., is a surgeon in private practice
and assistant clinical professor of surgery, Yale University
School of Medicine. In 1978 he originated the "Exceptional
Cancer Patient" group therapy which works with patients'
images and drawings, and has lectured and conducted
workshops across the country. He has written many articles
and is writing a book about his experiences (Harper and
Row), and has appeared on numerous television and radio
programs.

BARBARA H. SIEGEL, B.S., Dr. Siegel's wife, is editor, and co-author
of their articles and their five children. She is a former
schoolteacher.

HENRYK SKOLIMOWSKI, Ph.D., is Professor of Philosophy in the
Department of Humanities in the University of Michigan at
Ann Arbor. Author of *Eco-Philosophy: Designing New
Tactics for Living* (Marion Boyars Publishers), he promotes
Eco-Philosophy, which deals with the interaction of per-
sons with one another and with the environment. He is
also author of *Theatre of the Mind: Evolution in the Sensitive
Cosmos* (Theosophical Publishing House, 1984).

ROGER WALSH, M.D., is on the faculty of the Department of
Psychiatry and Human Behavior at the University of California, Irvine. His research interests include comparisons
and integrations among the major schools of psychology,
both Eastern and Western. He is also concerned with study-
ing contemporary global threats to human survival and well-
being (e.g. population pressures, starvation, ecological
degradation, and nuclear weapons) and with understanding

their psychological causes and the principles of effective response.

RENÉE WEBER, Ph.D., is Professor of Philosophy at Rutgers University and Chair of its Council for Integrative and Cross-disciplinary Studies. She received her doctorate from Columbia University. She has authored articles on esoteric and comparative East-West philosophy, on Plato, and on healing, many of which have appeared in *Main Currents in Modern Thought, Re-Vision, The American Theosophist,* and in anthologies. She has published interviews and dialogues with well-known scientists in *The Holographic Paradigm and Other Paradoxes,* edited by Ken Wilber (Shambhala), and elsewhere.

JOHN WELWOOD, Ph.D., is a clinical psychologist with a private psychotherapy practice in San Francisco. He is a Professor of Psychology at the California Institute of Integral Studies and Associate Editor of the *Journal of Transpersonal Psychology.* He has published numerous articles on East/West psychology, psychotherapy, consciousness, and personal growth, as well as three books: *The Meeting of the Ways: Explorations in East/West Psychology* (Schocken). *Awakening the Heart: East/West Approaches to Psychotherapy and the Healing Relationship* (Shambhala), and *Challenge of the Heart: Love, Sex, and Intimacy in Changing Times* (Shambhala). He is a long-time student of Buddhism and Eastern religions.

I

Healing as a World View

Is healing a process related to the nature of the cosmos? The authors in this section, a physician and two professors of philosophy, argue that it is: "We interact with the universe in ways that are profound" (Dossey). "A person becomes whole physically, emotionally, mentally and at deeper levels, resulting ideally in an integration with the underlying inward powers of the universe" (Weber). "To be whole is to be encompassed by the sense of the divine in the divine cosmos" (Skolimowski). Thus health and disease are placed in a cosmic setting.

These authors point to the crucial role of consciousness, both in the universe and in an individual, and its powerful effect on matter. They sense wholeness at some essential level and see this as "the foundation in which well-being is embedded" (Skolimowski). They support the concept of oneness and whole-ness of the universe by references to philosophers East and West and to modern physics.

Dynamism and change are also important aspects of the cosmos that bear on healing. According to Weber, disease occurs when one is disconnected from the flow and rhythm of the whole. Skolimowski feels healing can best be understood by integrating a view of the universe as in a state of flux and trans-formation with one founded on a pre-established harmony based on spiritual laws that give meaning to the flux.

1

In the picture of the world painted by Dossey and Weber, time is not just linear and one-directional, moving us inexorably toward extinction, but also boundless and n-dimensional as experienced by the mystics. This view allows for completeness in the present moment, even in the midst of illness (Dossey), and can account for the rare cases of instantaneous healing (Weber). Weber attributes these and also lesser healings to "pure spiritual energy beyond time and space where healing power originates."

These authors move us toward an expanded view of the world to accommodate an expanding view of the mystery of healing.

1

The Future of Medicine

LARRY DOSSEY, M.D.

I believe that the concept of health and illness as isolated phenomena that can be confined to single individuals is hopelessly outmoded, and no longer fits with emerging clinical data in medicine. Medicine, thus, has its own correlates to a principle that has arisen from many areas of modern science: the world cannot be fragmented into bits and pieces.

We have seen this attempt fail at the microscopic level, where the notion of isolated, noninteracting, billiard ball-like atoms has been abandoned. Distinctions between the observer and the observed are not as crisp as they once were thought to be, and the universe is viewed by some physicists today as a gigantic "participatory" event. In biology the strict separations between the individual and the environment are fading, and the natural world is no longer seen as a mere physical container into which we have been haplessly thrust. It is clear that the interaction between individual and environment shapes the evolution of both, that one does not stand apart from the other.

The common message is that the traditional idea of an "out there" world is no longer appropriate. We interact with the universe in ways that are profound. Isolation, the view of the world as a collection and assembly of units, is being transcended in favor of a perspective that emphasizes dynamism and interaction—the notion with which our age, as Bronowski put it, is aflame.

This view is surfacing today in modern medicine. Disease and health can be viewed as isolated events, it seems to me, *only* for the sake of convenience. They are not external processes that we "catch," as we frequently speak of infectious diseases, or that we "acquire," as we often say about health. In medicine, increasingly, interaction seems paramount.

An example is that the death rate in surviving spouses— widows and widowers—is two to three times higher than the average for the age-matched married population. In some way the experience of a spouse's death translates into physical illness for the survivor, and can even be a matter of life or death. The fact that illness seems to be shared is not trivial, it is not merely a picturesque or freakish event.

From a physician's point of view, inexplicable findings under the old separatist model sometimes seem to be better interpreted using the hypothesis of the oneness of humanity. One such explanation which doctors confront every day is the unexpected cure, the unanticipated positive turn of events. This is attributed to what we euphemistically call the "natural course of the disease." This concept has no explanatory meaning at all, and says only that "that which happens, happens." It says less about the natural course of illness than about the natural state of our ignorance. I suspect that many unexpected turns in the course of illness can be better explained by invoking field factors than relying on solutions based solely on intra-person effects, or on interactions between person and drug, or person and surgery.

Another event confronting us is what we call human variability. We confront this every time we give a patient a medication: we see varying responses to what is administered, even in surgery. Another example is the placebo response. And, although I may be pilloried by my colleagues for mentioning this one, I think the phenomenon of psychic healing is an event which we are very hard-pressed to explain in ordinary terms. I suspect that we will have to face the possibility that human consciousness is a potent factor in health and illness if we are ever to arrive at a satisfying hypothesis that accounts for these kinds of observations in medicine. There is some consolation, it seems to me, that other disciplines—notably modern physics—have been forced to do the same, although the verdict on the precise role of consciousness in modern physical theory is by no means in.

Modern physics acknowledges that in some way consciousness does interface with the physical world, albeit in degrees upon which physicists cannot agree. But the notion of a purely objective world that follows strict causal chains of connections simply is not tenable in modern physics any more. We get into conceptual trouble in modern medicine because we still adhere to a belief in a rigid causal chain that leaves no place for consciousness. Because we do, we limit the potential for explaining many phenomena, among which may be those I mentioned. My point is that, if our most accurate science, modern physics, has begun at least to acknowledge the *possibility* that consciousness may be important in the evolution of what we count as real, medicine may at least begin to entertain the same possibility.

A basic goal in medicine is to know how healing occurs. At present we have no satisfactory explanation about what does the healing in many instances. We have managed to convince ourselves, of course, that "the treatment" is responsible, by which we ordinarily mean drugs or surgical procedures. But the new view says that consciousness may modulate, in some degree, the effect of *all* kinds of medical interventions. The clinical data now shows that in some instances this effect may be profound.

Consciousness operates not only *within* a person, such as when persons lower their cholesterol level by meditation; it also operates *between* individuals, as we have seen from studies showing that bereaved spouses have an increased death rate. States of consciousness either help or hinder health. Rarely, I suspect, are they ever neutral factors.

We are one human family and, although we may be indifferent to starvation or suffering somewhere on the globe, if we were sensitive enough to the reality of our interconnections we would know we're losing a member of our family when someone dies. The field effects I have been discussing seem to mandate the possibility, at least, of this extraordinary level of awareness. At present, I think our tools for demonstrating our far-reaching associations are lacking, although we *can* demonstrate the significance of certain shared events that are not too spatially isolated, such as between husband and wife. What troubles me in medicine is the generalization that on the ordinary day-to-day physical level these fields don't exist. Although Western common sense tells us that we are separate, we know that historically the mystics would tell us with a single voice that our way of sensing isolation is an illusion. Certainly the capacity lies within our species to perceive this oneness. I think that the appreciation of our essential interaction with the universe will lead to a heightened ability to sense and actually experience our oneness with each other, an ability which, in medicine, might well be a therapeutic breakthrough.

We can be hopeful that awareness of group consciousness will evolve, and that the concept of "the family of man" will be a living reality. This will mandate a radically new way of looking at moral responsibility. Whereas it has been thought that only through philosophy or a spiritual and mystical state could one grasp shared destiny—the brotherhood of humanity—that message is now coming through at all levels. The old separatist philosophical notions stem from a time in history where our knowledge of physiology and biochemistry was naive and unsophisticated. Today we know that one cannot act in the world without affecting others—a fact that extends, even, to affecting their physiological functioning.

My perception of your caring (or callousness) toward me creates an *avalanche* of biochemical changes in my own body. Neural and hormonal events follow in a cascade fashion from my felt sense of how we interact. These are not remote or abstract philosophical issues, but concrete physiological consequences. This is vastly under-valued, I feel, and generally goes unnoticed not only by philosophers but by scientists and treating physicians as well.

There is, to put it plainly, a physiology of humaneness. If I treat you with kindness and compassion you are able to evoke a generally more healthy state. Let me give you an example of how this might happen clinically. In a recent study that was done at Harvard's teaching hospital, a group of patients were brought to the hospital for reasons of truly life-threatening cardiac arrhythmias—disorders of the electrical rhythms of the heart. In the twenty-four hours preceding the onset of these problems, fully twenty-five percent of these people experienced profound emotional upheavals, including anger, fear, and hostility. And, one has to ask, in response to what? To whom?

We can begin to talk about a social nexus even when dealing with something that traditionally has been considered totally objective, such as electrophysiological events in the heart. Proper therapy would be not only to administer whatever is necessary to quell the arrhythmia in the crisis period, but to look beyond. Are we going to send that patient, once the acute problem is treated, back to the same difficult environment? Is there any responsibility on the part of the significant others in social or family relations? This serves as another example that health is a shared phenomenon, with roots extending outside ourselves. We do live in each other's fields. Any theory of medicine that does not acknowledge that is bound to be, at best, incomplete. We would be shocked if a person were admitted to a hospital with malaria or plague, then treated successfully only to be released without any word whatsoever on how the disease was spread and contracted. Such an omission would be tantamount to malpractice. Yet when it comes to dealing with analogous interactions between humans which can deleteriously affect health, such as in the example of the emotionally induced cardiac arrhythmias, we suddenly become hesitant and frequently ignore life-or-death issues. We are frequently much more open to talking about (in malaria and plague) mosquito-human or rat-human interactions than about human-human dynamics.

Part of the hesitancy depends, of course, on an engrained idea that the noxious effects of one human on another are largely trivial. As such, they can be ignored, and no harm is done. We are discovering that this is far from true.

In the example I mentioned, the interchanges between the people around these cardiac patients literally had consequences in the invisible fields, the emotional and the mental. This broke through into the physical field as a crisis that was life-threatening. Our way of talking about the crisis, the cardiac event, has been to consider the heart as a self-contained, isolated organ. In the past few years we have found that this is far from true. There are actual anatomic neural pathways that connect the brain and heart, and the heart can be manipulated toward either greater or lesser electrical stability by events in what are referred to as higher central nervous system centers. Thus bioscientists now are able to talk of a larger field than just the heart, a field which now includes the brain.

Since we now know of these kinds of physiological inter-connections which include the brain in the picture, we have to ask, what changes the state of the higher nervous system centers themselves? We know we can't isolate them as we did the heart: they are responsive to events in the world. In fact, human beings having a brain, elegant sensing capacities, and consciousness are perhaps the most *un*-isolable things we know. So by our own innate capacities we are tied, hand in glove, to the world around us—a fact which has enormous repercussions in clinical medicine.

Because of our intimate associations with others and with the world, I see no way to avoid invoking concepts of ethics and responsibility in a comprehensive theory of health and illness. We are all, so to speak, cells of one gigantic organism in which you can't draw an artificial boundary any more between inside and outside, between visible and invisible, between physiology, emotion, intent, and even words and action. Because we affect each other, responsibilities follow.

Even though we have singled out the heart as an easy organ to talk about, we must also recognize the groundbreaking work that has been done in identifying connections between higher central nervous system centers and other systems in the body, such as the immune system. It is established that neural and hormonal connections unite the immune system (which was once thought to be autonomous) with the brain. My prediction is that we will eventually be able to specify how the brain plays a fulcrum role in influencing *most* of the activities of the body.

The complexities of our interaction are so intricate that logistically we cannot possibly keep track of what we are doing to each other and to ourselves. The key may be simply to have good intent and to bear in mind that we do affect each other, that interaction is the rule. My hope is that this understanding will lead to a sense of caring and regard for our fellow human beings, a factor which is de-emphasized under an isolationist model of health.

A further key to actualizing the ideal state of well-being will be to redefine what we mean by health. Oddly, we conceive of health as something that never changes—some stage of youth where we are perpetually unblemished and lovely and in perfect function. We reduce the dynamic harmony of function in the body to some static concept which biologically and physiologically has no correlate. We need to go beyond this naive notion of health. Ironically, when we renounce our preoccupation with health—the maniacal drive to possess or acquire it—the stage is set for becoming healthier. There is a sense of letting go that is important, and we can frequently realize healthiness by ceasing to strive to acquire it—for anxiety *about* health, anxiety about *any*thing, has been shown to be a factor in promoting illness.

Implicit in letting go is the notion that health is a natural state for most human beings. The fact is that most persons spend the bulk of their lives entirely healthy. We *aren't* sick most of the time. The body is astonishingly wise. As Lewis Thomas has pointed out, most of the bacteria that inhabit us are our friends, not our enemies, and the occurrence of an infectious disease is almost an anomaly when one thinks about all the different kinds and incredible number of bacteria that exist on the face of the earth and in and on ourselves. The fact, even, that we are here as survivors amid this enormous bacterial population somehow attests that health for us is a natural state.

In *Space, Time and Medicine* I talked a great deal about time and the eternal present, the time and space of the mystic. This state of timelessness—the absence of hurry and self-induced stress—is the state in which we flower optimally health-wise, physically and psychologically. Modern medicine has demonstrated the correlation of anxiety with illness. If we dissect what anxiety really stems from we can see that the ultimate anxiety—our fear of death—depends on our notion of linear time.

In nonlinear time, death is a concept that makes very little sense. One cannot talk seriously about finalities such as death in a non-flowing time, because it is not possible to establish ultimate demarcations in the way that one can in linear time. So if anxiety, which is based upon a linear concept of time, makes us ill, we can ask whether or not an experience of non-linear time makes us healthy.

Linear time is the time of day-to-day experience, the time that we segment into a past, present, and future. Experientially, it is the notion that time flows, that there is an external real time that is moving and that forms a backdrop against which, and in which, events in life happen and are anchored. Implicit in this idea is the fear that the flow of this river of time carries us downstream and hurtles us inexorably toward extinction—an obviously frightening and threatening model of time. The primary reasons I disagree with this model are, as the British physicist and mathematician P.C.W. Davies has said, there has never been any physical experiment to demonstrate a flowing time; and that the most sensitive representatives of our species, the mystics, who with a single voice in the written record talk about an experience of boundless, nonlinear time. To their observations we can add those of the most accurate science we have ever had, modern physics, which also speaks of non-flowing, nonlinear time. The physicists tell us that things do not *happen,* they simply *are.* And while there may not be total unanimity about what time actually is in physics, it does not seem likely that it will ever adopt the old classical idea that time is an external flowing substance.

We arrive eventually at the notion of completeness: there is really nothing to achieve—things are complete and perfect in *this* very moment, the only one there is. To speak of "becoming" ill, "getting" sick, "regaining" health, or "staying" well are concepts that depend on linear time. If all things exist in the moment, we must begin to question our common sense ways of setting health and illness in inevitable opposition to each other. We must begin to realize that they do not exist serially and in succession, as we always suppose. Thus we can say that health should not be thought of as a state to be acquired. Health somehow exists in the now, and thus at *all* times. We can begin to emphasize the timeless, experiential quality of health that, like time, transcends the purely objective qualities with which we have always invested it.

The criteria of health cannot be measured in terms of longevity. It may not even be accurate to regard health in terms of properly functioning body organs. For if we anchor health in experience, there comes a point where one's experience may override such a criterion.

Consider, e.g., pain. We know that pain is relative from person to person; it is perceived in astonishingly broad levels of intensity or tolerance so that it has virtually no meaning aside from experience. It is possible, in the same relativistic way, to experience health in the midst of illness, analogous to being in the eye of the hurricane and not be touched by it.

This idea of health does not depend on self-deception, on tricking ourselves into thinking we're healthy when we're really not. It hinges on wholeness at some essential level of our being. This wholeness permits, I feel, a transcendence of the ordinary indices of health such as lab tests, x-rays, even pain and suffering. It does not *exclude* them, necessarily, but enfolds them in a ground from which grander meanings emerge, to borrow the physicist David Bohm's terminology. From this larger experiential perspective our ordinary measures of health begin to seem trivial— not inconsequential, mind you, but profoundly less important.

I recall clinical encounters with patients I've cared for in a crisis period who, while lying in a critical care bed with monitors, with tubes coming out of every orifice, with multiple drugs going into their bodies, simultaneously have smiles on their faces. They seem to be totally unmoved by the devastation that is going on in their body. How can I make an allowance for that as a physician? I feel it is facile and wrong to say that they are "too sick" to understand what is happening.

Some of those people seem to be going through something of a mystical experience. They act with a clarity of understanding that has broken through in the midst of grave physical illness. They seem to express health, paradoxically, even in the midst of illness.

Most of us are not able to fully experience or understand the reality of nonlinear time, and we certainly are not all able to live always in the present moment. So we sense ourselves being assaulted on every side by events which threaten an end to life—myocardial infarctions, vascular diseases such as stroke, and high blood pressure. Given our limitations, then, what should our health strategy be? I think we can opt for *complementary* approaches to health care and acknowledge the fact that most of us *do* feel pain, that most of us *are* frightened by death, that we *do* have a sense of linear time. I see no reason why we should not admit this and use the best of traditional medicine that is available. Complementary approaches, then, which emphasize both time and timelessness are not mutually exclusive. Both can be employed. Each has its place in a modern approach to health.

This leads us to consider how we shall practice medicine in the future. As a physician I still want to uphold good health practices: diet, exercise, periodic exams, and so on. I think it would be negligent to abandon the best of orthodox medicine. I personally take great pride in the fact that children don't develop polio any more, that we have a vaccine. The use of many of our tools is humane, and I think it would add enormously and regrettably to the store of human misery if we were to desert them. In this regard, some of the tendencies of the holistic health care movement seem to border on anti-science and irresponsibility, and threaten to substitute certain naive methodologies for some of the powerful approaches we have in modern medicine. I have had occasion, for instance, to care for children whose mothers felt they did not need a vaccine, and I've seen those children die because of the development of an infectious disease that is completely preventable. An approach that would abandon the best of modern molecular medicine is foolish.

It is well known that it is possible for human beings to

achieve states of consciousness whereby one's actual physiology is changed. This can be done through many learned techniques: hypnosis, meditation, and biofeedback are examples. The effects of these "consciousness therapies" are as real as those of any drug or surgical procedure. Thus, they can be seen on one level as tools for change. I hope that we will one day recognize that the medicines we use that are contingent only on molecular interventions are in many instances a secondary approach—second lines of defense, if you will—because they can be supplanted frequently in specific situations by "consciousness therapies" which are effective and which have no side effects. Hopefully we will evolve into a balanced view wherein we realize that it is appropriate to use *both* approaches, depending on the situation, the person's individual capabilities, and his or her needs at the time.

In the medicine of the future it may well be that in planning treatment a physician will have to assess the extent of the person's "consciousness abilities" and then use "consciousness therapies" accordingly—in addition to or instead of the more traditional molecular medical approaches. This is happening already, and is actually a medicine of the present.

Meditation will eventually be viewed as a process which could be a powerful tool in restoring health. The goal in therapy has always been to use a technique that is capable of bringing about actual concrete change in the body. We know beyond question that meditative disciplines evoke such changes. Thus, meditation is entirely defensible as a therapeutic intervention, and will be increasingly recognized as such. This is a delightful marriage of the old and the new. It is exciting to see this fusion of science and the oldest traditions being played out in medicine in ways that will lead to a medicine of the future that is more potent and comprehensive than when either approach is used alone.

2

Wholeness, Hippocrates and Ancient Philosophy

HENRYK SKOLIMOWSKI, Ph.D.

*Rejoice at your life for the time is more advanced than you
     would think.*
*Rejoice at your inner powers for they are the makers of
     wholeness and holiness in you.*
*Rejoice at seeing the light of the day for seeing is a pre-
     condition of truth and beauty.*

Hippocrates was one of the sages of antiquity. He was born in
460 B.C. on the Island of Kos and died on the same island in
377 B.C. Blessed with illustrious ancestors, he was the eighteenth descendent of the God of medicine, Escalapus, on the
side of his father and the twentieth descendent of Heracles
on the side of his mother. He lived in the most glorious period
of Greek history when everything worthy of the human mind
came to fruition. It was his historic mission to lay the foundations of scientific medicine, yet we have to pause here. For the
term *scientific* covers a multitude of sins nowadays (in addition
to a multitude of virtues). Therefore it would be more apt to
say that Hippocrates was the father of systematic medicine;
and something else should not be denied to him—he was the
father of holistic medicine.

Scientific knowledge, in our sense, was but in infancy in the
fifth century B.C. Surprisingly, however, Hippocrates somehow

avoided making statements which scientific medicine would consider "dreadful mistakes." What saved him was philosophy (a right kind of philosophy), and there was plenty of it in his time. Hippocrates's pronouncements were often as philosophical as they were medical.

Yet we must not exaggerate. Hippocrates was a supreme and consummate practitioner of medicine, not just a philosopher. He spent twelve years visiting all the renowned medical centers of the world of his time. He pursued every line of empirical inquiry that was opened to him. In his Esclapeion in Kos, some 6,000 medical herbs were recognized and used. The knowledge of the organism and its reactions to herbs must have been gloriously studied.

The Esclapeion was a place of healing as well as a place of learning of medicine, a combined medical academy and a hospital, or a university hospital. But these terms of ours do injustice to the original conception of the Esclapeion. While our medical centers are places of sterility, places which we want to leave as soon as possible, it was quite the opposite with the esclepia of Ancient Greece. There were some three hundred of them, but those at Epidaurus and at Kos were the most famous. Situated in inspiring surroundings, sheltered by classical buildings and temples, an esclapeion was a place you wanted to stay, not to leave as soon as possible. The healing surrounding of the place was one of its primary assets. You can still feel it, after twenty-four centuries of destruction, when you find yourself at Epidaurus, at Delphi or at the esclapeion of Kos.

The physical quality of the environment of the esclapeion was immensely important, but it is only one aspect of it. Each esclapeion was dedicated to the god Escalapus; each was adorned with various temples, which were an integral part of the healing process. Thus the spiritual aspects of healing and of life were viewed as inherent parts of the tapestry of living.

Ancient wisdom was lacking in the knowledge of detail; but, it did not pervert the meaning of the whole for the sake of detail, as we have done in recent times. For the ancients, to restore meant to restore the whole; whereas we are still obsessed with details and want to be holistic via piecemeal strategies. The diseased empiricist mind is still ticking away in its clock-like discreteness within the Newtonian paradigm, oblivious of the holistic nature of all reality.

The main problem with our fractured existence and our fractured health is not the unhealthy social and physical environment in which we live, but the clinical, fractured environment of our mind, which we recognize as pathological in our instinct and in our intuitions, but to which we nevertheless succumb in our institutional and public life; the coercion of the public life becomes the curse of our individual existence.

Hippocrates was worshipped in his time, and the aureole of glory is still upon him after centuries of spectacular advances in scientific medicine. He was made an honorary citizen of Athens after he contained the plague of 430 B.C. So great was his esteem that Alcibiades, after he destroyed Kos in 411 B.C. for its insubordination to the Athenian Alliance, was instantly ordered by Athens to rebuild the city for the sake of Hippocrates and his son Thessalos.

Later on, the king of Persia, Artaxerxes, requested that Hippocrates come to Persia to fight an epidemic raging there; in return, Artaxerxes offered to Hippocrates as much gold as he would request. But the feeling among the Greeks toward the Persians was still hot and hostile. Hippocrates replied thus: "Thank you, Artaxerxes, for the honor and confidence placed in me. However, it is impossible for me to help a declared foe of my country. Consequently, both the gold and the disease are yours to keep."

Artaxerxes got furious at this reply. He sent a message to the people of Kos telling them to surrender Hippocrates or their entire polis would be so devastated that it would be impossible afterwards to distinguish the inhabited areas from the surrounding deserts and the sea. To this message the inhabitants of Kos replied. "Artaxerxes, the people of Kos will never do anything unworthy which would offend their divine ancestors and Hippocrates, who is the glory of this island. We shall not hand him over to you, no matter if this decision were to entail the most terrible consequences. The gods will not abandon us."

The Gods indeed were with the people of Kos. Artaxerxes got apoplexy when he read this insulting reply and died instantly.

Among the precepts which Hippocrates advocated were:

1. Nature is the cure of illness.
2. Leave thy drugs in the chemist's pot if thou can't heal the patient with food.

These precepts are so simple that they sound naive, but this simplicity was born of deep reflection and of study of the philosophy of the time. One of the great influences on Hippocrates was that of Heraclitus who lived from 544 to 484 B.C. The legacy of Heraclitean thought was still alive. The story has it that Heraclitus offered his papyri to the gods at the Esclapeion at Ephesos. And this is where Hippocrates went to study them. This is an interesting conjunction: a philosopher offering his scrolls to the gods to be kept at an esclapeion; and a medical practitioner going there to study them: an expression of a wonderful unity of things.

From Heraclitus, Hippocrates learned the fundamental lesson that *all wears out,* that "Nothing in this world remains unchanged but for one moment only. Everything changes aspect. It dissolves, merges with other elements and displays a new aspect, different from the previous one. This last appearance is to remain for another moment, then it dissolves, but nothing is lost. . . . " Thus all is in flux, in continuous transformation.

Heraclitus was not the only major influence on Hippocrates. Equally profound was the impact of Pythagoras (580-490 B.C.). From Pythagoras, Hippocrates learned that health, as wholeness, means that the body and the soul must be examined together, that there are spiritual laws which human beings can ignore but only at their own peril, that human will ensures and completes the harmony between body, mind and soul, that complete human beings are those who have grasped the sense of this harmony and implemented it in their own lives, and this harmony means thinking correctly, and living correctly—according to the law. The ancient people appreciated the value of philosophy for their own life. For Pythagoras, *harmony* was the key term, harmony holds it all, or nothing is held.

I should mention at this point that the notion of harmony

was known to Hippocrates before he went to study Pythagorean thought. The idea of harmony indeed pervaded all of Greek culture; yet, Hippocrates was immensely pleased and strengthened in his beliefs when he found that such an illustrious philosopher as Pythagoras upheld notions similar to his.

Yet another philosopher who made his mark on Hippocrates was Anaxagoras (500-428 B.C.), who represented the transition from Pythagoras to Socrates.

This was the philosophical world in which Hippocrates lived. You might say, "What a galaxy of minds to be surrounded with!" Indeed. Add to them Socrates who was Hippocrates's friend, and you will receive a picture of a time of enlightenment unmatched by any period of Western history.

Hippocrates marks a milestone in the history of Western medicine and Western thought, not because he was an industrious observer who also managed to amass more medical knowledge than anyone else at the time, but *because he could see the wholeness of the human condition; he clearly realized that philosophy is not an entertaining intellectual game but the foundation in which our well-being is embedded.* By extending this insight ever so slightly, we might say that illness is the result of holding a wrong philosophy, one which permits one to behave foolishly and disharmoniously, one which does not help one to perceive the body and the mind as a whole. The right philosophy, on the other hand, must aid one in the quest for deeper meaning, which in turn is a constituent of our overall wholeness.

One of Hippocrates's specific triumphs, of which we are usually unaware, was his ability to integrate the two divergent strands of Greek thought—the Heraclitean and the Pythagorean. One insists that everything is in flux and transformation, and the latter insists that there is a pre-established harmony. These two strands have never been properly integrated in Western thought since Plato. Our culture has become transfixed with "being" at the expense of understanding the deeper nature of "becoming." Plato has overshadowed Heraclitus. Therein lies the source of one of our deepest conceptual and spiritual troubles. We are unable to live with the flux and with uncertainty; we demand clarity, which in turn requires separation and cutting things into distinct slices; our analytical science has been an expression of this quest for clarity. Strange as it may sound, Newtonian physics is much closer to the Pythagorean view of the world than we usually credit it for. After all, at the threshold of the Newtonian era stands Galileo with his Pythagorean dream of reading the book of nature written in the language of mathematics.

Our minds are too fragmented to allow us to see that cosmology is relevant for correct thinking and good health. The tragedy of Western philosophy, and of the Western mind since the Renaissance (perhaps since Aristotle), has been our inability to generate cosmologies which are life-enhancing and supportive of our daily struggles, including the care for our health and our wholeness; Eastern philosophies have never lost sight of those supreme tasks, hence their enduring strength.

One of the great tasks on the agenda of the meaningful future is to find a new form of integration for Heraclitus and Pythagoras. The supreme secret of life-evolving lies in our understanding that we are dealing not with a static harmony but Dynamic Harmony. If we recognize Dynamic Harmony, we then recognize that all things are in flux, in transformation, in the process of becoming; at the same time we recognize the permanency of some spiritual laws which give meaning to the flux. The creation of a new cosmology that will accommodate the Heraclitean and the Pythagorean traditions and will fuse them together in a new understanding of the Cosmos is not only a precondition of our health but a precondition of the survival of the Planet, as well as a precondition of our coherent understanding of the world, which has been so fractured in modern times. In the twentieth century, Teilhard de Chardin towers over the horizon as the man who was able to combine Heraclitus and Pythagoras in a magnificent new synthesis.

Let us ask ourselves in the end: What is wholeness? The answer is "You know it when you have got it." Such a rendering may sound a bit vulgar; however, the essential point about wholeness is that it is not a description of the state of things, but a description—rather an experience—of the state of being.

We tend to think of wholeness as a property of an aggregate of things outside ourselves, while in fact it is a highly subjective concept describing individually and existentially the state of our being. It is in this sense that Ravi Ravindra maintains:

> It is also good to remind ourselves that any real reconciliation of the demands of the spirit and those of the body is not a matter of general mental abstractions such as "science" and "religion." It is only in a unique particular in an individual's soul that any such reconciliation has any meaning. It is only in the concrete existential situation in which I simultaneously experience and intentionally embrace the different forces of the two realms of spirit and body or religion and science that I have a possibility of wholeness. Otherwise, one remains fragmented, thinking about or wishing for wholeness.[*]

So once again what does it mean to be whole? It is to be on good terms with the cosmos, which means understanding and respecting the *laws,* as Pythagoras conceived of them. Or to put it in Plato's terms: "Health is a consummation of a love affair of the organs of the body." Wholeness works like a magnet: you must be whole to enable the other to become whole; your magnet of wholeness activates the potential for wholeness in the other. Writing and reading poetry is good for one's wholeness. Finally, to be whole is to be encompassed by the sense of the divine in the divine cosmos. If all these "definitions" do not begin to convey what we feel and recognize upon instinct as the wholeness of our being, then we have to resort to silence. "From the springs of silence comes all understanding. All great truths were conceived and recovered in silence."

Rejoice at listening to silence for it is the begetter of enlightenment.

Rejoice at your inner powers for they are the makers of wholeness and holiness in you.

Rejoice at your large philosophies for they are the foundations of your well-being and a precondition of correct thinking, correct acting and good health.

Rejoice at the joy of existence for it is the hidden source of your well-being.

---

[*]"Science and the Ancient Tradition." *The American Theosophist,* Special Issue, Fall, 1982, p. 352.

3

Philosophical Foundations and Frameworks for Healing

RENÉE WEBER, Ph.D.

The whole universe is one mathematical and symphonic expression, made up of finite representations of the infinite.
F.L. Kunz

I should confess at the outset of this essay that we do not as yet have a clear theory accounting for spiritual healing. An ideal and rigorous explanation resembling a scientific law seems presently beyond our reach. We must be content, therefore, with some philosophical frameworks *compatible* with the phenomenon of healing. Interestingly, these frameworks, though drawn from diverse cultures and epochs separated in time, cohere and thus possess certain common denominators. These denominators consist in a basic shared foundation, however varied may be the structures built thereon. By "healing" I refer to a process in which a person becomes *whole* physically, emotionally, mentally and at deeper levels, resulting ideally in an integration with the underlying inward power of the universe.

Consequently, the ensuing discussion will try to establish that the Healing Hypothesis is bound up with a major and majestic aim, transcending the mere utilitarian absence of bodily disease. Hopefully, this exploration will contribute

toward an eventual Theory of Healing, despite the fact that
our present attempts are necessarily rudimentary and pro-
visional.

The theoretical and philosophical frameworks compatible
with the Healing Hypothesis can sound the *direction* in which
our further search and research must move, and some of the
rich details embedded in these frameworks may turn out to be
useful in this endeavor. The major task, however, still lies
ahead. It consists in discovering and clearly formulating the
foundation for the dynamics of healing as such; a single
principle of potent explanatory and predictive scope. This
task awaits a creative breakthrough in which a new paradigm
of space, time, matter, energy, life and consciousness will be
forged within a unified field of knower and known.

While scientific validation of the Healing Hypothesis remains an abiding goal that constitutes a challenge, we must
be aware that we are dealing with a domain in which too rigid
a form of the positivist-physicalist model of proof may not be
appropriate. New paradigms of proof and explanation may
have to be evolved, combining rigor of mind with intuitive
sensitivity to subtler realms of being. An unquestioning ad-
herence at the outset to materialistic frameworks and assumptions about the nature of reality will tend to bar its adherents
from investigating any forms of spiritual healing, be this therapeutic touch, laying on of hands, or distant healing.

THE HEALING HYPOTHESIS

Throughout this essay I shall use the term the "Healing Hypothesis" to refer to a total context or syndrome of factors
that seem interwoven with healing. Among these are the claim
that energy and consciousness exist in various states, qualitatively differentiated, and with supremacy over gross physical matter; the irrelevance of physical contiguity to healing,
involving us instead in novel concepts of space, time, and
energy; the relativity of time in various dimensions of space
and its absence from the n-dimensional space of pure spiritual
energy where the healing power originates; its increasing
physicality and density as it enters the space-time sphere of

organisms, a process in which the healer acts as a conduit. The claim of the Healing Hypothesis further involves the power of intentionality of unbounded, living systems such as ourselves, ceaselessly interpenetrating one another, rather than being restricted to the discernible boundaries of our bodies and personalities; and the resultant interchange of qualitatively charged energies among all organisms in the universe, resulting either in creative or in destructive consequences for the cosmic ecology, spreading order or disorder depending on the wholeness or fragmentation of those energies. Finally, it may be stated that this universal healing energy is not neutral nor value-free, but an energy of order and compassion. (Bohm, 1978; Weber, 1978).

INCOMPATIBLE FRAMEWORKS

A useful preliminary consideration is to examine some frameworks that *cannot* be invoked to explain healing. Some of these are: materialism, positivism, reductionism, behaviorism and other crude versions of physicalism. Their fundamental incompatibility with the Healing Hypothesis is that their very foundation contradicts a healing thesis as such. The central assumption shared by those movements is a selective empiricism based on eighteenth and nineteenth century materialistic physics. Ironically, that version of physics has now been repudiated by advances in twentieth century physics, and thus seems no longer warranted even by current developments within science. (Bohm, 1978; Capra, 1975; Weber, 1975: 1978).

In spite of this, eighteenth and nineteenth century views about the nature of matter and energy persist, especially in the life sciences, and these reductionistic and mechanistic views continue to dominate most biologists and psychologists, dictating a model of organisms that seems outmoded even by the rigorous standards of physics itself. Simply stated, the foundation uniting these various frameworks is that nature is inert, that gross visible matter is ultimate, that matter and consciousness are irrevocably sundered—or, alternately, that consciousness is nothing in its own right and can be reduced to and explained solely through the laws of matter; life and mind being "nothing but" combinations of inert atoms, random and isolated from all other atoms. Thinkers adhering to this view maintain that the complex world of organisms is built up from "the outside in," as it were, through accretions of matter and its eventual adaptation to the environment, in a process characterized by Darwin as "the survival of the fittest," and by Monod (1970) as "chance and necessity." The corollary to those views is that consciousness— including the artistic, philosophic, and religious capacities of man—is *nothing but* the consequence of the organization of matter and motion, animated at most by a vital thrust. No purpose but survival ultimately informs these particles.

HOLISTIC FOUNDATIONS

We can discern some basic principles that by contrast with materialistic positions are philosophically compatible with healing, furnishing a theoretical foundation for the Healing Hypothesis.

The most fundamental of these principles is the claim that there is but *one* reality. This strict non-dualistic basis for the entire cosmos is the starting-point for any explanation of healing. It postulates an organic unity beneath the multiplicity evident to our senses, a unity that is primary and causal compared with the derivative and secondary status of the manifested things in the world (i.e., the objects of our sense-perceptions) (Kunz, 1963). That being the case, matter and consciousness are but two expressions of the one unbroken reality. They differ at best in degree and in function but not in kind. On the surface, this position may also sound reductionistic and hence reminiscent of the very behaviorism rejected earlier in this discussion. In fact, the present view is diametrically distinct from the Cartesian-Skinnerian one, since the interconnected oneness proclaimed here is a living force that unites all beings *through integration, not reduction* (Weber, 1975). Any apparent "reductionism" found here favors consciousness as the primary nature of reality, a consciousness in which the universe becomes unified. Consciousness thus is no incidental factor, an "epiphenomenon" or by-product as in Skinner, but an integral feature of being (Koestler, Smythies, *et al.*, 1969). The cosmos is alive throughout, from the lowliest atom to the highest human (or even meta-human) manifestations. Life is a continuum, expressing in endlessly diverse dimensions the inner pulse that gave it impetus toward manifestation. "Consciousness" may have different meanings at different levels and in the various orders of being, but this is due to diversity in complexity and organization, and in the subtlety of its substance. Beneath all life beats a unified rhythm, interconnecting every being as an expression of the same conscious, non-material reality (Kunz, 1963).

Matter and energy are equivalent, two interchangeable facets of one ground, as Einstein, echoing the ancient metaphysics, was to assert in our own era. The universe, far from being a machine or composed of atomistic, separate, and random particles as alleged by physicalism, is in fact one integral whole in which the parts—interconnected deep within this ocean of oneness—all bear directly on one another, exerting mutual influence and interdependence in all directions and dimensions, as is the case with any living organism. These contrasting claims form, by way of example, two distinct frameworks: the Platonic and the Skinnerian.

Plato, in *Timaeus,* describes the universe as a living organism, "endowed with intelligence and a soul," which "God fashioned . . . by form and number" and whose "body was harmonized by proportion." Skinner (1948), by contrast, depicts nature as an alien realm that must be conquered ("Triumph over nature"), and the most recurrent word in *Walden Two,* his blueprint for a future utopia, is the word "control," wielded over the natural world by technocrats intent on a single goal: the satisfaction of their desires.

CONFLICTING ANATOMIES OF REALITY

The single most significant feature of the Healing Hypothesis revolves around the issue of purposiveness, intelligence, and vision imputed to the universe, or rather to its underlying spiritual reality by Eastern and Platonic philosophy;

by contrast to the haphazard, blind, value-free events attributed to it by the various mechanistic versions. As in the case
of other features claimed by these latter, if the mechanistic
characterization of reality were correct, spiritual healing
would have no legitimate foundation and would thus be impossible: an illusion due to a crass so-called placebo-effect. Those
engaged in it would be self-deluded at best, fraudulent at
worst. (The "placebo-effect," itself a complex and poorly
understood phenomenon that may well be related to healing,
lies beyond the scope of my discussion.)

Thus, the question as to the kind of cosmos in which we
live is crucial to our assessment of the healing phenomenon.
The mechanistic-materialistic-behavioristic hypothesis ren-
ders spiritual healing impossible for, as has been pointed out,
it is inconsistent with the very nature of the universe in which
those systems claim we live. If, on the contrary, the holistic-
spiritual-vitalistic thesis is right, the Healing Hypothesis is
vastly strengthened. It even becomes a natural outgrowth of
such a metaphysics, expressing in empirical ways a network of
forces embodying the principles whose existence those
systems assert. On this view, spiritual healing is a natural, not
supernatural, consequence of the anatomy of the universe.

The purposiveness or teleological approach of the latter
account of reality also entails certain subsidiary principles.
Among these are the view that the dynamism associated with
living systems rules out static passivity or inertness on the part
of any being in the universe. Such a dynamic and stirring sea of
energy, pushing *from within* (Kunz, 1970) toward ever greater
growth and self-awareness is most aptly grasped in terms of
evolution, a spiritually motivated thrust at all levels of
existence that culminates in an increasingly self-conscious
cosmos, akin to Teilhard de Chardin's *omega point* (1959), or
to the liberation of spirit slumbering within matter that has
become self-transparent. This last idea is widely shared in the
philosophies and religions of India, the ancient systems of
Egypt and Greece, and in theosophical concepts embodied
in the esoteric tradition of both East and West (Weber, 1975).
Consciousness, in short, is world-creating.

These   accounts—Sankhya-Yoga,   Buddhist,   Pythagorean

and Platonic, to name but a few—all agree on some basic assertions. Consciousness, being primary, conceives, constructs, and subsequently governs gross visible matter, including the physical body. Since the world works "from within without" (according to the ancient Hermetic principle), from the hidden spiritual domains outward toward the dense manifest material ones, consciousness "makes itself a body," as it were. Far from being subject to gross matter, consciousness is in every way its sovereign (Smith, 1975). Since consciousness is one at its source (Schrodinger, 1969) and is the root of the cosmic reality, consciousness at some deeper level is in direct and immediate contact both with itself, as humanity, and with its ground, the infinite source. This ancient claim has gained unexpected support in the recent work of London theoretical physicist David Bohm (1978), whose distinction between the implicate-explicate orders, or the manifest/non-manifest domains lends further credibility to the foundation under present discussion. If it is correct, Cartesian solipsism is an empirical as well as a logical error, an absurdity which belies and contradicts the way things really are, namely the universal unity of being.

HOLISTIC FRAMEWORKS

In all these theories, and at the furthest extreme of behaviorism, we find a model in which all entities are intimately in touch with and influenced by one another, attuned to the rhythms flowing through each and through the whole. In addition to interconnectedness, a second feature of this unity is its order. The universe tends *naturally* toward order, as Pythagoras and Plato observed some twenty-five centuries ago. In spite of surface manifestations to the contrary (earthquakes, and other cataclysmic events), even a pessimistic account of nature would have to concede the preponderance of orderly processes without which the profusion of thriving species governed by laws would not be in evidence today. Such an observation, to take an historical example, struck Plato so forcefully that he postulated an entire cosmos pervaded by purposiveness, i.e., a teleological universe (*telos,* the Greek for purpose, aim).

The telos of the universe is the expression of a spiritual force Plato termed "the good," which disposed all things toward their own maximum well-being, and provided a kind of cosmic model or blueprint toward which everything "aspires" or strives. This model, Plato's Forms, might be termed an invisible DNA or RNA on cosmic scale. Like the miniaturized models invoked by contemporary genetics, Plato's Forms are characterized by their capacity to impart order and intelligence to nature. They are the blueprints for the outer expression of the inner essence of things. Plato's philosophy thus has a natural affinity with healing theories. In both, the primary and natural state of entities is order and wholeness, linked by a rhythm attuning each entity to the rhythm of the universe, with salutary effects on the participants in the cosmic dance, reminiscent of the "dance of Shiva" in Hindu cosmology.

THE PRIMACY OF THE ABSTRACT

A contemporary scientific complement to this view, touched on above, is the holographic model of reality independently proposed by Bohm(1978) and by Stanford neuropsychologist Karl Pribram (1976, 1977, 1979). It states that *in-phase* experiencing of this rhythm is perceived by us as flow, joy, spontaneity, insight and intuition, intrinsic kinship with and hence compassion for all that lives. The resultant sense of well-being might even be taken as an ideal state of health for organisms, since it is derived from their harmony with the whole. Experience *out-of-phase* with the holomovement, on the other hand, blocks those positive and health-giving rhythms and in their stead substitutes *disrhythmias,* leading to disease, a term that holistic theories deem synonymous with disorder.

Consequently, the Holistic Hypothesis postulates as the primary cause of disease the disconnectedness from this flow and rhythm of the whole, both within the single organism and also among groups of organisms. Lest one conclude that such postulation is simple (or even simplistic), I must add that the actual *causes* for the disrhythmias are complex and multiple. They seem subtly interwoven with many secondary and contributory factors (genetic, environmental, etc.), which, given the primitive state of our knowledge concerning these matters, we can at present only partly understand. Among such factors are our emotions, habits, energy-expenditures, and values—patterns all capable of either squandering or preserving our organismic integrity. Additional variables are lifestyles, involving dietary or other excesses, and even antecedent conditions both recent and remote, known in Eastern philosophy as *karma*. Through any one or, as seems likely, through a combination of these, the organism ruptures the rhythms prescribed by its proper blueprint, adversely affecting the *chakras* (Leadbeater, 1927, Powell, 1969), within the etheric and other subtle energy-fields which basically govern our health. Malfunctioning of the chakras eventually becomes organic malfunction.

The theory of subtle energy-fields is indispensable and constitutes a crucial foundation for the Healing Hypothesis. The two frameworks in which this foundation is most explicitly elaborated are the Sankhya of classical Hindu philosophy and the Platonic cosmology of Greece. Since these are intricate and technical systems, here I can provide at best a glimpse into them. Sankhya and Plato are bound together by a common premise: the primacy of the abstract. This proclaims that invisible realities precede and in fact *beget* visible ones. Alternately phrased, this principle reappears in contemporary physics: subtler states of matter are more primary than gross physical ones, both in order of appearance and in sovereignty over the denser forms (Bohm, 1978). This ancient conception turns common sense naive realism (i.e., "seeing is believing") upside down. It substitutes in its stead an account of the world expressed most perfectly in Greek and Indian Idealism, and in the visionary physics of David Bohm's holomovement. Their basic thesis is that a spiritual reality underlies and gives rise to our physical one, which it also sustains and governs through universal laws. In Plato, this ultimate reality is termed "the good," an undefinable force that pervades the cosmos and can account for its most minute workings by means of a more proximate, non-material principle, namely the Forms. Embedded in and generated by the Platonic Forms are the archetypal, non-physical blueprints alluded to earlier in this discussion. Their status has puzzled scholars for over two thousand years. Somehow they seem to constitute the key to the existence and functioning of the multiplicity of physical entities in our visible world.

PLATONIC PHILOSOPHY

Without entering into the philosophical complexities of Plato's Theory, its noteworthy feature for our purposes can be summed up quite simply: the existence and nature of any given entity depends upon its correctly reproducing the eternal, essential Platonic Form in whose "image" it is made. In the case of living organisms, for example, proper "participation" (*methexis,* in Greek) in the Form translates into health, whereas faulty participation leads to illness. "Health" in Plato involves the spiritual well-being of the whole person.

The applicability of such a view to healing is evident, although its detailed workings-out are exceedingly difficult and subtle. However, the *direction* dictated by this theory falls quite easily into such healing principles as we presently possess, even at this rudimentary juncture in the state of the art. Plato assigns the primary power for health or illness not to the visible outgrowth, the consequence of the archetype in flesh, blood and other matter, as is the claim of the materialists or of common sense naive realists. In a bold inversion of causal connections, he instead attributes well-being to our unobstructed connectedness with the Forms in such a way that we can "translate" their patterns, first into the invisible, subtler "bodies" or energy-fields, and subsequently into the gross visible, denser and stabler forms of matter of which our physical bodies are composed. As in Bohm's implicate-explicate orders (1978), for Plato our relationships to these supersensible realities determine proper functioning. This is not the place to present the many details that lie scattered throughout the Platonic dialogues, which can be woven together into a coherent theory of health and healing. However, anyone embarked on such an enterprise gains increasing conviction that a Platonic theory of healing exists embedded in the opus as a whole, even though it must be carefully culled therefrom and made explicit.

The second and more important point is that Plato, even were he never to mention human health or disease, furnished an *indirect* framework for the Healing Hypothesis through his metaphysics as a whole. Reduced to its barest outline, Platonic metaphysics postulates an ideal, eternal, supersensible model, beyond space and time, and a material, spatio-temporal counterpart which without the archetypal supersensible entity cannot continue to be, let alone to flourish. To be hale or whole is therefore impossible without continuing interaction with the eternal and higher-dimensional realm, Plato's ideal, intelligible world. In that sense, it may rightfully be argued that lack of health is lack of wholeness, i.e., partiality, undue restrictedness, isolation from the cosmic matrix, and self-enclosure, diminishing the dynamic balance in which healthy entities exist, by cutting off their ontological circulation, as it were. This state of affairs is nowhere more powerfully presented than in Plato's Allegory of the Cave (*Republic VII*), where partiality and physicalism are equated with an imprisoned state of blindness, curable by the abandonment of the cave for the realm of light which alone can set man free and make him flourish.

One might sum up Plato's philosophy with the observation that *Platonic metaphysics as a whole is a model for healing.*

INDIAN PHILOSOPHY

The second metaphysical framework especially appropriate here is the Sankhya of sixth century B.C. India. In some ways it may be even more suitable to healing theories than the Platonic because it deals more extensively with biological organisms. These are the direct expression of Spirit (*purusha*) becoming unaccountably entangled with root-matter (*prakriti*), leading through a series of complex but plausible steps to cosmic consciousness (*mahat*). This field-like force ultimately localizes itself into an individuating capacity which provides the potential for self-consciousness, the "I-making" capacity (*ahamkara*). One manifestation of this personal focusing of universal consciousness is mind (*manas*) or mental field, an active energy that can only be understood teleologically, not mechanistically as in behavioristic accounts. (The alleged dualism of Sankhya will be ignored in this paper for the purpose of simplification). Thus in Sankhya, mind or intelligence is the impetus for generating the physical, emotional and vital (etheric) energy-fields by which individual self-consciousness ("personality," as we call it) expresses itself in the phenomenal-empirical space-time world. Mind, and ultimately spiritual consciousness, *makes* matter by precipitating itself, as it were, into dense and stable forms of substance. As in Plato, mind governs matter, a hierarchy or metaphysical "pecking-order" that seems attributable to its greater energy. In this lies its tremendous power, for good or for ill, to affect the destiny of the physical field, since an atom of subtler matter contains more energy, more wholeness and hence more power than one of dense physical matter (Kunz, 1977; Bohm, 1978).

Although this highly telescopic *precis* can do no more than evoke these bold and intriguing speculations, their implications can be spelled out, even if their richly elaborated details cannot in a paper so limited in scope. These implications lead to a sweeping yet minutely refined cosmology in which all beings fit into the interconnected whole adverted to elsewhere in this essay. This schema overlaps, as we have seen, with parts of our own scientific account, even though its metaphysical postulations would be unacceptable to science in its present state. To summarize the claims of Sankhya: the individual consciousness produces the structures necessary to its evolution in the world from the potential "elements" or abstract, nonmaterial genetic "seeds." These give rise, through a process of "condensation," to forms of increasingly gross physical matter, from atoms to molecules, (*shtula-bhutani,* literally "dense material particles"), which in turn behave much as do the molecules described by contemporary Western science. Molecules ultimately form organic compounds, these evolve to become plant and finally animal organisms, culminating in self-conscious beings like man (and in metahuman manifestations of consciousness). The convergence of Sankhya with contemporary Western science occurs therefore at the later stages of explanation of this process; a sharp divergence exists with respect to both the initial stages and the teleological tone of the Sankhya system, for Western science does not at present accept the idea of consciousness as the catalyst for the origin, development, and rationale of the physical world, nor for that matter the deeper purposive and holistic context in which Sankhya lies anchored.

It may be asked: what practical differences do the explanations presented thus far entail, and more specifically: what are their consequences for healing? We shall see that insofar as concerns both the possibility and the practice of healing, drastic practical differences do arise from such divergent views. In materialistic-physicalist philosophies, both functions and malfunctions are attributable to the workings of gross physical matter without recourse to consciousness. This observation still holds, even though the view is being increasingly eroded within the medical community itself, through the compelling experience of every medical practitioner that mind and emotions play a central role in so-called psychosomatic and perhaps in all diseases. However that may be, no good theoretical ground presently exists to deal with such findings. In our current transitional stage, the physician attempts to integrate the psychosomatic reality with which his clinical experience daily confronts him, into the physicalism that remains to this day the preeminent metaphysics of medicine. Treating the whole person still lies in the future.

By contrast, as we have seen, holistic philosophies attribute the primary power of both health and disease to consciousness within the gross physical field, i.e., to the manifestations of consciousness. We must of course realize that even the divisions I have pursued here are artificial ones which the spiritual traditions repudiate. We may discern differences at the phenomenal level between so-called matter and consciousness, but at their root they are one, parallel expressions of the indivisible and single reality that furnishes their foundation (Govinda, 1969).

THE YOGA OF PATANJALI

Such an outlook invites a non-dualistic orientation in both theory and practice. By way of example, the *Yoga Sutras of Patanjali,* the classical treatise on physiology and psychology built upon Sankhya theory, makes some penetrating clinical and therapeutic observations directly applicable to healing. I refer to Patanjali's theory of the *samskaras* or scars, which he claims play a prominent role in health and, disease (Taimni, 1975). These scars are *tracings* left on us by our experience, akin to energy patterns etched into our organism. Perhaps this occurs at the cellular, neuronal or at even deeper levels, preserving, by encoding, what have been termed *engrams* of energy, i.e., records of experience that become part and parcel of our very tissues. In ways not yet understood by modern neurophysiology nor sufficiently explained by Patanjali, these "furrows" or tracings persist throughout our lives, exercising enormous influence on our behavior by their very presence. Their influence on our energy-economy is for the most part destructive and maladaptive, in that traumas and disappointments rather than joyful and fulfilling experiences are retained and energized to our detriment, much as Freud and the twentieth century analytic schools have argued in their theories of an unconscious that dominates us. Since Patanjali, like the psychoanalytic therapists, was impressed by the widespread power and tenacity of these "scars," wreaking havoc with the entire psychosomatic edifice, his approach to their dissolution is radical and holistic rather than a piecemeal strategy, which he rejects as useless in coping with the roots and not the mere branches of the conflict.

Accordingly, Patanjali's advice for defusing and de-energizing their destructive effect falls under what we would today call a healing approach. He observes that mere verbal techniques—reasoning with the traumatic tracings or *willing* oneself to ignore their presence—are powerless in the face of the vitality with which the scars are endowed. If anything, such tactics tend to sustain them with renewed energy, by focusing on and thus continually reinforcing the tracings through a negative energy-pattern. Patanjali urges "starving" them at their root, withering their structure and leaving in their place an "extinct" and harmless scar sapped of its force and thus of its power to damage our lives.

This withdrawal of energy can come about in a variety of ways, some of them almost contemporary in their coherence, for example, with the Simonton (1976, 1978) approach to stress diseases and cancer therapy, and the work of Achterberg (1976) derived from it. Patanjali specifically advocates visualization. This operates through identification with certain images on which we meditate. Most powerful in rebalancing our energies are yoga and meditation, which are Patanjali's analogues to healing. Yoga, i.e., union, rejoins the part with the cosmic whole. In its highest expression, the culmination of the process known as *samadhi,* yoga actually integrates man into the universal healing power whose orderliness sweeps away the scars. Obliterating psycho-physical lesions by its very presence and power, it seems to *overwhelm* the disrhythmic patterns in favor of the health-giving rhythmic ones that wipe them out. Thus yoga, in the far-reaching sense envisioned by Patanjali, radically alters our pathological patterns by *erasing,* as it were, the garbled and twisted records furrowed within our energy-fields. In this novel and unorthodox account, Patanjali proves himself surprisingly modern, anticipating the avant-garde theories of physicists like Bohm (1978) and neuropsychologists like Pribram (1976, 1971, 1979).

Patanjali's outlook finds echoes in Western philosophies widely separated from him in space, time, and culture, where no direct historical influence can be demonstrated. There is, for example, a coherence of vision linking him with Pythagoras (6th c. B.C.), who precedes him by at least four centuries. The father of psychosomatic medicine in the West, Pythagoras prescribed music to restore the imbalanced frame to its *rightful* balance, "rightful" because Pythagoras taught that an unheard cosmic rhythm, the "music of the spheres," pervades the universe, undetected by us only due to the high velocity of its vibration, approaching the speed of light. This "music," composed of ratio, pattern, harmony, and mathematical proportion, as Pythagoras held, orders the life of both nature and man, whose intrinsic unity is proclaimed as the isomorphism of macrocosm and microcosm, the Hermetic dictum: "as above, so below." Man is but a finite mirror of the universe as a whole. A diseased organism has lost its harmonic character to the discordant rhythms already referred to, and hence Pythagorean therapy aims at restoring the proper harmonics and "musical" patterns to the patient's life-field. Plato, Pythagoras' greatest disciple, concurs with these concepts and draws on them in his theory of organismic and social justice in *The Republic,* where harmonics becomes the key to both health and wisdom.

SPINOZA

In the modern era of Western philosophy, the healing framework is powerfully revived by Spinoza, the 17th century Rationalist whose philosophy seeks to combat the dualism and general fragmentation of his predecessor, Descartes. Mind and body are not two distinct substances but two ways of describing one and the same spiritual substance which Spinoza (1677) terms God or Nature. To Spinoza, the insoluble Cartesian dilemma of mind-body interaction is a pseudo-problem, nothing more than conceptual and linguistic confusion bred by a misunderstanding of the nature of things. The metaphysical ground of our being is *one,* the seamless garment of nature expressing itself both as consciousness and as matter, the two attributes (out of the infinitely many) that can be known by man. It follows from Spinoza's premises that disorder in any part of our organism involves concomitant disorder in all of it, since the cosmic ecology is a single fabric. A healthy consciousness is reflected in a healthy body; the converse connection is equally valid. No interaction, no "influence" and no causal account are warranted or needed since all these falsely assume the separation of a unity which Spinoza sees as the primary fact of life. Along with Parmenides (5th c. B.C. Greece), he is the most thoroughgoing and radical monist within the Western tradition, holding tenaciously to his view despite the testimony of the senses which encourages conclusions to the contrary.

Moreover, Spinoza's denial of dualism furnishes the basis of a remarkably modern physiology and psychology, set forth in his great treatise, *Ethics* (Parts III, IV, V). In a theory that may well turn out to be prophetic— cohering with holographic concepts of modern physics and neurology mentioned earlier in this essay— Spinoza observes, for example, that negative emotions and thoughts damage the organism, leading not only to despair and depression but, as his monism requires, to physical deterioration as well. Specifically, Spinoza singles out such affects as hatred, fear, jealousy, envy, guilt, regret, pity, self-pity, ruminative and self-centered obsessive thinking, dwelling on real or imagined injuries received from others—all of them destructive to our health. His concept of the *conatus,* a psycho-physiological energy reminiscent of *prana* in Indian systems, cuts across all aspects of our constitution. A heightened *conatus* spells well-being, harmony with the cosmic flow whose presence we register as "joy" or "blessedness," the highest happiness human beings can experience. Spinoza tells us that compassion, affection, contemplation of the laws of the universe leading to a grasp of its grandeur—that all these heighten the vital energy (*conatus*) which holds the key to our health.

Accordingly Spinoza, like Pythagoras, Plato, Patanjali, Buddha and others within this tradition, counsels a life of measure and moderation, characterized by altruism, optimism, joyful participation in the cosmic order facilitated by, but also in turn reinforcing, a selfless and saintly life of simple happiness.

Many of these foregoing views—dormant during the long centuries in which atomistic, materialistic, or dualistic hypotheses gained ascendency in the scientific community—are now being revived within science itself. Most notable amidst these attempts is the holographic paradigm propounded by Bohm and Pribram. The holomovement, to use Bohm's term, is a spiritual, dynamic, unbroken reality in which all entities are embedded and interconnected. Although its full nature is inaccessible to our discursive mind, we can intuit its presence, particularly in meditative awareness, which may be described as a unitive, healing, direct experience of it. All our concepts concerning it are metaphorical, for the "ocean of energy" in which we are immersed lies beyond language. It can be apprehended, but not comprehended (Bohm, 1978).

THE ROLE OF THE HEALER

I have tried to present some highlights of philosophical frameworks hospitable to the Healing Hypothesis. The remaining task of this paper is to consider the role of the healer himself. From the discussion thus far, we may conclude that his role is at once modest and powerful. Since consciousness has been accorded a creative status in the scheme of things, its role is that of an *active energy* capable of balancing the gross physical and even the subtler realms of matter. This premise is required by the Healing Hypothesis, which holds that a consciously focused intent is a *force* rather than a fantasy. That force influences all dimensions of "matter," be they physical, etheric, emotional, mental, or spiritual, since all of these overlap in any event. The healer's intent forms an energy capable of affecting the disturbed patterns of the healee. We must, however, be clear on one crucial issue. *The universal healing power, not the healer's personal energy, accomplishes the healing.* The healer is akin to a channel, passively, yet paradoxically with discernment, permitting the cosmic energy to flow unobstructedly through his own fields into those of the healee. He must be sensitive to the disturbances within the healee and simultaneously aware of the healee's wholeness at higher levels of being, an art that demands both discrimination and intuition. In short, the healer constitutes the link between the universal and the particular analogous to an electrical transformer capable of stepping down the source, in this case the prodigious cosmic energy, into a form utilizable by our systems. But it must be emphasized that this is neither a mechanical nor an automatic process. The healer's intentionality—his desire to help and his compassion for the suffering Other—is a necessary not a sufficient condition for contact with the healing source. The sufficient condition (i.e., the factor in whose presence healing cannot fail to take place) remains largely a mystery at present.

A number of factors have been proposed in the attempt to probe its workings. Among these are individual susceptibility to the healing energy, and differences in our capacity to give up fundamental and familiar energy-patterns, overcoming the natural tendency to cling to their miscoded information through fear of change. Finally, the decisive factor may be an ideal synchronicity of all three fields: infinite source, healer, and healee. About this, the most interesting theory of all, we know very little as yet. Such synchronicity implies a "time" quite different from Newtonian or clock-time. The suspension of clock-time in favor of atemporality—the eternal moment— seems a basic part of the healing framework. It can account for the well-documented albeit rare cases of *instantaneous* and complete healing in certain individuals, apparently a sweeping restructuring and reintegration of all their energy-fields amounting, in addition to a physical cure, to a total transformation of the personality and its values (Kunz, 1977, 1978). In such an event, the pathological physical patterns are erased and realigned with their etheric and subtler fields much like the erasure of a distorted tape recording and its replacement by orderly instruction and information. In the absence of such ideal synchronicity, where the healing energy can only partly break through the disordered patterns (which tend to block its natural flow and dilute its impact), there seems to be partial and less dramatic restoration, less lasting because the patient's disturbed rhythms tend to reassert themselves, eventually repatterning the physical fields along the old "grooves" which led to the disease in the first place (Kunz, 1978; Meek, 1977; Tiller, 1977, 1975). The person is potentially but not actually whole. Lastly, our self-image bears crucially on our capacity to both heal and be healed.

As even this most cursory discussion has established, spiritual healing is a complex pattern of interactions between three unbounded fields of energy: the infinite source, the healer, and the healee. The latter two can, incidentally, often exchange roles, each guiding the other to seek renewed instruction from the source. This leads to the inference that the healer serves to *speed up* the healee's own innate capacity to contact the archetypal blueprint, enhancing the universal tendency toward order that is part and parcel of all life. The healer thus mediates between a finite field that has somehow "gone wrong," and the infinite ocean of energy from which we become estranged only at our peril.

HEALING AS MOVING MEDITATION

The experience of union with the source is most often associated with a centered state of being in which the universal energy can pour through us without obstruction. Our thoughts, emotions, memories, anxieties, i.e., the ego and its residues, are temporarily suspended, knocked out of commission as it were, and with it ordinary time and our confined spaces vanish. Centering ourselves in the universe as a whole rather than in any part of it, we enter a dimension beyond the limits of our daily life, an infinite or n-dimensional space-time continuum.

Paradoxically, although our consciousness has burst its empirical boundaries and flows in a vastly expanded space, we are simultaneously more unified, less fragmented and less scattered than before. A tremendous power has gathered our energies and heightened them, focusing them as through a prism, resulting in renewed and unsuspected energy, clarity, and compassion. This state ideally favors healing, and not surprisingly all healers center themselves through some sort of meditation before proceeding to heal. This centering seems to filter out the interfering impurities spoken of earlier, and to make the healer a proper, i.e., an *impersonal channel* for the universal energy, for which such impurities constitute a barrier to which it must adapt, losing some of its intensity by having to move around the obstacles.

Meditation thus conceived is an active and dynamic force in the world, not withdrawal from it to some distant cave of indifference. The healing centeredness is a mysterious combination of high energy and absolute calm. It is both active and passive, movement and stillness, purposiveness without purpose, effortless effort. In short, the act of healing is meditation in motion.

THE PHILOSOPHER AS HEALER

The model of the healer as reconciler between the finite and infinite dimensions of reality seems to have been instinctively understood by the holistic philosophical frameworks referred to in this essay. The metaphor of the physician-healer figures prominently in these intuitively grounded systems of both East and West. Buddha and Plato, in particular, repeatedly compare the true philosopher to the physician. The latter is no mere dispenser of medicine, manipulating molecules of matter in some sort of mechanical enterprise. The engineer, of the scientific or the "social" Skinnerian variety, who operates on levers and pulleys of a machine whose workings he conceives along mechanistic principles, though he may be of help to others, is not a healer. His mechanistic paradigm, faulty according to the Healing Hypothesis, is a symptom of fragmentation, the selfsame disorder as the disease. The physician-healer, by contrast, is the sage, conscious of the supersensible reality to which he lives attuned in thought, word, and deed. The consequent wholeness and harmony of his being make him the natural conduit for the healing energies of nature.

The Pythagorean-Platonic, Buddhist, or Spinozistic model of the philosopher has intuited not only the universal harmony but also—sage that he is—gained insight into the root causes of organismic disharmony. His prescription for health involves the restoration of harmony through right living (ethics), resulting in a life of altruism enhanced by moderation and balance. In the light of this, recovery from illness entails simultaneous recovery from philosophical blindness, symbolized by Plato's Cave, and by Buddha's metaphor of ignorance as a knife-wound in ailing humanity's back. To be sure, partial recovery is possible, as noted, but it can bring us only a diminished state of disease. In the esoteric tradition of philosophy, restoration to total health is return to a pristine state of wholeness involving all creation and, above all, union with the ultimate source. This state is the birth-right of the whole person, open to us all.

BIBLIOGRAPHY

Achterberg, J., O.C. Simonton, and S. Simonton. *Stress, Psychological Factors, and Cancer.* Fort Worth: New Medicine Press, 1976.

Bohm, David. The Enfolding-Unfolding Universe. *Revision: A Journal of Knowledge and Consciousness,* 1978, 1, 3-4; Also: personal communications 1979.

Capra, Fritjof. *The Tao of Physics.* Boulder: Shambhala, 1975.

Govinda, Lama Anagarika. *Foundations of Tibetan Mysticism.* New York: Samuel Weiser, Inc. 1969.

Koestler, Arthur, and J.R. Smythies. *Beyond Reductionism: New Perspectives in the Life of Sciences.* London: Hutchinson and Co., Ltd., 1969.

Kunz, Dora. Healing Workshops. Craryville, New York, 1976, 1977, 1978.

Kunz, F.L. The Reality of the Non-Material. *Main Currents in Modern Thought,* 20, 2, 1963.

Leadbeater, C.W. *The Chakras,* Adyar, India: Theosophical Publishing House, 1927.

Meek, George W. Toward a General Theory of Healing. *Healers and the Healing Process.* Wheaton, Illinois: Theosophical Publishing House, 1977.

Monod, Jacques. *Le hasard et la necessite.* Paris: Editions du Seuil, 1970.

Plato. *The Dialogues of Plato,* tr. B. Jowett. New York: Random House, 1937.

Powell, A.E. *The Etheric Double.* Wheaton, Illinois: Theosophical Publishing House, 1969.

Pribram, Karl. *Languages of the Brain,* Englewood Cliffs: Prentice Hall, 1971.

Pribram, Karl. Problems concerning the structure of consciousness. In G. Globus (Ed.), *Consciousness and the Brain.* New York: Plenum Press, 1976.

Pribram, Karl. Holographic memory: Karl Pribram interviewed by Daniel Coleman. *Psychology Today,* 12, 9, February 1979.

Schrodinger, Erwin. *What Is Life* and *Mind and Matter.* Cambridge: Cambridge University Press, 1969.

Simonton, O.C., S. Simonton, J. Creighton. *Getting Well Again.* Los Angeles: J.P. Tarcher, Inc. 1978.

Smith, E. Lester. *Intelligence Came First.* Wheaton, Illinois: Theosophical Publishing House, 1975.

Skinner, B.F. *Walden Two*. New York: MacMillan Publishing Co., 1948.

Spinoza, Baruch. *Ethics*. In John Wild (Ed.), *Spinoza Selections*. New York: Charles Scribner's Sons, 1930.

Teilhard de Chardin, P. *The Phenomenon of Man*. New York: Harper, 1959.

Tiller, William A. Theoretical Modeling on the Functioning of Man. In George W. Meek (Ed.), *Healers and the Healing Process*. Wheaton, Illinois: Theosophical Publishing House, 1977.

Tiller, William A. Radionics, Radiesthesia, and Physics. Sausalito: Big Sur Recordings, 1975.

Weber, Renée. The Reluctant Tradition: Esoteric Philosophy East and West. *Main Currents in Modern Thought*, 29, 1, 1972.

Weber, Renée. The Good, the True, the Beautiful: Are They Attributes of the Universe? *Main Currents in Modern Thought*, 32, November 1975.

Weber, Renée. The Enfolding-Unfolding Universe: Dialogue with David Bohm. *Revision: A Journal of Knowledge and Consciousness*, 1, 3-4, 1978.

Weber, Renée. Field Consciousness and Field Ethics. *Revision: A Journal of Knowledge and Consciousness*, 1, 3-4, 1978.

II

Unseen Sources
of Healing

The physicians and psychiatrists whose articles fall in this section agree that both illness and healing are not merely mechanical processes, that many nonphysical factors are involved. Hogben looks at illness as a maladaptive response to stress, while Edmunds sees it as a strain between mind and body calling for inner adjustment. Bendit, with Jung, sees illness as resulting from misalignment with one's spiritual nature. Siegel's view encompasses all of these within his view of disease as a message to change and redirect one's life.

All these authors recognize emotion, motivation, and attitude as central in both health and disease. Among disease-producing factors mentioned are stress, despair, deep unconscious fear, and spiritual emptiness that can lead to feelings of isolation, anxiety, guilt, and rage. Health-promoting factors include peace of mind, love, forgiveness, acceptance, elation, a sympathetic bridge between doctor and patient. Bengtsson points out the effectiveness of the deliberate use of one's power of thought in a positive, healthful way.

These medical practitioners all agree that there is a spiritual dimension in healing. They use the techniques of medicine to the best of their ability as well as common sense, but they perceive deeper streams flowing as the vital energies of patients are restored, along with psychological well-being. Some see the deep strata of the patient as the source of spiritual healing, while others attribute it to God. In both cases, they share the orientation of bringing spirituality into the healing process.

4

Spiritual Aspects
of the Healing Arts

BERNARD S. SIEGEL, M.D.,
WITH BARBARA H. SIEGEL

In an intuitive way, I believe from the time life begins one is aware of the true nature of healing, or the fact that it is not mechanical or remedy oriented. A mother's touch, kiss, or a doctor's phone call suddenly bring relief. We begin to become aware of the interplay of psyche and soma.

From the outset one must understand that all healing is scientific. The problem is science's inability to measure or document what occurs. A typical example is the so-called spontaneous remission of an incurable cancer. I would rather have this spontaneous event retitled creative or self-induced healing, or hard work miracle. The former title turns aside the health practitioner's curiosity since it doesn't fit his scientific knowledge or his belief system. Solzhenitsyn wrote of self-induced healing in *Cancer Ward* (Farrar, Straus, Giroux, 1969):

> Kostoglotov... [said] ... "we shouldn't behave like rabbits and put our complete trust in doctors. For instance, I'm reading this book." He picked up a large, open book from the window sill. "Abrikosov and Stryukov, *Pathological Anatomy,* medical school textbook. It says here that the link between the development of tumors and the central nervous system has so far been very little studied. And this link is an amazing thing! It's written here in so many words." He found the place. "' It happens rarely,

but there are cases of self-induced healing.' You see how it's
worded? Not recovery through treatment, but actual healing.
See?"
There was a stir throughout the ward. It was as though "self-
induced healing" had fluttered out of the great open book like
a rainbow-colored butterfly for everyone to see, and they all
held up their foreheads and cheeks for its healing touch as it
flew past.
"Self-induced," said Kostoglotov, laying aside his book. He
waved his hands, fingers splayed. . . . "That means that suddenly for some unexplained reason the tumor starts off in the
opposite direction! It gets smaller, resolves and finally disappears! See?"
They were all silent, gaping at the fairy tale. That a tumor, one's
own tumor, the destructive tumor which had mangled one's
whole life, should suddenly drain away, dry up and die by itself?
They were all silent, still holding their faces up to the butterfly.
It was only the gloomy Podduyev who made his bed creak and,
with a hopeless and obstinate expression on his face, croaked
out, "I suppose for that you need to have . . . a clear conscience."

To understand how to fit spirituality into the healing process
or to recognize its place, let me take a step back and describe
present medical training.

Young men and women are accepted into medical school
based upon their ability to take tests and accumulate knowledge. (Hopefully they also have an interest in people.) They
are then taught about disease and its treatment. Little if any
time is given to the study of their feelings and how to deal
with people.

They are oriented into a failure system, meaning, we fill
our time, offices, and hospitals with people who don't do well,
and we do more to them if their first treatment fails. We fight
disease with the poor patient as the battleground. If a patient
does well, we do not see him again, and if he gets well when
he is not supposed to, we tell him it isn't necessary for him to
return, or ignore his recovery as being mystical. Any good
business would study success, but medicine ignores it. We
should be knocking on survivors' doors saying, "Why didn't
you die when you were supposed to?" We should be teaching
the messages all surviors know. By survivors, I mean survivors

of disease, concentration camps, tragic life events, or other disasters.

The students become more mechanics than healers. They are taught what to do to people who are sick and little about why people get sick. They are, therefore, given the unspoken role of lifesavers. Again, this sets them up for failure, since everyone ultimately dies. The healthcare provider, therefore, withdraws from the patient so the eventual failures will be less painful. He, therefore, does not become aware of what truly occurs when one lives with disease. He has little contact with the healing process or its absence. The disease can never become a motivator for change in this setting.

I felt very unhappy as a mechanic-lifesaver. I knew from my childhood that there was more to the healing process. I knew doctors were not always right in sentencing people to death. My mother was told not to become pregnant or she would die. A case of hyperthyroidism had her weighing ninety pounds, and an obstetrician thought a pregnancy would be life threatening.

To make a long story short, she found another obstetrician who agreed to work with her if she gained weight. After she gained thirty pounds she conceived. I was born and the hyperthyroidism disappeared. It was hard for me to not be accepted and loved by my parents after a beginning like that. In any event, this love was a handicap for a doctor, as it didn't fit into the medical model to which I was exposed. Nowhere in medical school was any time spent discussing why one becomes a doctor. I practiced medicine for a decade with a heavy heart trying to fit love and spirituality into my practice. I inquired into other professions for a possible career change until a cancer patient made me aware of the people I was caring for. As strange as this may sound I saw diseases in the waiting room not people. Once I began to orient my practice to people, my life and my practice changed. Patients came in and said, "Now I can talk to you." When my belief system changed it was safe for them to talk about the spiritual and mystical events related to their illnesses.

Initially, I sent letters to one hundred patients inviting them to begin meeting in groups to deal with their lives with an holistic approach. I expected hundreds of responses and had only twelve. I realized that of the people I saw and see with chronic or catastrophic illness, about twenty percent are the truly exceptional patients or survivors. This may vary in different living areas depending on how independent and how used to participating in their own lives they are. The exceptional patient or survivor is willing to take responsibility for his problem.

To learn the kind of person I was dealing with I began to ask four simple questions. 1) Do you want to live to be 100? (A simple question about feeling in control and looking forward to life.) 2) What does your disease mean to you? (Is it a challenge or a death sentence?) 3) Why did you need the illness? (What is it providing you with? Nurturing and love as do our sick days at work?) 4) What happened in the year or two before you became sick? (This lets the patients know how they participate in an illness by not meeting their needs. It makes them responsible for change if they wish to accept the responsibility.)

The mechanic would treat the illness and not look at who was sick. The healer/teacher says who are you? Who were you? And what brings you to this point? We have the opportunity to lead people on new pathways to help them with their rebirth.

Illness or pain is a message to change. In an all inclusive way I used the phrase, "Everyone has his cancer, either emotional or physical." From this ground we have the option to either promote change and healing, or see it as a catastrophe or death sentence. I choose the former, and I offer it to my patients.

Since the medical profession is failure-oriented, it tends to say to people, "don't ask why you became ill"; it will make you feel that it is your fault, that you are a failure. I say the illness must be seen as a message to redirect your life, and, within this transformation, healing occurs.

I know the power of this transformation and the knowledge our inner voices, intuition, or unconscious minds can provide. For years I ignored it but kept getting a powerful personal message to uncover something. As a mechanic, therefore, I went to the barber and had my head shaved. Of course, having a bare head didn't solve the problem.

Two teachers helped me. (When you are ready a teacher will appear.) One was Elisabeth Kubler-Ross who, at a workshop, interpreted a spontaneous drawing of mine. It shows a fish out of water (a spiritual symbol) and a mountain covered with snow. (A white crayon utilized to portray snow on an already white piece of paper represents a symbolic cover-up.) What this drawing did was to show me what needed to be uncovered was not my head but my love and spirituality, and then I would no longer feel like a fish out of water. Prior to meeting Elisabeth, I attended a workshop with Carl and Stephanie Simonton and was told during a guided imagery exercise I would meet an inner guide. The mechanic in me said, "This is all ridiculous." And yet in the meditation along came George. George is a spiritual figure who guides me. Since then I have met other guides who have been seen by mediums. I only see the guides in imagery exercises and sense them around me, but mediums have seen them standing around me at my lectures or workshops. A new world opened up where a mechanic could exist no longer with his old belief system. By bringing this new belief system into my practice, my world, and the world of my patients changed. I realized that mind and body communicate by a symbolic language, and consequently I now utilize dreams and drawings as a regular part of my therapeutic and diagnostic approach. Mind, body, and spirit are considered as one unit. Being a highly skilled mechanic is important but true healing occurs only when psyche, soma, and spirit are integrated.

When you use this new approach patients begin to share with you the life events prior to their becoming ill. They realize the illness allows them to say no to demands they would have felt obligated to fulfill. However, when I offer people options for getting well most prefer the mechanical, "Cut it out I can get a babysitter" approach instead of one of changing their lifestyle. They say exercise and meditation may change family routine and the spouse will be angry.

> We would rather be ruined than changed.
> We would rather die in our dread

> than climb the cross of the moment and
> let our illusions die.
>
> W. H. Auden

The illness gives me a chance to teach people about un-conditional love: giving with no expectations because one chooses to give. Discipline and saying no are permitted between two people sharing this love. It is the conditional love upon which most of us are brought up, that leads to illness. We never *get* all the thank you's and praise we would like. It is having something to give that restores us and provides us with a reason for living, when what we are giving is unconditional love. Physical handicap or illness does not interfere with the ability to give love. Invariably the love is returned to us without our asking because people see the change and want to be closer to this new found peace.

Many of my patients who are physically quite ill, some near death, wonder why they still have so many visitors. I explain to them that their spirit is very much alive and that terminal is a state of mind. Their spirit and love attract others because the others see life not death and therefore are comfortable in their presence.

In 1926 Elida Evans in her book entitled *A Psychological Study of Cancer* said, "cancer is a symbol, as most illness is, of something going wrong in the patient's life, a warning to him to take another road." Those who take this new road find a new life, exceed expectations and sometimes are cured of incurable illness. The new lifestyle is the goal, not physical well-being. The latter is the traditional medical approach.

The physician can be a spiritual leader and help people be reborn. These same patients are not upset with you for not healing them physically, but they actually thank you for the new life and ability to love. They feel this way because you indeed have made them eternal in the only way possible.

The secret to being eternal is love. Thornton Wilder said, "and we ourselves shall be loved for a while and then forgotten but the love will have been enough, even memory is not necessary for love, there is a land of the living and a land of the dead and the bridge is love." It can be said in another way: to die but not to perish, that is eternity. Love teaches us how not to perish.

There is eternal life through love, yet part of the reason physicians have no need to deal with this problem is that unconsciously they believe doctors don't get sick or die. (This is an unconscious reason for many to become doctors, but it is never addressed during medical training.) There is a massive denial which keeps them from feeling what their patients feel and, therefore, from needing to face illness and death. For those who face these problems, the physician has little advice. When I asked God what to do when confronted with a patient with a serious illness whom I could help or God could heal, He said "Render unto the doctor what is the doctor's and unto God what is God's."

One patient, when confronted with a dismal future leading to the grave, asked her doctor (who made the prognosis), "But what can I do?" He replied, "You only have a hope and a prayer." She asked, "How do I hope and pray?" And he said, "I don't know, that's not my line." With my help she has learned to hope and pray. She has transcended her physical illness and her fears and now goes to her doctor to bring him life and love. He, incidentally, has become very busy making notes about her exceptional course.

Doctors' invulnerability is one aspect of the problem, and another is what I have labeled the "war and peace" aspect of medicine. The doctor sees God as coming in only when he feels helpless or hopeless, an unfortunate loss of the spiritual component of healing. Spirituality should not be relegated to "helpless" cases because it provides exceptional results and has cured the medically incurable.

Where can spirituality fit into a war on disease? How does the greatest healing power in the universe adjust to killing? Can healing occur in this environment? Listen to the language of medicine's war on illness: we kill, insult, assault, blast, and poison you and your body. All these are words with which doctors are comfortable. Tests have shown that eighty percent of all people are not comfortable killing, unless they have to kill to save the lives of loved ones. Neither are we comfortable in killing disease, since it is a part of us. There is only a small percentage of patients who are comfortable being aggressive towards something residing within.

The disease should be seen as a part of a personal growth process. We can use our white blood cells to consume the disease (nourish themselves on the disease) and we can grow psychologically because of the disease. This process then creates immune system changes which can lead us to healing and new life.

I believe diseases are a response to loss and have often thought of the comparison to a salamander. Salamanders, incidentally, have very few cancers but do have the ability to regenerate and we have the opposite potential.

If a salamander has a loss it grows a new part. If we have a loss we grow a cancer or generate a disease. As one of my patients said, "I grew it to fill the emptiness inside of me."

If a salamander has an extensive cancer and its tail is cut off a new tail grows and the cancer returns to normal cells. By instructing my patients to grow I hope to stop the growth within them, restore them to normal and open a pathway to physical, mental, and spiritual health.

My therapeutic goal has more to do with peace of mind than physical healing. Why? Because that is the stuff of which miracles are made. W.C. Ellerbroek, former surgeon and now psychiatrist, feels that cancer miracles occur only when people are moribund or practically so. That is when they give up the despair and the healing process begins. (He has over five dozen well documented cases at last communication.) How sad to wait until one is almost dead to resolve conflict.

I try to teach this message to my patients. *Live* with a sense of time limitation. Decide things based upon the value of your time. Say what needs to be said, resolve conflicts and share openly the love you feel. What happens then?

One of my hospitalized patients told me she felt like dying. I said, "That's all right but please share this feeling with your children and your parents. They don't know how badly you feel." I came back after the weekend to see her and she looked wonderful. She had on make-up, a suit and her wig. I said, "What happened?" She answered, "I told my children how I felt. I told my parents how I felt and then I felt so good I didn't want to die." She was discharged from the hospital. I have seen other patients expected to die resolve their conflicts and be discharged with, as one patient said, "incredible energy." That is the power of love which resides in each of us. I have watched those who have learned to live leave their bodies. It is a peaceful, pain free process in which no time is really spent dying. It is a letting go. For this to occur two basic conditions must be met. The lifesaver/doctor must be instructed when to stop, and loved ones must give permission to the individual with the illness to fight or not. Finally, those with the illness are given permission to die when they no longer feel they are "living." Their survivors share their love and grief and the knowledge that they will be able to go on because of the shared love. This allows the life and death decision to be made by the individual free from the "don't die" messages we often give each other. If we give "don't die" messages death becomes a failure, something that must occur in secret when the loved ones and lifesavers are not present.

This then allows the individual the choice of a time to die and people with whom the event is shared. It allows family members to say, "It's all right to go." It allows them to see their loved one take one breath and die.

Being present at such a death makes one aware that it is a transition. The spirit leaves the body, the cocoon, and moves on. Scientists will describe this as the parasympathetic nervous system slowing and stopping bodily functions, but it doesn't look scientific, it looks spiritual when you are there.

> We shall not cease from exploration and the end of all our exploring will be to arrive where we started from and know that place for the first time.
>
> T. S. Eliot

Just as Solzhenitsyn in his book *Cancer Ward* sees spontaneous healing as a rainbow colored butterfly, so his unconscious knows that to heal one must deal with one's life spectrum (the rainbow) and shed the cocoon and become a new person (a butterfly) with a "clear conscience" as Podduyef says in the book.

This spontaneous change can more easily occur when we open to God's healing energy. Once a patient of mine returned to the office free of an incurable cancer and said, "I left my troubles to God." I now had a therapy to share with others.

However, if God said to you "be happy!" what would most of us do? We would ask for an exception in our case. Why? Because if God only knew our life and troubles He wouldn't ask us to be happy; He would allow us to be victims and an exception to his rule of happiness.

If one conceives of God as an intelligent, loving light, and if one opens to this light, true healing of mind, body, and spirit can occur. My fantasy is that someday our nuclear physicists will become our theologists when they discover this ultimate source of intelligent, loving energy. A new specialty of theological physics will then exist.

I have long felt the absence of God from our hospitals. Notice the absence of signs of spirituality in a hospital not run by a religious order. One of my associates, Richard Selzer, a surgeon and writer, shares my feeling eloquently in his short story "Absence of Windows." He states, "I very much fear that, having bricked up our windows, we have lost more than the breeze; we have severed a celestial connection." In this article he was discussing the removal of the windows from the operating room.

How do we reestablish this connection? Obviously not by bringing windows back but by creating a healing, spiritual environment. I personally use music as a way of reestablishing this connection. Since biblical times this quality of music has been known. It creates a mental state conducive to healing, as well as a greater awareness of the true nature of healing and our common source.

It is my belief that music creates a healing rhythm within the body, a harmony of all parts. I believe dreams and drawings reveal the symbolism of this rhythm. Healthy organs have their natural vibration based upon their molecular structure.

Disease changes this rhythm; disharmony occurs and it registers in the mind. To convert this to mental awareness symbols are used. If we pay attention to these symbolic messages we can diagnose disease at an earlier stage and, hopefully, learn to send healing messages or symbols back to the body. Historically, Carl Jung diagnosed physical illness based upon patients' dreams. And I have been able to do so with dreams or drawings. Frequently the patients are already aware of the dream contents'meaning and are simply sharing it with me. My patients' dreams and drawings reveal our common or collective unconscious, our common origin, our shared beginning with all men, and so the source of healing is of the same origin for us all.

What are the changes which create this environment conducive to healing—the introduction of laughter, music, love, forgiveness and acceptance—all coming after a release of resentment, conflict and despair. Every cell in the body is then involved in the healing process. When we laugh every cell laughs. When we love, our immune system feels the most vibrant live message it can receive and fights for our life. I say choose this course not in an attempt to try to live forever, but because of the beauty it brings to your life. It is God's work. If you choose to love you are a success. You will have days when you will disappoint yourself for not loving enough, but forgive and go on. It is the pilgrimage which is important and what we encounter along the way; not the necessity of reaching "sainthood" but striving towards it.

Emmett Fox has said:

> There is no difficulty that enough love will not conquer; no disease that enough love will not heal; no door that enough love will not open; no gulf that enough love will not bridge; no wall that enough love will not throw down; no sin that enough love will not redeem. . . .
>
> It makes no difference how deeply seated may be the trouble; how hopeless the outlook; how muddled the tangle; how great the mistake. A sufficient realization of love will dissolve it all. If only you could love enough you would be the happiest and most powerful being in the world.

To me the last sentence is the key. Some of us may feel like failures if we don't accomplish everything he suggests, but it is the exceptional person who chooses to attempt it and knows how hard it is. Yet it is this difficulty that allows us through shared pain to help each other. The person who chooses to be the family failure or life's victim is no help to others. He is always dying. Lovers are always living and feeling. Rilke has said, "Do not believe that he who seeks to comfort you lives untroubled among the simple and quiet words that sometimes do you good. His life has much difficulty and sadness and remains far behind yours. Were it otherwise he would never have been able to find those words."

To choose love is to bring into effect the spiritual healing force and source of life. I choose to live by Teilhard de Chardin's words. "Someday, after we have mastered the winds, the waves, the tides, and gravity, we shall harness for God the energies of love. Then, for the second time in the history of the world man will have discovered fire."

One could go on quoting the great men of history referring to the power of love and not convince anyone. I say to all of you, believe and see the change that occurs in your lives, or spend a lifetime being convinced and never seeing.

Science teaches us to see in order to believe and the spirit says believe and you will see. I know the latter to be true.

In my early years of practice, patients did not share either their healing or out of body and life after life experiences, and I wondered if any of this was true. When I changed my patients changed. Of course it was my change. Now they were free to share with a believer: A blind patient seeing as he watched his own resuscitation—an amputee being whole again and describing the beauty of where we are all going. Many of my patients have shared these incredibly moving and beautiful experiences that again remove fear and fill their lives with love. Their bodies being God's gifts they use them to the fullest before choosing to move on.

One patient of mine, a physician, was naturally very scientific and found it all hard to believe. When I asked him one day in the hospital, when he was quite ill, if he were ready to die, he said, "Considering the alternative, no." Three months after his death, a student came to interview me and gave me a card containing a message. She said she had been at a healing circle and told everyone she was going to interview me the following day. The medium present asked if there were a message for Dr. Siegel, and she wrote out the message she received on the card. The card said, "To Bernie from Frank, love and peace. If I had known it were this easy I'd have bought the package a long time ago. I wouldn't have resisted so much." The language on the card was Frank's way of referring to my teachings. He had never "bought the package."

To be handed this note helped me to believe. I only ask others to be open to this in their own lives and to see what occurs. Let this intuitive guiding force lead you on the correct path. I instruct my students that when they are on this path they will know; elevator doors will open without pushing the button, and people will appear whom you plan to call.

One stops judging what I call "spiritual flat tires," which are those events that delay you in order for you to meet someone you wouldn't have met if you hadn't had the "flat tire" event. I ask you to believe and see what occurs in your life. Live with a sense of time limitation, and, because of it, feel comfortable to say no without guilt. Love, be selfless, childlike, and see the love returned.

I can say that my attempt to help twelve of my patients (disciples), in our first "exceptional cancer patient" group, has led me to receive love from several continents. I have had the opportunity to love and heal so many more, including medical students and physicians, who are opening to this new light all because I wanted to give something to the world.

I would like to continue to share with all of you but space obviously limits the number of anecdotes and metaphors that can be included. Let me close with two quotes by Carl Jung whose work I consider one of my greatest resources. "Your picture of God or your idea of immortality is atrophied, consequently your psychic metabolism is out of gear." "Every problem, therefore, brings the possibility of a widening of consciousness, but also the necessity of saying goodbye to childlike unconsciousness and trust in nature."

It is time for medicine to get its psychic metabolism in gear and cast aside the guilt caused by leaving the garden of eden (trust in nature). We must become a success oriented healing discipline using the patient's illness as the "ticket of admission." Then, not mechanics but healers and teachers will redirect their lives on a healing pathway. You might ask me why I am still a surgeon. I still see my mechanical skills as a way of buying time for the healing process to happen. I know I can operate on patients and see them have less pain and fewer complications when we are a healing team, utilizing faith in ourselves, our treatment and our spiritual faith. Despite all that has been said up to this point, as a surgeon my feet remain on the ground. Patients do have complications and do die, but in the process I still have something to offer them. The mechanic would be at a loss and would probably desert them.

In closing, let me share a few words from a traditional Indian saying that sums up my message. "When you were born, you cried and the whole world rejoiced. Live such a life, that when you die the whole world cries and you rejoice." To accomplish this requires only a short time. As long as one is alive it can be accomplished, change can occur. Richard Bach the author of *Jonathan Livingston Seagull* has said, "Here is a test to find if your mission on earth is finished. If you're alive it isn't." Many children who die give the gift of love to their parents and it lasts them a lifetime. Others choose a lifetime of hate because of a similar loss. I can only ask as the Bible does, for you to choose life.

> If I am not for myself, who will be?
> If I am only for myself, what am I?
> If not now, when?
>   Martin Buber

5

Many Doors to Healing

OTELIA J. BENGTSSON, M.D.

Looking back over the last nearly one hundred years, it is interesting to note how many new approaches to healing have been enthusiastically received, each being a center of greatest interest for its moment, and then lessening to be succeeded by another. But like the ripples caused by a stone dropped into a still lake, the waves of help from each have moved in ever widening circles for years thereafter. We recall the discoveries in bacteriology; in nutrition and the effects of vitamin deficiency, endocrine abnormalities, wonder drugs in internal medicine and psychiatry, and psychosomatic investigations.

In this same period there was the rise of osteopathy, Christian Science, and kindred movements. Especially since World War II, in this country, there has been a genuine and markedly growing interest in spiritual healing both in and outside of the orthodox churches. The enthusiasts of each group seem to feel strongly that their approach is the main one. But it is probably true that though one may be dominant in a situation, healing benefits from all. While the psychological attitudes in medicine and healing interest me most, I would like first to call attention to the debt we owe to so-called physical medicine. Examples could be given from each of the groups, but we will choose only one.

Years ago I knew two elderly sisters. In their youth they had
a home in the country. The younger one wrote poetry and was
a singer. Her fiancé was a composer and a pianist. To the delight of the whole family he accompanied her as she sang her
own poems which he had set to music. Then tragedy struck,
the parents, brother, older sister, and fiancé all developed
typhoid. Only the younger sister escaped, and all but the older
sister died. Supposing a healer could have come and saved the
family. What a miracle it would have seemed! Yet, have we
not in this part of the civilized world been recipients of as
great a miracle? With the discovery of the typhoid bacillus,
the methods of its communication, and modern sanitation,
typhoid fever and tragedies such as mentioned above have
been practically wiped out. Yet typhoid is still occasionally
contracted. Recently an eleven-year-old girl became des-
perately ill. When it was proved that the disease was typhoid,
she was given large doses of a specific antibiotic and in twenty-
four hours her temperature was normal. Her mother said "It
was a miracle!" In the two previous years there had been only
two cases of typhoid reported in New York City. The discovery
of specific antibiotics for specific bacteria is a part of the most
recent circle of widening good from the bacteriological discoveries of a century ago. Think how much and how many
folks have been involved in this kind of healing by prevention!

At times somewhat humorous situations are created by
proponents of two opposite theories. One Sunday years ago,
when I was an intern, the young resident of the Salvation
Army hospital across the street came over to seek help from
our resident. A postoperative patient had developed a severe
atony of the intestines. The distention was so great that they
feared for his life. "The Salvation Army officers are praying
on every floor," said the resident. "Have you tried eserine?"
asked our doctor, who had just completed an internship in our
largest city hospital. They had not. It was not in the pharmacy
of either of the hospitals, but was obtained from a nearby
druggist who kept open on Sundays. It worked like magic.
Within a short time the patient was resting comfortably. The
next morning the resident from across the street came over to
relate the happy result. She said in a disgusted voice, "The

Army says it was an answer to prayer but, of course, it was the eserine."

I wonder! Could it not be both? Think of all the people connected with that recovery before the eserine reached the patient. The eserine comes from the calabar bean grown on vines in West Africa. There are those who raise the vines, the shippers, the large drug companies who import it, the chemists who know how to extract the active principle and put it into a pill containing one sixtieth of a grain, the druggist who bought it from the wholesaler and who was interested enough to keep open on Sunday, the Salvation Army who owned and dedicated the hospital and, finally, the nurses and doctors. At exactly the time when the patient's condition was desperate, through the agencies of all of these and countless others, the medication that started out in a bean in Africa was available on East Fourteenth Street in New York. It reminds me of the New Testament saying, "The Father knoweth what ye have need of before ye ask," and also the advice of the Chinese philosopher to open our eyes to the wonder of living.

At one of the conferences on spiritual healing at Wainwright House in Rye, New York, there were people of various disciplines: psychics, clergy, leaders of healing prayer groups, doctors, and physicists. The question was asked: "Can members of such a mixed group agree on what is necessary for spiritual healing?" One man answered, "Teach people to love," and the definition of love was given: "To love is to set free." So many of the present day illnesses, so frequently dubbed "diseases of civilization" are due to the tensions and anxieties of our modern age. Tensions are expressions of open or hidden fears. Love is the antidote for fear, as the following case perhaps illustrates. Years ago a professor in one of the medical schools wrote an article in the *Journal of the American Medical Association* reporting the case of a young man who came to the cardiac clinic. The man was found to have rather serious valvular disease and was advised to limit his work. This he claimed he could not do because he had a wife and child to support. He agreed, however, to report regularly to the clinic for observation. He came every few months and no change was found in his condition. When his little son was two years old the mother died of pneumonia. The man had to continue to work full time in order to support his son and the one who took care of him. Year after year this went on with little or no change in the cardiac condition, to the amazement of the doctors in the cardiac clinic. When the son was nineteen years old he was killed by an automobile. The father's heart deteriorated rapidly and in a few months he was dead. Was the love for the boy the healing and sustaining element all those years?

Or, in another instance, was it the love of a daughter which made a mother receptive to spiritual healing? Long before the day of the "pusher" a young mother with a seven-year-old daughter had become addicted to drugs. She was most frightened by the effect on her child. In desperation she decided to commit suicide to free her daughter from these effects. She had planned to jump in front of an elevated train. As she was climbing the stairs, the Salvation Army Band started to play. She turned around and went to their meeting. At the close of the meeting a Salvation Army Lass approached her. Putting her arms around the young addict mother she said, "Jesus loves you, won't you open your heart to him?" Together they went up front. While they knelt there the mother completely lost her desire for the drug and was healed. From then on she worked with the Army. Years later, on a radio broadcast, I heard her give a very vivid account of her healing.

At present the drug addiction among the young is a matter of great concern. Recently I heard a speaker comment on the fact that those healers who brought a religious element to bear seemed to get a more sustaining result. Twice on the radio in the last few months I have heard the work of the Teen Challenge movement very favorably spoken of. In order to understand how Teen Challenge came about, I heartily recommend for its amazing interest and sincerity the book *The Cross and the Switchblade,* by David Wilkerson, its chief founder.

Nor should the magnificent work of Alcoholics Anonymous be passed over when mentioning the approaches to healing in our time. Thousands of people have been made whole again through the activity of this splendid movement.

I feel also that I should touch on the work that has been done by spiritualistic mediums in giving advice which, when followed, has led either to complete restoration of health or to great improvement. I myself know about two such cases.

Everyone has heard about the amazing immediate cures of hopeless diseases at the shrine at Lourdes. One patient, as reported in orthodox medical literature, had extensive cavitation of the lungs and discharging sinuses of the bones from active tuberculosis. He was sent home to die. Friends helped to get him to the Shrine. He was instantly healed. Subsequent X-rays showed clean lungs and normal bones. He had only a slight skin scar over one bone. The result seems absolutely unbelievable but it was well verified.

While the restoration to complete physical wholeness is something that we ardently and earnestly work for, regardless of the particular discipline that we follow, there is another type of healing that is truly beautiful and awe-inspiring to watch. That is when the patient cannot be healed of the physical condition but his spirit is so sustained that he triumphs completely over his handicap. Sometimes these patients seem to act as a kind of "vicarious atonement" for other people. In the clinic we had a lawyer who, until he was twenty-three years old, was sound in body and mind. On a bicycle tour with a friend he had a very serious accident which resulted in a severe spastic paralysis. One eyelid was ptosed. His forearms were fixed in different positions so that he could not feed or dress himself, or get tokens from his pockets for the subway. There was an injury to the heat regulating center of his body so that, in the coldest weather, his shirt was wet with perspiration. He could walk, but with a very peculiar gait. But he could speak and practice law. I was told that everyone in the Woolworth Building downtown knew him.

When this young man came to the allergy clinic the other patients watched him. "Does he have allergies, too?" they would ask. He was as serene as if he had been blessed by some secret angel, and he conveyed his gentle spirit to all who saw him. While he was in the room the other patients all seemed to lose their complaints. In his presence theirs seemed to be too minor to speak about. It was as though they were temporarily healed by his courageous endurance of a very severe affliction.

There is a beautiful illustration of what I am trying to convey in Lloyd Douglas' book, *The Robe*. The questioning Marcellus heard the inspiring singing of a young lady. He had heard also of the wondrous healings that had taken place. Perhaps, he thought, this girl had been healed and that was why she sang so movingly! He sought her out and discovered that both her legs were paralyzed. The Master had completely changed her outlook on life. In his presence she had felt the fruits of the spirit, love and joy, and these she could convey in her singing, even though her legs were not healed.

The intense specialization in modern orthodox medicine has led to many important discoveries. Many lives have been saved that could not have been saved even fifty years ago. Every positive good seems also to have a negative aspect. In overemphasis on specialization, the consideration of the person as a whole is apt to be lost. This is one of the reasons why people are so happy to learn about healers and to seek them out.

There are individuals who have the gift of revitalizing exhausted etheric bodies, and others who not only have this gift but also seem to have higher abilities to heal. Still others, by clairvoyant insight, can make more accurate diagnoses than our coarser physical methods can achieve. By this method, an associate of mine has helped many. She can see the psychosomatic connection. Sometimes the patients are not aware of the kinks in their thinking and feeling mechanism. These may be relatively simple but the habits created by their constant repetition may undermine the health of the individual. My co-worker can point these out. Sometimes she has to say the same thing in a half-dozen different ways before the patient will admit that she is right. There always seems to be a lighthearted humor about the atmosphere which "salts" down the observation until the patient acknowledges it. This is followed by careful advice, suited to the ability of the person to carry it out. Practically always the patient leaves in a happy frame of mind. I brought to my associate a chronically ill patient whom I had known for several years. She laughed when the interview was drawing to a close. I was astounded. I suddenly realized that I had never seen her smile or laugh before.

Most of us cannot do such remarkably helpful work or be healers. But there are things that each and every one of us can do. In *At The Feet of The Master* we are advised: "Use your thought-power every day for good purposes.... Think each day of someone whom you know to be in sorrow, or suffering or in need of help, and pour out loving thought upon him. Learn to distinguish the God in everyone. . . . You can help your brother through that which you have in common with him, and that is the Divine Life; learn how to arouse that in him, learn how to appeal to that in him; so shall you save your brother from wrong. When you pour out your strength to help, there must be a result whether you can see it or not; if you know the Law you know this must be so." And about our own aches and pains, let us remember the saying of one of George Eliot's characters: "We are children of a large family and must learn as such children do, not to expect that our hurts will be made much of, to be content with little nurture and caressing and to help each other the more."

6

The Influence of the Unconscious on Healing

H. TUDOR EDMUNDS, M.D.

It is well known that numerous anomalies arise when treating the sick, how a particular method used with success in one case fails in another similar one, while on the other hand completely different methods of treatment, both orthodox and unorthodox, may have their successes in treating the same ailment. It would seem therefore that there must be a common factor which influences success or failure, and which acts more deeply than the actual method of treatment used.

Consider two well-known methods of treatment such as homeopathy and orthodox medicine which are completely opposed to each other in conception and technique and yet have numerous successes. The former uses extremely minute amounts of active substances which are often diluted to such a high degree that it can be proved there is not one single atom or molecule of the original substance in the tablet or liquid given to the patient; while in orthodox medicine potent chemicals are used which alter the metabolism of the body, or attack invading organisms which are regarded as the cause of the illness.

In the school of osteopathy all illnesses are regarded as being due to minute displacements of the spinal vertebrae which press on nerves emerging from the spinal cord and interfere with the vitality of the organs they control. Treatment then consists of adjustment by spinal manipulation.

SUCCESSES WITH FUNDAMENTALLY DIFFERENT TREATMENTS

There are numerous other methods of treatment which have their advocates and can claim many successes. One of the most popular at the present time is radiesthesia in which the patient supplies a drop of dried blood or saliva on a piece of filter paper which the practitioner places in a piece of apparatus that he claims enables him to determine the specific vibrations of the disease which he can diagnose without the patient's being present. He then passes an electric current through his apparatus in a way that he claims will radiate healing forces to the patient. It is also claimed that by these methods incipient disease can be diagnosed before it has caused the patient any symptoms of any kind, and that healing radiations can be sent out to him at any distance, which will neutralize the disease before it has manifested itself. In this way it is claimed that a person who is perfectly healthy and active can be cured of a disease he has not yet developed but would in the future if he had not had radiesthesia treatment.

Among other popular healing systems based on different theories or beliefs are the ancient Chinese method of acupuncture, the wearing of different kinds of charms; or even the burying in the garden of a piece of bacon-rind at the exact moment of the full moon; but strange as these methods may seem, the interesting fact is that they all have their successes.

We must add to these the numerous cases on record where treatment has failed when carried out by clever physicians with considerable knowledge, that have later been cured by methods based on pure superstition.

These undisputed facts force us to look deeper for the causes of human ailments, but before the factors common to these very diverse methods of treatment can be ascertained, the constitution of Man in his totality must be studied.

H. Tudor Edmunds

THE EVOLUTIONARY PERFECTION OF THE PHYSICAL BODY

This takes us far back into the evolution of the animal kingdom which provided us with the physical bodies we inhabit today. The mammalian body is probably the most wonderful creation of evolution on this planet, and it has taken very many millions of years to reach this degree of perfection. The animal is remarkably complex yet works with such superb harmony that in its natural animal state it enjoys perfect unself-conscious health. All its functions are controlled by an elaborate system of reflexes, working on a plan of the utmost wisdom, which enables the animal to satisfy all its needs in the ever-changing environment in which it finds itself. If it is injured by accident or attack, its tissues and bones have latent powers of self-regeneration which come into play the moment an injury occurs. If harmful bacteria or viruses invade its body, its highly complex, and well organized, chemical system creates the exact specific antibody which will kill the invader but do no damage to its own living cells; moreover, once it has had such an experience, it stores up an excess of the antibodies it has manufactured, in order to be still more prepared for a future attack by similar microorganisms should such an attack occur.

If seasonal changes in an animal's environment necessitate *its* moving to other parts of the globe, the highly sensitive reflexes in its controlling nervous center cause it to migrate to those parts most suited to its needs.

And lastly, in order that its particular species shall not become extinct, elaborate systems of hormone stimuli enable it to reproduce its kind at times and in circumstances which give greatest protection to its young.

All these things take place instinctively, and unself-consciously, always adjusting themselves to fortuitous changes that may take place at any time, so any contingency that may arise—apart from something catastrophic—is provided for in a remarkably comprehensive way that only a tremendous intelligence could have devised.

At the same time as the physical body evolves, the animal

develops an emotional system which helps it to create the subtler reflexes needed for the finer adjustments of its daily life.

Such feelings as pain, fear, and alertness help to protect it from external dangers, while affection and protectiveness cause it to preserve the family unit. Nourishment and rest are controlled by hunger and fatigue, and the joy of living acts as a general incentive to healthy activity.

When this physical animal body with its attendant emotional mechanism finally reached perfection, man took charge of it for himself, and added to it his self-conscious mind—a mind having the power to overrule the natural instincts of the body. But whereas his body was the result of millions of years of experience, his mind was a new and untried instrument, lacking both wisdom and experience, and thus causing a state of unbalance from the very beginning of his existence.

CONFLICT BETWEEN BODY AND MIND

This struggle between mind and body still obtains today, and it seems that man's main purpose at this state of his cosmic evolution is to bring his conscious mind to the same state of perfection as that of his unconscious body, so that the two will work in harmony, and not as antagonists, as so frequently happens.

When there is strain between body and mind, the forces of life welling up deeply within are obstructed in varying degrees and at different levels as they flow outwards. Such impediments to the passage of vitality cause weakness and congestion at the sites of obstruction, giving rise to ill-health at those particular levels. Strains and impediments of this kind, between the body and its mento-emotional component, can be brought about in many different ways.

Man, with his perfect physical instrument, but untried mind, is impatient and anxious to exercise the latter's powers and experiment with life. Unfortunately he lacks wisdom and experience, and so does many foolish things, interfering with the harmony of himself and the surroundings in which he lives, indulging his sensations for the pleasure and excitement they bring, rather than using them as a guide to the needs of his body. This leads to pain and ill-health at the levels of his being where he has gone astray, and so the forces of reaction are called into play and gradually compel him to seek out his errors and remedy the disharmony he has created, thus bringing him back once more to a state of good health.

Now the very nature of the inertia and density of physical matter necessitates a great effort on the part of the spirit of man to bring about such an adjustment, and the magnitude of this effort impresses his inner nature with the importance of all the factors concerned, so that they become a permanent part of him—in fact, a small fragment of wisdom—and in this way he evolves.

ILLNESS IS BENEFICENT

Illness from the theosophical viewpoint is thus seen to be a beneficent, adjusting process of the inner man bringing about spiritual harmony, and not just bad luck or misfortune.

Health, like everything else in life, follows basic karmic laws, so it is impossible to go against these laws and then think that some new healing method, or wonder drug, will quickly restore good health and excuse one from dealing with the original mistakes. Nature cannot be deceived or bribed; but she welcomes cooperation in her work.

It follows from this that all disease is psychosomatic when viewed cosmically, though this is by no means always apparent, owing to the difficulty at times of discerning at what level of man's complex being the flow of life has been obstructed and has led to the manifestation of a particular illness.

Yet the list of physical ailments recognized by orthodox medicine as being psychosomatic, grows longer almost daily as the relationship between man's psyche and his ailments continues to become clearer.

In mentioning a few of these common complaints, gastric and duodenal ulcers, caused by prolonged anxiety, perhaps head the list. Asthma and eczema are often due to deep *unconscious* fear of some aspect of life, while a raised blood pressure with its secondary ill effects of hemorrhage and paralysis can be brought about by prolonged worry at the conscious level; and even simple obesity often results from seeking, by overeating, a happiness in life that is otherwise lacking.

In all these cases so far we have been considering *chronic* diseases, but when we look at *acute* infections, they seem to be distinctly physical, without any traces of mental origins. However, on deeper consideration we find that the continuous ignoring of simple laws of health such as overworking, over-indulgence, lack of fresh air or exercise, will ultimately bring about an acute illness owing to the accumulation of toxic products in the system. In such attacks, pathogenic micro-organisms of various kinds may take an active part by living on these accumulated waste products, and in turn add their own toxic substances to the total mass of poisons. Immediate treatment in such cases is often begun by administering remedies and antibiotics and similar substances to destroy the infecting bacteria, or to hold up their rapid multiplication, until the body has had time to develop its defenses. In this way a severe case of pneumonia may be prevented from reaching a fatal termination by the administration of penicillin in the early stages, but the fact that the penicillin has not *cured* the disease can be seen by the long convalescense which follows —it has simply gained time by stopping a rapid chain reaction.

CHRONIC PSYCHOSOMATIC DISEASES

Returning to *chronic* psychosomatic cases, the cooperation of the patient is vital if a cure is to be effected. With a certain amount of self-examination and sympathetic assistance from the healer, the patient may often discover some habit, or rigid attitude of mind, or discord in his life, which is acting as a vital obstruction which is the main cause of his trouble. By altering such a condition, or if that is beyond his power, adjusting himself to it, the illness will gradually disappear.

There are times, however when a man finds the difficulties of life too great to bear in their fullness and unconsciously seeks escape from the responsibility of dealing with more than he can stand. This fear of the burden of living can interfere with the flow of vitality at the mento-emotional level and so bring about some *chronic* physical ailment which will lessen his everyday responsibilities, and relieve him of his more subtle fears. Such an illness can only be cured when he has grown in strength sufficiently to face life's problems in their totality. Until that time arrives, no method of treatment will cure him, though it may bring some degree of relief.

There is another factor to be borne in mind in cases of chronic ill-health, especially when it occurs early in life, and probable causes cannot be found. In such an instance, the karmic forces which brought about the present illness probably had their origin in a previous existence where circumstances were such that the process of readjustment did not have sufficient time to complete its work, which had to be continued in the present incarnation.

The time taken for an illness of this kind to be cured may last from a few months to a whole lifetime, depending on the magnitude of the original forces of disharmony which were generated. The treatment, however, will still be the same as if those forces had had their origin in the present incarnation, though they will probably be more deep-seated, and so more difficult to eradicate.

THERE IS NO PANACEA

We see therefore that the process of healing is the relieving of these obstructions, and is not dependent on any particular system such as homoeopathy, allopathy, or osteopathy. *Any* treatment, whether orthodox or unorthodox, which will bring about this release of vitality at the required level in a particular case will also bring about a healing result, provided the patient is willing to be cured deep down within himself, and gives his cooperation.

The *causes* of disease can be placed under four main headings:

Accidents and Mistakes: When something harmful is done inadvertently.

Ignorance: Probably the greatest cause of all, due to the limitations of the mind with its lack of wisdom.

Fear: When appearing as a normal function, and without

exaggeration, it is essentially protective and beneficent. But when it is the result of ignorance, it tends to grow out of all proportion, causing vital restriction and tension at the emotional level, which in turn is reflected in the physical body, bringing about disorders of various systems and organs. Paralysis and various forms of heart strain are common examples, as are probably all neuroses.

Self-indulgence: This, like exaggerated fear, is a subtle form of ignorance, for if man were completely wise, he would enjoy his bodily functions without ever carrying them to excess, knowing that Nature cannot be tricked and would exact a painful price sooner or later if he went beyond his instinctive needs. Self-indulgence may have a known harmful element from the first, such as the use of tobacco, alcohol, and other pleasurable drugs; of this fact the victim is aware, but considers the pleasure obtained worth the price he later has to pay, or he thinks he may be lucky in some way in avoiding it. On the other hand his indulgence may be of a harmless nature, except when carried to excess as in overeating or overactivity.

In all these cases there is a common belief that one can escape from the law of karma by paying a chemist or doctor to supply a medication which will neutralize all evil consequences. Such a belief is illusory, for the remedies can only ease symptoms, not remove the results of one's actions.

The frequent refusal of man to accept the responsibility for his own actions is well illustrated by the person who deludes himself that his overweight and breathing difficulties are due to some capriciousness of nature, and so willingly goes to a nursing home to be starved for a fee, rather than admit his responsibility and starve at home for nothing!

RELIEF IS MORE COMMON THAN CURE

Thus it will be seen that the healer is often restricted by the patient's attitude of mind as to how much help he can give, and has to be satisfied with giving some degree of relief, rather than bring about a radical cure. Even the great healer of the New Testament, who was ever ready to help suffering humanity, recognized this limitation, never trying to force his curative powers on the sick, but said to everyone in need, "I stand at the door and knock." Thereafter it was the patient himself who had to do the initial opening.

In all matters of therapy one great fact must constantly be borne in mind: that it is nature that does the actual healing; man can merely ease nature's way by cooperating with her, just as a gardener creates the best conditions of soil and environment for his plants to grow to the most perfect expression of what is inherent in them. But however hard he may try, he cannot create a new rose or lily from chemicals and soil.

The greatest of surgeons, performing a very delicate operation, does not cure the patient but simply prepares the ground by removing diseased tissues, or by re-adjusting those which are displaced, and so leaving them in the most suitable condition for nature to carry out her healing processes.

There are various ways in which a physician can help his patient. Sometimes by simple advice, but much more often by sympathetic and compassionate understanding. Such an attitude brings about an atmosphere of harmony on all levels of consciousness, enabling the sufferer to relax inwardly and often release some of the tension causing his illness, without realizing what has happened. But more than this, the healer will have created a bridge between himself and the patient along which the healer's own harmonizing forces can travel to the sufferer and reinforce the latter's curative powers.

THE SYMPATHETIC BRIDGE

This sympathetic bridge between doctor and patient is probably the most important factor in personal healing of any kind. It inspires faith in the patient, and enhances the effect of any physical remedy that may be used, whether the latter has useful powers of its own as in medicines, massage, radiant heat, and things of like nature, or in itself is useless but is believed by both to be efficacious. It is this sympathetic bridge-factor which sometimes appears to cause a useless remedy to bring about a cure when a more reliable remedy has failed, the healing power being not in the remedy used, but in the sympathetic understanding created, and the positive desire to help on the part of the healer. This enables the latter to help on the subtler planes of consciousness, and also makes of him a channel for some of nature's healing forces to pass through to the patient.

Since this sincere wish to help can act equally well at a distance once the bridge of sympathy has been established, and the patient fully wishes to cooperate, the process can be carried on continuously and the results may often be spectacular.

It can now be seen why the same ailment may appear to be cured in one case by the use of a box which is supposed to radiate health; in another by a drug; in another by an inert tablet; and in a fourth by prayer.

The remedy used may be simply a dramatic means of gaining the faith and cooperation of the patient, or it may in addition have some curative or alleviating action in itself such as the application of warmth, or an injection of a pain-relieving drug.

Sometimes the remedies have to be administered in stages as when dealing with a severe emotional conflict. In such a case it may be impossible to create a sympathetic rapport with the patient owing to his preoccupying agitation, until he has first of all been given a sedative. Then when he is calmer it will be possible to communicate with him and proceed with a deeper treatment. If a cure results, the patient is quite likely to be mistakenly led into thinking that the success of his treatment was due to the drug that was used rather than the resolution of his emotional difficulties.

DANGERS OF NON-SEQUITUR REASONING

This non-sequitur reasoning is extremely common in health matters, and has to be guarded against with the utmost diligence when seeking the true causes of illness and their most suitable treatments. There is a great temptation to jump to general conclusions from a single success, especially when the treatment has been a little unusual.

Chronic diseases particularly lend themselves to this fallacy when a number of remedies have failed and a final one seems to succeed.

We may take, for example, a chronic skin disease like psoriasis for which there is no known medical cure, but only medical alleviation. It is a distressing disease aesthetically, for although not painful or infectious large dry, scaly patches appear on the arms, legs and body, and may last from a few weeks to a few years. It has one redeeming feature, however, in that sooner or later it disappears *spontaneously*.

It does not take much imagination to realize how frustrated a young person of either sex must feel on being unable to go swimming or sunbathing or to play tennis, and, in the case of a woman, to wear evening dress. A young girl suffering from psoriasis, and having tried orthodox remedies without success, is likely to turn to magazine advertisements and quack remedies for help. When these in turn fail she is likely to feel desperate. If at that time it should happen that a gypsy met her and promised to cure her for a small remuneration, one would not be surprised if she jumped at the chance. Supposing the gypsy then told her with great seriousness that she was to put a spot of honey, which must be heather honey, on the rim of her left ear when going to bed each night, and that she was then to go to sleep on her right side, and that in a little while the skin would become normal, she would almost certainly do as she was told.

If, to her delight and amazement, the psoriasis disappeared during the next three or four weeks it would be natural for her to give entire credit to the gypsy for her cure. Yet what would actually have happened is that the disease had run its course and would have disappeared at that time in any case, whether treated or not, but probably no one would ever be able to convince that girl that the honey had nothing to do with it, especially when a particular honey had been recommended; for as Poobah remarked in "The Mikado," the introduction of such a detail "is intended to give artistic verisimilitude to an otherwise bald and unconvincing narrative!"

I think we can now see that the work of the ideal healer is threefold.

In the first place he tries to discover the level in the patient's consciousness of the causal obstruction, and its exact nature, and then helps the patient, if possible, to resolve it. This as a rule is a very difficult process and takes a long time, so that his immediate concern is to alleviate the pain and discomfort caused by the ailment.

Because of the difficulties of everyday life this *concentration on the relief of unpleasant symptoms is the chief method of treatment today,* and it is only when the patient can spare the time, and is willing to give his full cooperation in a spirit of optimism, that the deeper causes of chronic sickness can be dealt with and a complete cure brought about.

NATURE—THE REAL HEALER

Lastly, the therapist uses his knowledge and skill to assist nature—the real healer—to have the best possible conditions for her work of reconstruction.

These three factors are so intimately connected that success in one helps the others. Even the simple treatment of unpleasant symptoms will often enable the patient to examine his own mind and personality more clearly than he could when distracted by suffering. In such a case the administration of a powerful and crude sedative such as morphia, though poisonous, may do far more good in the early stages than more delicate and refined treatments which would fail while the patient was wracked with pain, or in a state of severe mental agitation.

When we consider common remedies in use today, we find that many of them come under the category of relievers of pain and distress, rather than methods of cure, and in judging their usefulness it is most important to avoid non sequitur conclusions, by testing each remedy over and over again.

THE POWER OF SUGGESTION

The power of suggestion in man is highly developed, as every witch doctor or advertiser of commercial products is well aware, and it is a common experience that when a new method of treatment is put on the market, it always has numerous successes in its early days, even though at a later date it may be found to be useless or even harmful.

An interesting experiment illustrating this principle was done by the Royal College of General Practitioners in England a little while ago in connection with plantar warts, those most annoying and painful nodules which school children often get in the soles of their feet. They are not at all serious, but they are very incapacitating.

One hundred and twenty people of various ages, suffering from plantar warts (veruccas), were divided into three equal groups. The first group was given formalin lotion to apply daily (this being the favorite treatment at the time); the second group was given a lotion to apply daily, consisting of plain water; and the third group was given an inert tablet to take daily. They were not told the nature of their respective remedies and were asked to continue treatment for six weeks and then return for examination. At the subsequent examination it was found that 60 percent had recovered in each group. And so one is forced to conclude that in this particular experiment either the power of suggestion, or the natural rate of spontaneous recovery, not the remedy, was responsible for the cure.

Of course, many remedies do have alleviating properties of their own, and are useful for relieving the symptoms of everyday minor illnesses, but one must be careful to bear in mind that a treatment is not more efficacious because it is mysterious, or unusual, such as treatment by honey—especially heather honey! A sprained ankle is better treated with a cold compress, and perhaps gentle massage, than with colored light administered by a clairvoyant!

LACK OF PREJUDICE ESSENTIAL

It is all a matter of common sense and the willingness to use any remedy one thinks is best in all the circumstances. It is also quite fallacious to believe that the particular system one happens to favor is better than all others, because by doing so the patient is denied the fullest degree of help to which he is entitled.

One can sum up by saying that in all cases of illness that are really cured, it is the patient himself, working in cooperation with nature, and perhaps with the assistance of others, who actually brings about the resolution of his own ailment. Without his cooperation and desire to get well, *all* methods of healing will fail.

On the other hand, if for any of these reasons it is not possible to bring about a complete cure, it is usually possible to give him considerable relief, and make his life much happier and easier.

Fortunately for all of us, there are also great and wise beings who watch closely over the welfare of the human race, and who are ever ready to pour their healing forces into us whenever we turn our attention towards them.

Sometimes these harmonizing forces are directed to us through the compassion of our fellow men; at other times they well up within us from the depths of our being. But however they arrive we can take heart from the fact that the guardians of humanity are always near those who suffer, ever ready to bring them ease and comfort in their distress, when possible.

So in spite of our follies, our perversities, and rebellious minds, we will always be helped by those wiser than we are, until such time as we ourselves will have grown in wisdom and spiritual stature and cause sickness to be banished forever.

7

Spiritual Awareness as a Healing Process

GEORGE L. HOGBEN, M.D.

Every day, during my hospital visits and office hours, I see people with a variety of physical and mental conditions. Some have severe catastrophic reactions which threaten imminent death. Others endure chronic degenerative diseases which slowly destroy the individual's will. Many experience physical symptoms without distinct anatomical changes.

Each person, no matter how severe the condition, relates a history of stress generated by the usual temporal stressors: loss of a loved one; job failure; career success; marriage; relocation; divorce; and so forth. The stress provokes an intense maladaptive physical-mental reaction leading ultimately to the disease state.

However, as the ill person and I work through the role of the stress in the illness, we invariably become aware of something within the person which is more fundamental to his becoming ill than the stress itself. This internal state seems to prepare the individual to react to the temporal stress with illness. It may explain why the same stress provokes illness in one person and growth in another.

SPIRITUAL EMPTINESS: THE GROUND OF ILLNESS

The internal state is characterized by an essential lifelessness at the core of the individual's being. It is as if a light or primary energy had been extinguished or perhaps never burned at all. The individual's vital state must not be confused with other facets of the personality such as lightheartedness or apathy in daily life. Ill individuals seem to have an existential weariness which is independent of spirit in daily living.

Let me present a brief sketch of a woman who exemplifies the inner state I am describing. This woman has high energy in conducting her daily affairs. She has a busy schedule and does not tire easily. She is always warm and friendly. Blessed with a good sense of humor, she laughs readily. Her mood is no playacting as everyone feels her genuineness. Yet she claims she feels flat inside. "It seems as if some vital part of me is missing, but I'm not tired or depressed. Just flat. I feel so aimless. I wonder if it's all worthwhile."

This woman is healing from a life-threatening chronic illness and her inner state may have resulted from the condition itself. She does not think so though, since she had flashes of awareness of the feeling prior to her overt sickness. Other people I talk to have also reported the same emptiness before major illness.

The inner state seems related to emptiness in the person's spirituality. Many sick people I have seen do not have an intimate relationship with God. They do not believe that God is in them through each breath they take, waking or sleeping, working or recreating, even during the most mundane activities. They do not sense the Spirit working within them. Even sick people who are strongly religious may be empty of Spirit because for them God is "up there" until the next life. They do not experience the movement of God *now*! Moreover, people with no religious conviction, or those who do not believe in God may, nevertheless, perceive the reality of Spirit.

I have observed that many factors participate in a person's spiritual emptiness. Most children have a rich and complex spiritual life. Children converse directly with God and see God or, in some direct way, experience God within them. Gradually, as children become older, their consciousness "materializes" and they lose that direct link with God.

No doubt the culture plays a role in this process. The

underlying metapsychological assumptions of our culture are rooted in scientific-materialism. Only that which has substance exists for our culture and something that cannot be perceived by the five senses does not exist. Also, intuition, faith, imagination, forgiveness and love, the tools of the soul, are non-rational and, as such, are often ridiculed by our culture.

DEVELOPMENT OF SPIRITUAL EMPTINESS

There are also personal experiences which turn growing children away from their spiritual life. Growing up saddles adolescents with increasingly worldly responsibilities. These new burdens unnecessarily compete with spirituality for available developmental energy. All too often, young adults ignore their spirituality when they don't see adult role models who exhibit a blending of active spirituality and adult responsibility. Moreover, many people have had cruel experiences with spiritual leaders. At vulnerable times during development, when it is important to teach the healing properties of God's Spirit, clergy have acted in ways which portray God as cold, harsh, judgmental and punitive. Young people actively reject their spiritual nature after negative experiences in the confessional or the failure of spiritual teachers to provide healing empathy rooted in the Spirit.

Without experiencing the flow of God's Spirit within us, we perceive ourselves as alone in the world. This percept of aloneness forms our self-image. The absence of the energy and guiding hand of God becomes the animating motif of our consciousness. The consciousness that develops under this condition is one of scarcity, isolation, egocentricity and meaning restricted to the transitory and material. This kind of consciousness spawns a social ethic of closed communication and no-holds-barred competitiveness. It generates affects of fear and anxiety, guilt, anger and rage.

Let us examine briefly, in a very simplified way, the process many people demonstrate in developing the consciousness of scarcity and its negative consequences. When we are alone and isolated from an indwelling spiritual life, we define reality with our senses. The senses deal with the tangible, and the material of the world becomes identified as reality. We see only the surface of our skin, empty space and objects beyond the space. We touch an object outside ourselves, a ball or a friend, and it seems separate. We learn we can move some objects or manipulate them in some way. We experience energy and will only as they relate to the objects.

Gradually, we come to feel our energy and actions effect whatever changes we witness within the environment. Thus, we assume total responsibility for the events which surround us and in which we are involved. We place ourselves at the center of the world and become God-like in our evaluation of our importance in daily life. I can't tell you how many times I have heard, "I can't leave my job now, they can't get along without me. This is the wrong time, maybe later."

ANXIETY, GUILT AND RAGE: THE EMOTIONS OF SPIRITUAL ALONENESS

But the material world is transitory and things happen. Objects break, friends move away, financial statements show downward trends. People who do not experience the permanence of the Spirit become terrified lest anything go "wrong" and guilt-ridden at all that does go "wrong." Terror and guilt over loss burns deeply within the individual even though the feelings may exist outside of awareness.

The egocentric person also demands God-like responsibility from others and exists in a near constant state of anger and rage at being "let down" by others. In some, loss may also provoke the thought that the resources of the world are limited thereby evoking intense competitive drives to control them.

Perhaps the most destructive aspect of the consciousness being described is the lack of meaning the individual may experience in relation to his or her life. Many people grow despondent after achieving some long sought-after goal in the material world. This depression expresses the individual's awareness, either consciously or unconsciously, that the quest was undertaken to correct a feeling of inner emptiness rather than as a creative expression of the Spirit flowing within.

Constant feelings of anger, fear and guilt take a heavy toll on the individual over time. Spiritually, the negative feelings increase the separation from God and a vicious circle between estrangement and anger, fear and guilt ensues. Mental attitude and self-esteem suffer. Pessimism, thoughts of self-defeat and personal impotence, and feelings of self-loathing and worthlessness abound. The chronic stress of rage, fear and guilt lead to prolonged bodily tension and a multitude of negative physical reactions. These physical states are not identifiable as distinct anatomical pathological reactions. Rather, they are dysfunctional processes such as muscular tension which force different parts of the body to function in non-physiological ways. Ultimately, these states lead to distinct anatomical changes and overt illness.

Illness comes to the progressively deteriorating condition as a beacon illuminating the individual's mindless approach to life. It makes manifest in a physical sign that major dysfunction and fragmentation exist on all levels of being, spiritual, mental and physical. Illness urges the person to stop pushing out of awareness spiritual isolation and emptiness and their numerous mental and physical concomitants.

Often, the illness provides information which can point out the path an individual may take for healing. It simultaneously expresses the breakdown in an individual's consciousness and contains the seeds for its healing.

My own illness is an example of this. I had been working in a competitive academic institution that pursued hard science and ignored, even actively criticized, spiritual approaches to healing. I had a rich spiritual life during my early development but gradually denied it by turning to a scientific materialism which was foreign to my nature. In this context I developed severe spinal arthritis with reactive spasm of the back muscle. This was so severe I had trouble getting out of bed in the morning. In fact, I had to kneel next to the bed and push myself up. I also had trouble driving to work because I could not turn my neck to see the traffic clearly. As I worked through the meaning of my illness, I recognized how I had turned away from my true nature, the spiritual life. I saw that to heal myself, I had to leave the job where I was not growing spiritually and begin to kneel in earnest.

HEALING OF CONSCIOUSNESS

Many, many concepts and techniques exist to help an individual heal. These techniques focus on different aspects of the individual's nature ranging from concentrating on the physical through the mental to the spiritual aspects of life—nutritional methods, exercise, massage, acupressure, imagery, meditation, laying on of hands, prayer, healing of the memories, etc. Although numerous methods may be employed by an individual, healing occurs primarily in consciousness.

Healing may be defined as a miraculous unfolding of consciousness for one's being in the world. We learn who we are, what and who really matter to us, how to express ourselves fully and openly. Ultimately, the healing journey leads to an intimate union with God through the experience of the flow of God's spirit within. It is a slow, arduous passage, unique for each individual, filled with danger and risk, triumph and joy, and finally, peace, trust, awe, reverence, love, tenderness.

Healing of consciousness develops from the dialogue between ourselves and our illness, and the actions we take to make whole our broken bodies, our pain, our sorrow, and our suffering. The dialogue begins in assessing what is wrong and what the disease means about how we are leading our lives. I encourage people who consult with me to use several different approaches in assessment such as descriptions of the phenomena of dis-ease and the context in which it develops, imagination, dreams, examination of metaphors about one's disease harvested from drawings or figures of speech, and reading about the illness in specialized texts. The information generated by these inquiries stimulates insights which develop the person's awareness of him/herself.

The developing consciousness in itself is healing and provides a basis for determining what a person can do to continue the healing process. In the beginning of a healing journey, unless an individual is sophisticated in matters of mind and spirit, most people select physical approaches to follow over time such as nutrition, exercise, massage, etc. As the person works with the healing program, I instruct him/her in being conscious of the changes experienced not only in the body but also the mind and spirit. I also attempt to educate the person on the relationship of mind and spirit to his healing.

Eventually, the person slows down and detoxifies from long-standing abuse. Calming and detoxification are important, not only from the physical need of ridding the body from stress, but also in preparing the person to fully appreciate mind and to hear the call of God's Spirit within. Many people are just too overrun with fear, tension, anger and pain to practice the quiet necessary to explore mind and spirit. However, the insights and relaxed state that emerge from basic dietary changes often permit the person to continue on the healing path and explore mind and spirit.

GOD'S SPIRIT: THE HEALING FORCE

The spiritual nature of the individual is an essential part of the healing process. Whether we know it or not, God is our healer and God's Spirit is the energy for our healing. The various healing techniques we employ all act by channeling the energy of the Spirit in our behalf. Moreover, we cannot completely give up the anger, fear, guilt and terror of our aloneness and the accompanying stress and tension until we experience the steady deep power of the flowing Spirit within. The healing force of God's Spirit transforms suffering and pain to love and compassion. The experience of God dwelling within provides enduring meaning to our lives. It transforms consciousness from one of constantly worrying about competing for limited material goods to one of awe and reverence for the limitless creativity of the Spirit.

While occasionally an individual's consciousness is transformed completely instantaneously, most of us labor along satisfied with modest, but nonetheless meaningful gains. We work at opening our consciousness by continually examining our dis-ease, acting toward wholeness and being conscious of our experience.

It is important that spirituality be brought into the healing process as soon as possible. Even a faint glimpse of the beauty of non-material reality can provide a person with the meaning necessary to continue a healing path. I have seen many a nutritional regime fail because it was not based in a healing consciousness which included the whole person. Advising someone to "give up" sugar is often seen by them from the consciousness of scarcity and only serves to aggravate the already rampant feelings of guilt and resentment.

In the course of a healing, many changes in a person's life and their attitudes about life are necessary. Dietary changes, work habits and attitudes toward spirituality name just a few of the many areas that undergo revision. These changes are extremely difficult to make inasmuch as they often require people to act differently from their internalized image of themselves or the established routines and values within the family and society. The energy of the Spirit can sustain an individual through anxiety-provoking healing change.

Spirit is also crucial in healing distorted, broken self-image. Self-image develops slowly during the course of an individual's life. Unless one is imbued with a sense of union with God, self-image is formed from the feelings of anger, guilt and fear which flow from the percept of aloneness. Self-image is at the very deepest levels of our being and permeates all aspects of our lives. It is essential that self-image be transformed in healing, yet we are powerless by ourselves to change it. God's spirit is necessary to penetrate to the depths of our being with the love essential for altering our fundamental image of ourselves.

In the final analysis, healing is the experience of the love and forgiveness from the working of God's Spirit. Each time we give up pain and feel the love from God's Spirit rushing in to take its place, we learn that God's love is here *now*. Gradually, we learn to accept the love and claim it for ourselves. This teaches us that we commune with all that is through the Spirit. Any ideas of separateness between people were tricks played on us by our limited consciousness. We become able to love others and forgive just as we are loved and forgiven by the Spirit.

SPIRITUALITY: CHALLENGE TO THE HEALING ARTS

The great challenge facing the healing arts is to bring spirituality openly and consciously into our work with people. It is not enough to mouth vague theoretical ideas like "holistic health is being healthy in the Spirit" or "holistic health treats the whole person" and then proceed with business as usual. How do we move from concepts of spirituality and health to working models that fully liberate us from dis-ease?

Healing of consciousness may be practiced by everyone in the healing arts no matter what one's basic approach. It is not necessary to be a rabbi, Zen monk or cloistered nun to foster health through spiritual awakening. Every methodology from physical examination to healing prayer groups provides opportunities to show the healing power of God's Spirit.

In order to help another person heal in consciousness, it is crucial that the healing arts practitioner be immersed in his or her own spiritual journey. Developing awareness for the relation between sickness-wellness and spirituality requires direct experience. Matters of the Spirit are non-rational and non-material. One flash of feeling the love of God's Spirit undoing the tension from years of stress is worth more than all the books on the subject. By working on spiritual consciousness, the practitioner develops models to use in healing encounters.

Becoming whole requires role models that show how to live in the Spirit and how this life style promotes wellness. Practitioners who talk about spiritual health without being radiant with their own spirituality do not make their point. Consciousness of God's Spirit develops through love and love heals the pain of dis-ease and the confused twisted inner state that causes it. We heal others when we share the love we receive from God's Spirit.

Practitioners who grow in personal knowledge of the healing power of God's Spirit become emboldened to teach others about it. Very often, sharing knowledge about health and spirituality can lead to profound healing. I have found that many people are struggling to establish an intimate relationship with God but feel awkward and alone in their search because they lack information about the spiritual quests of others. Furthermore, many have been led to believe that a direct experience of God's Spirit is impossible or wrong. Discussing these issues openly with others frequently brings a flood of relief in discovering that they are not alone or crazed.

People who follow a spiritual path may be faced with taking seemingly great risks in their lives and work. As consciousness changes and individuals move closer to God, they may be stimulated to act in ways foreign to their old consciousness. When we work with the Spirit we realize we do not do the healing work but act as channels for the activity of Spirit. This realization causes us to open ourselves to the Spirit without setting limits.

When I first began committing myself to the spiritual aspects of healing, I intellectually understood the need to be open and not hold back in transmitting the action of the Spirit. This was relatively easy until one day I was confronted to act on this concept rather than intellectualize about it. As I sat talking with a client, I became aware of an intense electrical activity in the room. The patient had been suffering from a severe prolonged cold which had defied conventional remedies. I intuited I should stop our conversation and make the client aware of the energy so that together we could meditate on it quietly. I was made quite anxious by this awareness since it was outside of anything I had experienced previously. Nevertheless, I acted on my intuition and we meditated for some time, both gripped by a strong and deeply moving power flowing within us. After the experience the client felt dramatically better and within hours the cold was gone.

Although our society is trying its best to deny it, we are whole people with spiritual as well as physical and mental natures. Spirituality plays a major role in some forms of healing within our society. However, many healing arts are not practiced with spiritual consciousness. This is unfortunate since healing that does not awaken the individual to the health-giving fire of God's Spirit is incomplete. Hopefully, the growing consciousness for living in the Spirit will develop our knowledge and acceptance of spirituality in the healing arts.

8

The Spirit in Health and Disease

LAURENCE J. BENDIT, M.D.

"I was so much hoping I could have spiritual healing and not go to an osteopath. It would be so much cheaper," said a patient who had come for diagnosis by a competent clairvoyant.

I mention this to indicate the confusion in which the whole matter of "spiritual" healing, and even the idea of "spirit," exists in the minds of many people. One finds what is at best spiritualistic healing taken to be genuine spiritual healing; and I say "at best" because so many spiritualistic healers produce no results, are self-deceived and, without intending to, deceive others because they have not the least idea of the meaning of the word "spiritual." It is not the same as "psychic," which refers to another and much more personal level of the human being. It is because of this that I have chosen this subject so as to try to make things a little clearer.

Basically, every student of what some people call "the wisdom" must sooner or later find himself in broad accord with the general principles adumbrated in such books as those of classical Theosophy, Huxley's *Perennial Philosophy,* and Saint Paul. The latter says that man consists of body (*soma*), soul (*psyche,* which is also called mind), and spirit (*pneuma,*

Essence, or *nous*); and this is the way most people would see things. The esotericist differs in that when he begins to penetrate into the human being, he is bound to reverse the order while preserving the triple categories. He realizes that man is spirit, and that, for evolutionary purposes, he has, attached to this Essence, a personality, which consists of mind, or psyche, and body. Body is cogged into the physical world and its rigid space-time continuum. Spirit exists out of this continuum, hence the extraordinary difference in consciousness which man has in what the late Abraham Maslow called moments of "peak experience," or transcendence. Mind or psyche lies between the two, so that one experiences space-time in the flexible, plastic form we know best in dreams, and also in some extrasensory experiences, where the plasticity is apt to prove very confusing to both the sporadic experiencer and to the professed and not properly trained "psychic."

It is against this background that we can consider the subject of this essay on health and disease. At this point I should like to ask the reader to place a hyphen in his mind in that word "disease," for it covers not only ill-health within the body but all forms of unease between oneself and one's environment, in social relations and everything else that is uncomfortable. Health, on the other hand, means an integration, a "wholeness," a "holiness," in the individual from moment to moment.

It was C.G. Jung who first put forward directly the principle that all our problems—all our dis-eases—are the result of maladjustment to our spiritual being. Each of us, for the most part as yet only in the spiritual superconsciousness, knows the path we should tread. If we feel disease, it is because somewhere we are going astray. This may be between ourselves and others, or it may be in our bodies. In both cases, the unease is both a signal to ourselves, a warning light, and a kind of riddle which contains its own answer. That answer is how to return to health, to find "healing" insofar as we have not already damaged the physical body beyond repair—for this life-time.

Healing is basically the result of putting right our wrong relation to our body, to other people and—I will not go further into this than to mention it—to our own complicated minds, with their emotions and instincts at war with one another and not properly understood and accepted by what we call "I" or "me." The process is one of reorganization, reintegration of things which have come apart. The healthy person finds his environment a happy one—even if it is not perfect—and, while minding his own business, calling on him to improve it. But he is healthy also in his organism at the physical level. As he is not yet perfect, from one moment to the next something may hit him: some unpleasant adventure, some virus or microbic or metabolic disease. If he is spiritually aware even to a small degree, he will look for the cause within himself, not blame fate or others, or accident. The word "accident" means "something which happens to one"—whether pleasant or unpleasant—from outside the field of what one calls "oneself." But he may not be capable of doing anything about it without help from others. From this he learns, if need be, that no individual exists otherwise than in the context of his fellows and, beyond them, that of the whole of life. Retreat into a hermitage, an *ashram,* into meditation of the kind practiced so widely today may be useful for a time provided it is not an attempt to escape from living, but it needs to be followed by a commonsense return to contact with one's fellows. Moreover, it means also a proper and commonsense relationship to the physical organism, which has to be fed, kept clean, and otherwise treated with the love—and, I hope, respect—one feels for one's animal pets. One cannot be spiritually healthy if he neglects or suppresses any single part of his total make-up as a human being.

I should add parenthetically that exaggerated attention to health, diet, self-adornment, and beautification is in itself a sign of disease. One can be obsessed by one's body, and this is on a par with the people who make too much of their dogs or cats, to the detriment of the pets as well as to their own.

Passing on from these generalizations, let us consider what healing or therapy means. For details of methods, as well as an elaboration of principles, I recommend the book produced by the Medical Group of the Theosophical Research Center in

England, *The Mystery of Healing* (Wheaton, Illinois: Theosophical Publishing House, 1977). Far more important is the
principle of healing itself, in general, that is, the realization
that restoration of health is a permissive, not an active thing.
Whatever the external methods used, whether psychological,
chemical (pills or medicines) or manipulative, nobody and
nothing heals a person otherwise than by releasing the things
which have prevented him from healing himself. In other
words, if there are vital energies pent up and causing disease
by their being so pent up, the external factors used or applied
result in release of these forces, and health returns to the extent that physical laws allow damaged tissue to grow again,
to be absorbed or resolved.

This brings us to the question of the place of the healer (and
under that title I include doctors, dentists, vets, and all who
have, as it were, made it their life's work to treat the sick). I do
not include those who call themselves "healer" out of vanity,
just as some preen themselves on being "psychic" and "so
sensitive," but only those who are genuinely trying to do something for others, not to acquire a reputation or court publicity
or raise money.

At first one might feel inclined to say, "If a person suffers, it
is his karma, and one shouldn't interfere." But a little more
insight shows us a principle long since known to the Taoists, in
particular, and which Dr. Carl Jung has called, in western
language, "synchronicity." This tells us that the immediate
situation, the "now," is the crucial point in all one's actions,
mental or physical. One has to do the right thing, appropriate
to every "now." Couple that with the idea of the unity of everyone with the whole of humanity, already expressed, and it
follows that at any "now" there is a proper action toward those
in one's immediate environment.

This means that if a person is in distress, the one brought
into the picture, or who sees it for himself, has a part to play
in the whole cross-section of that moment. If a person is ill
or hurt, a trained "healer"—provided he does not rush in un-
invited, or without sufficient knowledge—has his role to play,
and will do what he can for the other person. He is in the
other's momentary world-picture, but so is that other's

existence part of his own momentary view of things. So it is karmically right that the two world-pictures should interact at that moment. In short, it is not interfering with karma to help a person in difficulties, provided the proper mutual consents are given, verbally or tacitly.

The spiritualized healer will never wantonly rush in and mind more than his business, unless in some way invited to do so. Nor, however, will he stand back when his services could be of value, whether or not he expects to get paid for them on however small a scale. Spirituality asks no return.

From this we can draw a light picture of the true spiritual healer. For there is no doubt that such exist, and, moreover, that they sometimes work miracles. But they are humble, unobtrusive people who claim nothing and may assert that it was Christ, or perhaps some other great Being who used them; they are more likely to say nothing, lest they give the impression that they believe themselves to be special people, chosen for the work. One who fits into this category is a doctor among my friends who has a true charismatic power which his sensitive patients feel; but his methods are those of straight orthodox medicine, applied with a discrimination which many of his colleagues lack. To meet him one would scarcely notice him more than anyone else in the room, and it is perhaps only in private, and with certain people, that he is willing to talk of such delicate matters as his philosophy of spirit. He is and works under the banner of Christianity, but he may quietly admit that his skill comes from the far past and, if pressed further, that he believes himself to have been trained in the Aesclapian Schools of ancient Greece. Humility is a marked characteristic of this man—as indeed of all truly spiritualized people.

I have drawn this picture to show a contrast with the self-advertising, crowd-attracting "healers," if only because, when one seriously investigates their work, one finds endless disappointment. True, there may be some temporary and showy results, largely due to suggestion, but they do not last. If one should find anything really strange to have happened, it is probably in the minute proportion of the medically verified miracles at Lourdes: one in several millions of the pilgrims who have been going there over many decades.

If one is seriously in search of the spiritual outlook, and wishes for help of the deep and right kind, he needs to develop the right attitude of mind. The woman whose comment stands at the head of this article evidently had no clue to the truth. She wanted something for herself, as cheaply in terms of money as possible. She may be an extreme case, but many are in some degree like her. This is the reason why the true cure is rare; however saintly the doctor or healer, he can only evoke the true healing power from a patient whose attitude is somewhere oriented in the right direction. The Roman Church insists on confession before being able to absolve a penitent. Crude as the idea has become, it suggests that people have to mean seriously to change themselves before the absolution can be effective. The same principle applies to the sick person. Self-seeking stands in the way of the deep spiritual transformation which brings about real cure. It is true that a bottle of medicine may "cure" certain symptoms, but others will replace them and need more superficial treatment. On the other hand, it may be a touch of spiritual insight which persuades a person to use common sense, take a simple remedy or have an operation or anything else when needed. There is nothing "high-falutin'" about spirit. It stands for common sense as well as uncommon sense.

In conclusion, we may go still deeper, if briefly, into the question of health and disease. I suggested earlier that there were occasions when one might consider disease as a problem containing its own answer. Nowadays, a number of medical philosophers are telling us what we call and feel as *disease may in reality be itself a healing crisis.* The word "healing" here needs to be taken in very wide and long terms. Not only may a fever or a skin eruption be a crisis of elimination of some chemical or viral toxin, but even so dread a state as the schizophrenic breakdown is now seen as at least potentially therapeutic. As the child with measles develops immunity to that disease, so the schizophrenic may so change inside that he emerges from the ordeal not a wreck but a new man, more integrated to his own deeper nature, more spiritualized.

And this applies also to death: physical death may result from the release of the healing forces inside a patient. It is not then a tragedy but a triumph for the healing powers. Everybody must die physically sooner or later, but few—especially the bereaved—see death in its true colors. Moreover, even Theosophists who use ideas of reincarnation as a comforting thought, often fail to learn the lesson of how to prepare themselves to die. They want their little egos to persist. Even people of great insight sometimes wish to let go of their bodies but feel that somehow they have not learned the proper knack, the proper mental attitude which will allow them to do so. But the more we learn the laws of the spiritual life, the easier should be our progress, not only through a lifetime, but also through the transition between one incarnation and the (probable) next.

III

New Dimensions in
Health Practices

Man is a multidimensional being consisting of several grades of energy-matter ranging from the physical body to tenuous and rarefied inner spiritual levels. This is the claim of teachers such as Patanjali, Aurobindo, H.P. Blavatsky, and of many spiritual traditions. Chernin and the Greens present such a model in this section and show that the energies it implies are becoming credible scientifically.

In such an expanded context, illness and health involve the whole spectrum of consciousness. True healing art as Quinn defines it facilitates integration, harmony, and balance of all levels: body, mind, and spirit. Peper and Kushel extend this concept to include the individual's local network of relations and his or her belief system.

Technology from modern medicine can be integrated with that of much older traditions (such as Ayurveda and acupuncture) to provide a wide range of psychospiritual dimensions to treatment (Chernin and Quinn). Treatment at any one level has repercussions at other levels. For example, biofeedback training can have impact on the whole family as the patient learns to control his or her symptoms (Peper and Kushel). Such simple physical training can even lead to opening the inner doors of awareness at transpersonal and

99

spiritual levels within (Green and Green). At its best, healing can facilitate the integration of the personal and trans-personal aspects of one's being.

9

Holistic Medicine: Its Goals, Models, and Historical Roots

DENNIS K. CHERNIN, M.D.

According to the concept of *holistic medicine,* health and wholeness imply the integration of the physical, mental, and spiritual levels of being. From this perspective man is more than a machine that can be serviced like the family automobile. He is a person with spiritual and social aspects whose well-being is as much a reflection of the health of his psyche as it is a reflection of his physical health. Man is meant to function as a totally integrated being, and any medical system of analysis or diagnosis that effectively treats him must also be complete.

Holistic practitioners feel that modern medicine has done well in treating many illnesses and containing infectious diseases but has not gone far enough in defining and teaching the principles of health and in creating an atmosphere of wholeness. We physicians have been given the opportunity to explore the meaning of health and disease. Our traditional medical training, with all the sophistication that modern technology provides, has helped us to understand anatomy, physiology, biochemistry, and pathology. However, it is necessary to expand that knowledge in order to gain a greater

Several passages in this article also appeared in Dennis Chernin and Gregory Manteuffel, *Health: A Holistic Approach* (Wheaton, Illinois: Theosophical Publishing House, 1984).

understanding of the seemingly subtle influences that underlie the body's physiochemistry and orchestrate integration of
the human being. The desire to blend scientific training with
that which can only be experienced intuitively and instinctively has led to the exploration of alternative philosophical
systems. We have studied systems of health care, both modern
and ancient, that facilitate an understanding that body, mind,
and spirit are interdependent. And we have found some com-
monalities, some unifying principles, behind the fundamental
teachings of different medical and philosophical systems
studied.

Holism spans past, present, and future as it is based on
ancient tenets, recent changes in orthodox medicine, and on
future ideals. The integration of technology with the psychospiritual dimensions of man underlies this approach. In
holism, ancient and modern systems and technologies can
complement one another in a cohesive and universal manner.

Holism does not necessarily imply alternative modes of
treatment, for these methods can often be superficial, non-
verifiable, or unidimensional. Nor does it imply that traditional
physicians could not be holistic. What is most important is
for the practitioner of holism to create an atmosphere where
mind and body are seen to be interconnected and the psychological and spiritual dimensions of physical illness are
consistently acknowledged.

In the following discussions three aspects of holistic medicine will be presented: 1) its goals and responsibilities, 2) a
model for the cause and treatment of disease, and 3) its
historical roots.

GOALS AND RESPONSIBILITIES
FOR THE HOLISTIC PHYSICIAN

The role of the holistic physician includes open and effective
communication with patients. He° demystifies medical care
by explaining both theory and treatment. Also he stresses
individualized treatment, which requires that he know each

°The masculine pronoun is used only for convenience and is intended to
include women as well.

patient individually. To give the most intelligent and effective service, he must keep up with advances, both in orthodox medicine and in new findings concerning ancient methods and theories, and he must be thoroughly familiar with well-proven alternative methods of healing. Also he must know when it is necessary to refer patients to appropriate specialists.

Perhaps the most unique feature of the holistic practitioner is that he himself becomes a role model, inspiring patients to live holistically. This means that he must practice approaches inherent in holism, being personally a practitioner of health as well as a healer.

The holistic physician treats all aspects in the health of an individual and family. This includes: 1) treating acute illnesses, and 2) chronic diseases, 3) promoting prevention, and 4) teaching self-care techniques and procedures.

1) Acute illnesses are treated by almost all physicians, though the scope and seriousness of the acute process may necessitate more in-depth treatment by specialists or hospitals. A practitioner of holistic medicine may also choose to use modalities of therapy that may be less conventional. This might include, for example, Vitamin C for upper respiratory infections, lactobacillus acidophilus for diarrhea, comfrey root herb for loose coughs, breathing and relaxation techniques for asthma, or homeopathic remedies instead of drugs.

2) Chronic diseases are also treated by many primary care physicians, but here again the depth and scope of treatment of the holistic doctor is potentially more extensive. A greater emphasis is placed on nutrition, relaxation, and exercise. An orthodox physician, for example, might treat hypertension with drugs, mostly through beta blockers, diuretics, or methyldopa derivatives. Some superficial mention of the importance of weight reduction and exercise might also be involved in treatment. On the other hand, a holistic doctor would strongly encourage preventive and self-care techniques and add medications only if blood pressure remained high or if debility, defensiveness, or resistance caused the patient to be unable to follow the nonmedicinal therapies.

3) Prevention is an integral component for the holistic practitioner. Here the divergence from the more orthodox

approaches can more readily be seen. Three stages of prevention must be promoted.[1] *Primary* prevention is used before a
problem begins. Therapies used might include immunization,
nutrition, exercise, relaxation techniques, evaluation of sleep
patterns, or psychotherapy related to growth and creativity.
Secondary prevention involves early detection before illness
symptoms arise (as in high blood pressure, which is often at
first asymptomatic). This approach prevents an extension of
illness or injury. *Tertiary* prevention prevents the deterioration of a chronic condition and improves life within the limits
of the illness. These last two areas of prevention involve more
than the use of drugs and surgery. Knowledge of the family's
socioeconomic situation, for example, is important in understanding the limits of curability, as are stresses that might
inhibit improvement and attitudes about life and death.

4) Self-care techniques are a mandatory component for
all people practicing holism. Recognizing the need for education and the importance of fostering self-responsibility is
essential. Self-care is still the predominant mode of health
care.[2] In fact, it has never been proven that people who live
in rural areas (who have adequate nutrition and sanitation)
and groups like the Christian Scientists, who see physicians
much less often than their urban, doctor-going cousins, have
any more health problems than the average population.[3] Both
groups use many self-care techniques and rarely go to doctors
for trivial problems.

Patients should be helped to see that they are the initiators
of their medical care rather than passive recipients of the provider's actions. It is important to recognize the great healing
potential of one's body and that many illnesses are self-limited
and can be handled by simple home procedures. This approach would decrease doctor overload and save the community and patient considerable expenditure. Some practical
educational techniques include teaching high blood pressure
patients to use the sphygmomanometer (blood pressure cuff),
mothers to use otoscopes to see if their children have ear
infections, using hemoccult (a test that is sensitive to the
presence of blood) for checking blood in stool samplings,

and offering classes on the home use of safe yet effective herbal or homeopathic remedies.

A MODEL FOR THE CAUSE
AND TREATMENT OF DISEASE

A model of holistic medicine that illustrates the cause and treatment of disease incorporates the principle that man is a multidimensional being whose existence permeates many levels of consciousness. Man, according to this idea, is a composite of the body, mind, and spirit. If he exists on these levels, then it follows that disease is also involved with these levels and that diagnosis and treatment should be focused at the appropriate level.

A very useful paradigm that expresses these ideas is rooted in the Vedanta and Samkhya philosophies, which are based on the ancient *Upanishads* and *Yoga Sutras* of India. The Kabbalistic tradition of the Hebraic people also has concepts similar to this model. Man is described as existing on several levels: physical, energy, conscious mind, unconscious mind, superconscious mind, and the Self or the center of consciousness.[4] The following diagram exemplifies this model.

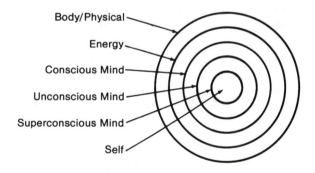

The levels of consciousness are conceptualized as existing from gross external levels to more subtle internal ones, the outer being more dense and obscuring the finer, less material inner layers. Associated with each level is a specific type of awareness. These levels of consciousness are called sheaths because of their concentric arrangement, although they interpenetrate one another. The more external layers are less permanent and more susceptible to change. The inner layers control the layers external to themselves, with the Center of Consciousness, which is permanent and immutable, integrating all the other layers.

The philosophy of sheaths represents a model of preventive and holistic health which offers both conceptual theory and pragmatic treatment approaches into which various other therapeutic systems of healing can be integrated.

Therapeutic interventions can be organized following this scheme. Outlined below are only therapies that have been well proven over time or are verified by precise scientific methodology.

BODY

1) Diet
   Protein, fat
      carbohydrate
      intake
   Vitamins
   Minerals
   Fasting
2) Exercise
   Aerobic
   Passive
      Martial Art
      Hatha Yoga

   Physical Therapy
   Manipulation
   Massage
3) Herbs
4) Drugs
   Immunization
5) Surgery
6) Preventive
   Seat belts
   Helmets
   Sanitation
   Hygiene

ENERGY

1) Biofeedback
2) Breathing and Relaxation
3) Chinese Medicine
   Acupuncture
4) Homeopathy

MIND - SELF

1) Psychotherapy
2) Dream Analysis
3) Contemplation
4) Meditation
5) Death Counseling
6) Spiritual Guidance

While each treatment focuses on one level, there are many overlapping effects. For example, a diet high in sugar may cause physical symptoms of hypoglycemia with weakness or palpitations as well as the mental symptoms of anxiety and confusion.

BODY: *Diet* as an approach to therapy can be either preventive or treatment oriented. Although the uses of nutrition in prevention are well established by orthodox physicians, unfortunately few practitioners promote dietary changes. There are many examples of the relationship between food and disease, especially chronic diseases: fats and salt in cardiovascular disease, refined carbohydrates and high fat in colon cancer, animal fat in breast cancer, thiamine (Vitamin B$_1$) in beriberi, niacin (Vitamin B$_3$) in pellagra, ascorbic acid (Vitamin C) in scurvy, and Vitamin A in night blindness. Experimental research and clinical experience have shown how dietary alternatives can be used to treat a myriad of disorders and often can be used in an advantageous way so that drugs may not be needed. For example, eliminating dairy products for allergic and asthmatic people decreases mucus production and viscosity (stickiness). Nongluten grains can also be helpful in these conditions. Constipation is greatly aided by high fiber diets. Diarrhea can effectively be treated by drinking soup made from grated carrots, by unripened bananas (overripe bananas conversely aggravate diarrhea), and by replacing lost colon bacteria with lactobacillus acidophilus cultures found in yogurt. Tryptophan (an amino acid) can help induce sleep in insomniacs. Vitamin B$_6$, if taken at night, can help a person remember dreams, and Vitamin E can help diminish hot flashes.

Exercise closely parallels nutrition in well-known yet often overlooked benefits, both in preventive and therapeutic applications. Aerobic exercise has certainly been implicated in positive cardiovascular health. Kenneth Cooper in his book *Aerobics* actually systematized how long and how fast a person must exercise to get maximum cardiovascular stimulation. He compares such exercises as jogging, walking, swimming, and bicycling.[5] Active exercise has also been used by many psychiatrists as a therapy for depression and is often heralded as being as effective as psychotherapy and medication in many cases. Passive stretching such as hatha yoga is another therapy that can be used preventively and therapeutically. By assuming specific body postures, endocrine glands can be stimulated, and this can help in such conditions as hypothyroidism, menopause, and adult-onset diabetes. Muscular and skeletal problems result in a great number of visits to primary care physicians,[6] and many of these disorders can be both prevented and healed more quickly by the increased flexibility, balance, suppleness, and grace that exercises like hatha yoga promote.

Physical therapy can also be used effectively by the holistic doctor. For example, cases of carpel tunnel syndrome (numbness in the hand from a nerve being pinched) can be well treated by specific wrist stretching, often along with Vitamin B12 injections, so that surgery can sometimes be avoided. Osteopathic and chiropractic manipulation can be used with great therapeutic benefit in cases of sacroiliac dysfunction and sciatica, two major forms of back morbidity.

I personally have met several hatha "yogis" in their late 70s and late 80s whose strength, flexibility, and muscle tone were much greater than that of people in their 20s and 30s. One man can do over one thousand consecutive push-ups, break chains, and is so relaxed that he can fall asleep in advanced yoga postures. What this seems to indicate is not that senescence (the association between degeneration and aging) does not occur, but that through diligent practice and dedication the aging process can be substantially slowed.

Drugs and *surgery* are also areas used by holistic physicians. The doctor who treats the whole person doesn't neglect more modern pharmacologic advances and surgical interventions and accordingly must be well aware of new developments. Yet the holistic practitioner realizes that the risk of iatrogenic (doctor induced) disease is also increased by powerful drugs and surgery and always attempts first to use simple, effective or alternative approaches if possible. These methods usually are a combination of indigenous botanical medicine, nutrition, exercise, or stress reduction techniques.

The holistic doctor should always be keenly aware of the

preventive aspects of health. This includes the encouragement of personal hygiene and cleanliness and the use of safety devices such as seat belts and motorcycle helmets. Education is as important as treatment.

ENERGY: The energy level found in this model refers to an area not clearly defined by orthodox medicine. Subatomic and quantum physics approaches this idea of fields. Einstein's theory of the interconvertibility of energy and matter can also have applications to medicine and healing. Technology based on these concepts is, of course, already in application in the areas of lasers, X-rays, nuclear medicine, CAT scans, and nuclear magnetic resonance. In addition, it would seem to follow that if one can treat matter (body), then one can also treat the energy aspect (since they are interconvertible), so long as one can diagnose and perceive illness on this level. Several traditions and medical theories have actually developed around the concept of energy, including homeopathy, Chinese medicine, and the Ayurvedic system of ancient India.

Acupuncture works on the principle of the flow of chi (energy) along meridians which have no parallel in the physiology of the human body. According to this model, blocks and disruptions can occur along these pathways, and through stimulation and pacification of the energy flows, adjustments and balancing can be achieved. Practitioners of anesthesia through acupuncture explain it through energy transmission, although Western science has attempted to present alternative theoretical models (such as the "spinal gate theory" and endorphin release).

Homeopathic medicine is based on the concept of vital force, an energy that gives life its animation and underlies the body's defense mechanisms and metabolic processes. In health this force functions smoothly, but it is disrupted in illness. Medicines that have been diluted and activated (potentized) to liberate kinetic energy from potential energy are used to catalyze the body/mind complex (through its energy medium) to rebalance and strengthen the patient.

Breathing exercises might be taught by a holistic practitioner. All theories of medicine based on the energetic concept hold that the breath is the main vehicle for transmitting energy. There are specific breathing exercises that have been developed in yoga that can be used prophylactically and therapeutically for asthma, sinusitis, and bronchitis. Other breathing exercises can be helpful in thyroid problems or chronic tonsillitis.

Biofeedback has been called the yoga of the West. By learning to relax and by getting feedback on muscle tension or the degree of warmth of the skin, a person learns to recognize how certain emotions, thoughts, memories, breathing patterns, or physical sensations affect muscular tension or skin temperature. The biofeedback signal is given by translating muscular tension or skin temperature into electrical energy impulses, and then externalizing these into audio or visual signals.

MENTAL AND SPIRITUAL: The mental and spiritual dimensions in holistic medicine are of paramount importance. A doctor focusing on self-care believes that true health is never established unless the mind and emotions are balanced. The holistic doctor sees the intimate relationship between the body and mind and sees that almost all disease involves an emotional component. Practitioners will be interested not only in a person's sore throat or ulcer but also in why that person got sick and what contributed to the over-susceptibility, on both the physical and emotional levels. The techniques of psychotherapy, counseling, and dream analysis can be used to help a patient become aware of repressed anger, sadness, or guilt that may underlie disease of psyche or soma. The field of psychosomatic medicine, an offshoot of Freudian analytic schools, has shown that certain personality configurations are associated with certain physical diseases such as in diabetes, rheumatoid arthritis, ulcerative colitis, and hypertension (high blood pressure). A holistic physician, understanding these interconnections and utilizing psychotherapeutic techniques to diagnose and treat these afflicted people, could greatly enhance growth and creativity as well as alleviating distress.

In addition to technical skills and knowledge, compassion, caring, and understanding are essential to any healer. This is apparent in anthropological research in situations where people who live in an indigenous area do not respond to the appropriate Western medication until the local doctor/ shaman, who understands the people's belief system of disease causation, is consulted and gives his herbal medicine or counseling.

HISTORICAL ROOTS OF HOLISTIC MEDICINE

Something of the development of holistic medicine may have become apparent through the previous discussion, but added information is needed. Following is a list of factors in the medical field that contributed to the rise of holism:

1. The rise of self-help groups (well exemplified by the La Leche League)
2. The increasing exposure to ancient systems of healing
3. The rise in chronic disease
4. Mounting stress in modern society
5. Increased medical subspecialization
6. Rise in iatrogenic (doctor induced) disease
7. Increased concern over social injustice and the importance of the individual

1) Self-help groups fill an important gap in the network making up our health care system. Their rise constitutes a social movement initiated by consumers. Such groups provide assistance, encouragement, and needed services for chronic disabling conditions.[7]

Self-help groups can also be used to educate patients on improved care for themselves. In fact, "self-care is clearly the predominant mode of health care for the common complaints. Studies . . . suggested that as much as 75% of health care is undertaken without intervention by professional providers of health care."[8]

An example of a successful self-care group is the La Leche League, founded in 1956 by mothers who believed that the then-current mode of infant bottle-feeding was negative in health consequences. At that time there was a widespread antipathy towards breast-feeding, and the League mothers worried about the physical and emotional deprivation that bottle-feeding imposed upon mothers and their babies. They had meetings, encouraged research, wrote books, and organized at the grass-roots level. Their efforts were focused on raising the eight percent of mothers who nurse to a much higher percentage. They argued, and researchers who did studies for them, found that breastfeeding was easier, caused less infections, caused less overweight in infants, and protected the infant from milk (cow's) allergy. The La Leche League efforts were paramount in influencing the great rise in breast-feeding and in inducing the American Academy of Pediatrics finally to endorse nursing in 1979 as being of superior nutrition.[9]

2) Ancient systems of medicine have provided another important foundation of the holistic paradigm. Western interest in Eastern modes of philosophy and healing dates back many centuries. The Persians and Greeks interacted with Indian Ayurvedic physicians for hundreds of years in ancient times. With Marco Polo's journeys, China was opened to Western scrutiny. Healing knowledge and techniques are found in these great traditions. In the Ayurvedic texts called the *Caraka,* many drugs, physical therapies, and surgical procedures are described, showing advanced and sophisticated diagnostic techniques and instrumentation. These theories view disease as a result of the imbalance of the basic elements that underlie all life. Health can be reinstated by careful attention to the natural cycles and inner biorhythms inherent in man and his environment.

In the United States the great philosopher/poets Emerson, Thoreau, and Whitman were students of the Orient and influenced many philosophically minded doctors. Carl Jung recognized and interpreted many unconscious conflicts in terms of universal metaphors and symbols that have been systematized in the philosophies of the East for thousands of years. Writers such as Arthur Avalon, Christopher Isherwood, and Paul Brunton used their skills to interpret Vedantic, Buddhist, and Taoist texts into modern understanding. All these influences fascinated some Western physicians and created a desire to study the practical wisdom inherent in the Eastern systems. Yoga philosophy and meditation are more recent stimuli to the holistic movement that have roots in ancient systems. Many young admirers of yoga saw its potential advantages in health and creativity and began to practice more advanced yoga techniques and to look for health-care providers who share their views.

3) Chronic diseases have replaced infectious diseases as the major factor in mortality. This is because of safer water and milk supplies, improved personal and food hygiene, and efficient disposal of water. Older people especially are subject to chronic diseases: "Eighty percent have one or more chronic conditions and their medical treatment accounts for about 30% of the nation's health care expenditures . . . But a large portion of chronic activity limitation stems from respiratory conditions such as chronic bronchitis and emphysema."[10] In this context, health-promoting techniques—such as good nutrition, cigarette smoking cessation, and exercise, which could decrease chronic disease incidence like heart disease or emphysema and save the national expenditures—are often sought through holistic practitioners.

4) In the last few years stress has been implicated as a major factor in disease initiation. The holistic movement has attempted not only to expose this problem and explain it scientifically, but also to offer effective techniques of stress reduction. "Studies indicate that up to 80% of serious physical illnesses seems to develop at a time when the individual feels helpless or hopeless."[11] Many people suffering stress-related diseases have been seeking the therapeutic techniques that the holistic doctor teaches and advocates.

5) Consumers often worry that only a certain part of their body is being treated while they as the whole person are neglected. This results from increased medical subspecialization. Surgeons who cut open the body often neglect the emotional ramifications. Psychiatrists who describe situations as psychosomatic often overlook true physical suffering. Cardiologists treat the patient's heart with drugs and use sophisticated diagnostic devices but tend to forget about diet, exercise, and relaxation, which could have prevented the coronary artery disease in the first place or could prevent further extension of the disease. Also the use of primary care doctors has decreased from 95% in 1931 to 38% in 1975. Since

holistic doctors are often general practitioners, family physicians, internists, or pediatricians, all of whom do primary care, holism may fill an important gap.

6) The rise in iatrogenic (doctor induced) disease has become a serious concern. The more technology and the more money third party insurance companies pay providers such as hospitals and physicians, the more potential there is for dangerous procedures being done. The following quotes illustrate these points. "In the late 1960s, the rate of surgical intervention in the U.S. was double that of England and Wales. We would expect to see higher mortality rates in England and Wales in potentially fatal disorders. But this is not so . . . One major difference between the two areas is the method by which the hospital physician is paid: fee per service in the U.S. as against salary in England and Wales."[12] "The CDC [Center for Disease Control] estimates that just under 4% of all patients admitted to general hospitals develop a new infection while being treated."[13] "One analysis . . . concluded that only about one-half of some 7,000 surgeries to remove ovaries from women could be thoroughly justified."[14] "During the 1970s a series of reports linked cyclamates with bladder cancer in rats and breast cancer was attributed to reserpine, etc."[15] All these situations point to the great need for moderation and alternative techniques that the holistic practitioners can offer.

7) Increased concern with individual rights and the ethical and legal issues of all people—regardless of class, race, or socioeconomic status—contributes heavily to the rise in holistic medicine. All holistic physicians believe in preventive medicine. This position has been stated well: "1) It is immoral to permit unnecessary illness or premature death. 2) In preventing adverse influences on health, we can exercise such powers as society wishes to grant us. 3) In exercising the powers granted to us, the rights of the individual are to be protected and preserved."[16]

Holistic medicine encourages the attempt to integrate the apparent materialistic world with the spiritual, to see the interconnection between psyche and soma, and to promote with integrity the equality of all mankind. One final feature that sets off holistic approach from conventional medicine should be mentioned. It is that both physician and patient must share the conviction that a person can grow and learn from illness as well as from health. They must look at pain and suffering as leading to greater awareness and compassion, as catalysts to both insight and action—all of which leads to physical, emotional, and spiritual freedom. Thus "getting well" is only the beginning of a life-long journey toward wholeness and health at all levels, spirit, mind, and body. This approach holds the hope that all humans can learn to live in peace, maximize their potential, and create a healthy and dynamic world.

REFERENCES

1. Burkett, Ann: Health Education. p. 38 in *Community Health.*

2. Lough, C. and Stewart, B.: *Self-Care as a Health Service.* Chapter 8 from *National Priorities for Health: Past, Present, and Projected.* R.F. Rushmer, Editor, N.Y., John Wiley and Sons, 1980, p. 307.

3. Ibid, 302.

4. Ajaya, S., Ballentine, R., and Rama, S.: *Yoga and Psychotherapy.* Himalayan Institute, Honesdale, PA, 1976, p. XXIV.

5. Cooper, Kenneth, M.D. *Aerobics.*

6. Williams, S.J.: Ambulatory and Community Health Services. Ch. 4 in *Introduction to Health Services.* S.J. Williams and P.J. Torrens, Ed. N.Y., John Wiley and Sons, 1980, p. 99.

7. Gusson, Z. and Tracey: The Role of Self-help Clubs in Adaptation to Chronic Illness and Disability, *Soc. Sci. and Med.,* 10:407, 1976.

8. Op. cit. Lough, p. 301.

9. La Leche League International, *The Womanly Art of Breast-feeding,* La Leche League International, Franklin Park, Il. 1981.

10. Health People: *The Surgeon General's Report on Health Promotion and Disease Prevention,* 1979. DHEW (PHS) Publ. No. 79-5507, p. 74, 1979.

11. Ibid, p. 71.

12. Gulyer, A.J.: Public or Private Health Services? *J Pol Analysis and Management,* 2:397-98, 1983.

13. F.J. Thompson: Health Policies and the Bureaucracy: Politics and Implementation, Cambridge, MA, MIT Press, p. 44, 1983.

14. Ibid, p. 46.

15. Smith, T.: Are the Drug Regulatory Agencies Paper Villains. *Brit Med J,* 281:1333 (Nov 15) 1980.

16. Shindell, S.: Legal and Ethical Aspects of Public Health, p. 1845 in Maxcy-Rosenau.

10

The Healing Arts
in Modern Health Care

JANET F. QUINN, Ph.D., R.N.

As I began to think about the preparation of this paper, two questions consistently appeared, in my stream of consciousness. Both questions were related quite specifically to the title of this issue, and refused to be ignored. The first question was whether or not our modern health care system includes, or at least allows for, the practice of "healing arts." The second question was whether or not, in the practice of these healing arts, there are always spiritual aspects. As I considered these questions, it became clear that only the first required answering, for the answer to the second question may be found in the definition of "healing arts."

HEALING ARTS

If we think of health as wholeness, which is consistent with the origins of the word, then we may conceptualize healing as a process which facilitates health, and thus wholeness. The next step would seem to be to define wholeness, a task considerably more difficult than the former, at least to this writer. Volumes have been written on the subject from a variety of perspectives including religious, philosophic, psychologic and physical, and yet the term wholeness seems to defy objective definition. As a working definition, admittedly over-simplified, let us consider wholeness to mean integration, harmony and balance of mind-body-spirit in interaction with the totality of one's environment. A healing art may thus be conceptualized, again over-simplistically, as a skillful practice which facilitates the integration, harmony and balance of mind-body-spirit in the recipient. Given this set of definitions, one cannot practice a healing art without attending to the spiritual nature and needs of the recipient. Thus, the second question is answered.

Now the question is whether or not our modern health care system includes, or at least allows for, the practice of healing arts. Although the question is certainly debatable, I shall argue that, except in rare instances, it does not. My argument is based on the following two observations:

1. The focus of our health care system is the curing of disease, rather than the healing of whole persons.
2. The spiritual nature and needs of people are virtually ignored in our health care system, while mind and body are usually considered to be separate entities.

HEALING VERSUS CURING

Curing may be conceptualized as the elimination of the signs and symptoms of disease. Typically, people enter the health care system when indicators of illness can no longer be ignored. The signs and symptoms will be treated with medication, or if the signs and symptoms are severe enough, hospitalization will ensue. If, after a certain course of treatment by surgery and/or drug therapy, the signs and symptoms no longer exist, then we say that the person has been cured. A good deal of satisfaction is derived from this process by both the health care providers and the recipients, for the system has functioned as it was intended to function. Modern medical science has cured the disease. However, if the signs and symptoms cannot be eliminated, then the health care system is judged a failure. It is all very clear—success is the elimination of the disease, and failure the inability to do so. Notice that one need never discuss the person with the disease to adjudge the treatment as a success or a failure. The old joke that "the surgery was a success but the patient died" seems alarmingly close to the truth when viewed in this context.

While the process of curing disease should not be under-rated in importance, it is at best only a small part of the larger process of healing. Modern medicine does some things very well, but it simply does not go far enough. For, while signs and symptoms of disease might be eliminated, our system of health care does little to facilitate people's wholeness. If any-thing, modern medicine impedes the healing process by fostering the idea of separateness between mind-body-spirit.

BODY-MIND-SPIRIT

Much has been written of late about the separation of mind and body in the practice of modern medicine. (For excellent discussions of this issue, the reader is referred to the bib-liography at the end of this article.) Briefly, modern medicine is based on a philosophical view which is both dualistic and reductionistic. Dualism is the perspective that the mind and the body are separate and distinct entities. This view was put forth by Descartes in the 17th century and has prevailed ever since. Reductionism, simply, is the belief that understanding of any system may be gained by reducing the system to its simplest or smallest part. One need only examine the organiza-tion of health care services to have these philosophic perspec-tives demonstrated quite vividly.

Generally, we have two broad classifications of disease—physical and mental—each with its own specialists. Within the broad specialty of physical illness, practitioners further specialize in diseases of a particular body part, so that one can consult a specialist in eye, ear, nose, and throat, another in neurology, another in cardiology, etc. Within the specialty of cardiology, there are cardiac surgeons and medical cardiolo-gists, providing yet another specialization. Each of these speci-alties is typically located in its own area of a hospital, so that there are eye units, heart units, kidney units and so on. The mental ill-ness specialists, too, have their own units in the hospital.

There does exist within this model some acknowledgement that in physical illness one must also address the psychological status of the patient. Nurses are taught, for example, to be aware of the "psychological implications of the patient's physical illness" in planning nursing care. On the surface, this would appear to bridge the separation of mind and body. Upon deeper analysis, however, one realizes that this is not the case. For in attending to the "psychological implications of physical illness" there are the same dualistic assumptions at work. Implicit in the phrase is the assumption that the body is sick, and the mind/emotion has a reaction to this. For one part to react to another, separateness must be assumed to exist between the parts. Also implicit in the phrase is that the causes or origins of the physical problem can be found in a malfunction of that part of the whole, and that mind simply watches this process, a non-contributor and helpless.

The question of the role of the mind and emotions in the origin of physical illness is seldom addressed. Only after the fact of physical illness do we usually consider the psychological implications and then only as a secondary concern. The primary concern continues to be the elimination of the signs and symptoms of the physical disease. Even when we acknowledge the mental and emotional factors in the origin of some physical illnesses, such as gastric ulcers, colitis or tension headaches, we continue to treat the physical with physical interventions, while advising the patients to decrease the stress in their lives. This advice is often accompanied with a prescription for sedatives or tranquilizers. Again, the treatment is dualistic and fragmented.

There was certainly a time in human history when spirit was a central, not peripheral, focus in matters of health and illness and healing. With the advent of science, this perspective changed. The realm of spirit was relegated to religion and philosophy, which were other than science. Science is the measurable, the observable, the impersonal, the objective, the rational. It is opposite of the unmeasurable, the unobservable, the ineffable, the personal, the subjective, the intuitive. Somewhere along the way, it was decided that health, illness and healing had much more to do with the former than the latter.

The spiritual nature and needs of patients are virtually ignored in our modern health care practices. While mind and
body each have health care specialists, care of the spirit is
usually entrusted to the Chaplain on duty. Again, there exists
in practice an acknowledgement of the spiritual needs of sick
persons. Interestingly, the appreciation of spiritual needs
seems to increase as the likelihood of cure decreases. Nurses
are probably more appreciative than physicians of the spiritual
needs of their patients, for they are taught to be so in their
educational programs. In the course of practice, however,
this appreciation usually gets translated into little more than
respecting a patient's religious orientation, and calling the
appropriate Chaplain.

Occasionally, one can hear health care providers lament
that their ministrations are not working because the patient
has a "broken spirit" or has "lost the will to live." It is doubtful,
however, that even in these instances any true appreciation
for the power of spirit and of the spiritual aspects of life is
being expressed. It is more often a judgement which proclaims the patient guilty and the health care providers
innocent. "It is not our fault; if he doesn't want to live, we
cannot help him."

Perhaps the problem is in defining "spiritual" and "spiritual
nature" broadly enough to be acceptable to most health care
practitioners and recipients and yet specifically enough to
provide direction for useful and appropriate interventions.
This is a difficult task indeed. It is clearly a much less complicated matter to identify and label disturbances from the
normal in the physical and mental nature than to discern
actual or potential disturbances of the spirit. After all, one can
at least locate the physical, no matter how small, and one can
observe the mental/emotional functioning of a person. But
where does one's "spiritual nature" reside? Where do we
begin to look for this nature? How do we know when we've
found it, and once we've found it, what do we do with it? How
do we determine if it is in need of intervention, and what
interventions can we use?

Given all of the above, it thus appears that our modern

health care system, except in rare instances, does not include the practice of healing arts. However, the fact that there are indeed rare instances, in spite of the prevailing medical model which mitigates against the practice of healing arts, is cause for celebration. Further, the rare instances appear to be increasing in number, and this provides cause for great hope. Perhaps the most significant indicator that change is occurring in the direction of an increasing practice of healing arts has been the enormous popularity of the Holistic Health movement. While imperfect and sometimes misconceptualized, the Holistic Health movement represents a quantum leap away from the prevailing medical model.

HOLISTIC HEALTH

Heralded as a radically new approach to health care, with ancient origins, the Holistic Health care movement has as a central theme the inseparability of mind-body-spirit in health, illness and healing. Briefly, the Holistic Health perspective acknowledges the fundamental wholeness, unity and integrity of the individual in interaction with the environment. Body-mind-spirit are viewed as inseparable and interdependent dimensions of being. All behaviors, including health and illness, are manifestations of the life process of the whole person. An holistic approach emphasizes self-determination of health care goals and self-responsibility for goal attainment. Health care interventions are chosen for their appropriateness to, and in the context of, the needs of the total person. Although relief/cure of physical signs and symptoms of disease is attempted, the underlying meanings of the symptoms and the ultimate alteration of (antecedent) life patterns are of equal, or prime, importance.

The Holistic Health movement is neither perfect nor complete in its evolution. There are some major flaws in thought and action which will require correcting before the concept of Holistic Health can be incorporated into our mainstream health care system. One major flaw involves the assumption that Holistic Health care is equivalent to the use of alternative forms of care.

HOLISTIC CARE VERSUS
ALTERNATIVE FORMS OF CARE

The past decade has brought with it an enormous interest in and promotion of "Holistic Health" ideas. There has been a proliferation of articles on Holistic Health in both the lay and professional literature, and whole new publications have come into being with Holistic Health as their focus. In most bookstores one can now find a section entitled "Holistic Health." Within this section are dozens of books dealing with nontraditional or alternative forms of health care, such as Reflexology, Biofeedback, Iridology, Herbal Remedies, Acupressure, Massage, Polarity Therapy, to name but a few. Conferences and workshops with an holistic theme abound and usually include presentations related to one or more alternate forms of care as mentioned above. Radio and television talk shows feature Holistic Health practitioners discussing various new age interventions, while wellness centers and Holistic Health clinics seem to spring up virtually overnight.

What reason is there to suggest that, simply because one is receiving Acupressure or Reflexology, or is taking herbal and homeopathic remedies, one is being assisted toward greater wholeness of body-mind-spirit? There is no reason, and yet this assumption appears rampant within Holistic Health circles, as the foregoing discussion suggests. The issue is one of form versus context; of confusing the tools of care with the approach to care.

Health care providers carry on their practice by utilizing an Holistic or a Reductionistic (described earlier) *approach* to care. Within a given approach, health care providers choose traditional (usually medication and/or surgery) or alternative *forms* of care as the tools of intervention. Usually, traditional forms of care are selected as tools by those subscribing to a Reductionist approach, while those subscribing to an Holistic approach are more likely to choose alternative forms. However, these facts must not be interpreted to mean that the use of alternative forms automatically makes the care Holistic. Nor should it be assumed that the use of traditional forms automatically makes the care reductionistic or un-Holistic. Further, it should not be assumed that, in practicing an alternative form of care, one is engaged in a healing art. If one administers the alternative form of care with the same traditional goal of simply removing signs and symptoms, a healing art is not being practiced. Unfortunately, much of what is practiced in Holistic Health today fits this description. There is no such thing as an inherently Holistic or Reductionistic intervention. The care which is provided is Holistic or Reductionistic based on the approach to that care, not the tools of care.

There is an implicit assumption which derives from the confusion of approaches to care with tools of care. The assumption is that traditional forms of care are always un-Holistic, therefore "bad" and therefore to be avoided by those who hold an Holistic perspective. This assumption is not only erroneous, but potentially quite dangerous. As stated earlier, there are some things which traditional, reductionistic medicine does very well, and subscribing to an Holistic perspective should not prevent people from seeking and receiving this care where indicated.

FUTURE DIRECTIONS

Without question, the Holistic Health framework provides an environment, a context in which true healing arts might flourish. But, as with most radical change, the pendulum has swung a bit too far in the opposite direction, and we are in danger of throwing out the baby with the bathwater. I have great hope, indeed expectations, that the pendulum will eventually swing back and settle somewhere closer to the middle. When this happens, we should see a merging and blending of the best that both traditional medicine and Holistic Health have to offer. But when the Holistic Health fanfare dies down, and the faddists have moved on to the next bandwagon, there will remain an enormous amount of work to be done by committed health care professionals. I would suggest that much of that work will be on the self as the practitioner of a healing art. For it would seem that in this dimension of wholeness, and particularly spirit, our machines are useless, our laboratories still, and science fails us. We are left with what our ancestors had to work with not so very long ago. We are left with ourselves; just our imperfect, fallible selves. It is the use of self, in a loving and compassionate way, which provides us with our most powerful instrument for healing. The simplicity of this fact is truly elegant, yet its complexity cannot be overstated.

The author acknowledges the contributions of Dora Kunz, Dolores Krieger, Martha Rogers, and Renée Weber, among others, in the evolution of the thoughts and ideas contained herein.

BIBLIOGRAPHY

Dossey, L. *Space, Time and Medicine.* Boulder: Shambhala Publications, 1982.

Hastings, A.C., Fadiman, J., Gordon, J.S. (Eds.). *Health for the Whole Person.* Boulder: Westview Press, 1980.

Krieger, D. *Foundations for Holistic Health Nursing Practices: The Renaissance Nurse.* Philadelphia: J.B. Lippincott Company, 1981.

LeShan, L. *The Mechanic and the Gardener: Making the most of the Holistic Revolution in Medicine.* New York: Holt, Rinehart and Winston, 1982.

Otto, H.A., Knight, J.W., (Eds.). *Dimensions in Wholistic Healing: New Frontiers in the Treatment of the Whole Person.* Chicago: Nelson-Hall, 1979.

Pelletier, K. *Holistic Medicine.* New York: Dell Publishing Company, 1979.

11

A *Holistic Merger of Biofeedback and Family Therapy*

ERIK PEPER, Ph.D., AND CASI KUSHEL, M.S., M.F.C.C.

This article is a positive consideration of the integration of self-regulation skills (biofeedback and autogenic training), and family therapy in order to create a holistic approach which includes the individual, the family, the social network and the belief system within which one lives. We believe that the same tenets provide the foundations for health in both approaches.

Traditionally, biofeedback has focused on the individual and his power to self-regulate or self-heal. That is, biofeedback has assumed that it is possible to learn to control physiological functions such as body temperature, heart rate, or muscle tension, which were previously thought to be beyond conscious control. Such control is accomplished through the use of electrical instruments which detect a body function, amplify it, and then communicate it (feed it back), through a tone, light, or meter.

Family therapy, or systems work, as it is sometimes called, has focused its attention on the family unit as a whole, and considers the interaction between family members as the key to change. The goal here has been to restructure the family and to interrupt and redirect the flow of dysfunctional communication and behavior.

Both approaches, although relatively young in the field of health care, have had some exciting successes in relieving pain (either physical or emotional), and in opening the options for life-enhancing, health-giving changes. Much of our most significant learning comes not from these successes, however, but from trying to explain the failures, the cases for which these approaches did not work.

In searching for the answer to why certain people did not respond to one of our therapeutic disciplines, we began to discover the obvious. Family therapy would benefit immensely from the application of biofeedback learning to enhance the self-regulation potential of individuals in the family by allowing them to control their own symptoms; and inversely, biofeedback practitioners would gain much by becoming aware of and integrating the adjustment of family interactional patterns, especially since most successful biofeedback training programs include home practice. Doing "homework" means the individual will affect his own social network.

The bridge we found to integrate self-regulation skills and family therapy was this use of home practice. Family therapy has also long made use of "homework" and self-regulation added a new dimension to the potential for developing a sense of competency and a sense of relaxation that is so often missing in the dysfunctional or illness-prone family. Equally hopeful was the fact that all families could benefit from exercises and games designed to increase a sense of peace and closeness in the family and at the same time positively affect their way of interacting. This article will include a working definition of biofeedback and family therapies, provide a number of ground rules for holistic combinations of both approaches, and will include a series of home practices.

We will define family therapy and systems work under one philosophical and functional umbrella. This model emphasizes the importance of the way family members act, speak, and feel about each other and believes that a circular motion of action and interaction exists which can be either healthy or in some way dysfunctional. Healthy systems produce individuals who are both autonomous and who have a sense of belonging or identification with the family and the world around them. These functional families communicate clearly and congruently. They encourage independence and provide loving support for their young. They are consistent with discipline and encourage appropriate responsibility. Most important, they allow for individual differences and are willing to make appropriate changes in family rules as children grow and circumstances change. Often these healthy families are supported by shared spiritual values or community involvement.

This view is a revolutionary change from the psychodynamic model which sees sickness and health as a product of the individual's internal mental/emotional process. While family therapy respects the importance of the individual and recognizes that there are large areas where he/she transcends the family system, the emphasis is on joining the family system and effectively altering poorly functioning patterns of interaction.

This view of man in context extends to the social network around families, including schools, churches and work situations. In the beginning years of family work, it was common to work with the entire family at once. Pioneer family therapists such as Jay Haley, Don Jackson, Virginia Satir, and Salvador Minuchin directed their energy toward changing the organization of the whole family, and believed that if the therapist could help change the way family members behaved, they would change the way they felt. Those beliefs are still accepted, but it is becoming more common to work with only one or two family members on the theory that it is possible to affect the entire system by shifting the way in which one of its members behaves. Often this shift is facilitated by changing the way in which that one member perceives him/herself.

Biofeedback is an effective way of facilitating this change of perception. Biofeedback is information about something that has just taken place in the body. By paying attention to this feedback about internal states, most people can learn control over functions previously thought to be beyond our conscious control. These automatic or autonomic functions may include body temperature, heart rate, muscle tension, brain waves, and more. Biofeedback consists of displaying normally unnoticed physiological information about an organism back to itself. With such a psychophysiological mirror, a person may become more self aware and/or be able to change his/her own psychophysiology. The information displayed plays the role of an unbiased observer—the information is neutral. How a person uses this information depends on the set and on the setting.

The basic steps in feedback learning are:

1. Monitoring the physiological system to feedback changes in that system, since information only exists if there is change.

2. Becoming aware of the feedback and objectively or subjectively linking it to some internal or external sensation. In some cases a person needs to become aware that, for instance, each time the phone rings, he/she frowns.

3. Controlling the physiological system with the help of the feedback signal.

4. Maintaining the psychophysiological control without feedback; which means that the person has to internalize the learning process.

As a tool of self-regulation, biofeedback can be extremely useful for self-healing. Its clinical applications have included treatment of headaches, Raynaud's disease, cardiac arrhythmia, epilepsy, essential hypertension, migraines, and backaches, as well as many other stress-related diseases. Clinical success is highly related to the amount of home practice done. The more the patient integrates the learned skills into daily life, the more likely is clinical success.

Although biofeedback offers a promise for health, in many cases clinical success does not occur if autonomic self-regulation is done outside a holistic context. For example, in 1971 we first worked with a patient who had Raynaud's disease, a vasoconstrictive disease. Although she had learned how to warm her hands (decrease symptomatic arousal), we did not account for the fact that she would not practice at home in the presence of her husband. In this sense, we had to say about our work that "the operation was a success but the patient died." We had not considered teaching her assertiveness skills or other tools with which she could change her family pattern—the patient must learn to develop a responsibility for health within the family network.

If a broader holistic perspective is used, a number of chronic illnesses may be reversed. An important step in this process is belief in the patient's potential. This attitude is discussed in a study by Peper, Robinson, Craig and Jampolsky (1979) involving nineteen patients with open-angle glaucoma (average age 53.6 years; mean years of disease 12.1). Their training included a variety of self-healing approaches, including biofeedback and guided visualization, a process which inevitably involved the individual in self-awareness, growth, and profound personal experience. At the end of the ten-week training period, the eye pressure dropped significantly for ten of the subjects. Their eye pressure continued to remain low after a 1.6 year follow up as shown in Figure 1 (Peper, Pelletier, & Tandy, 1979). For many of the trainees, this program has changed their lives. We have found that these experiences create a marked transformation of the personality. Evoked

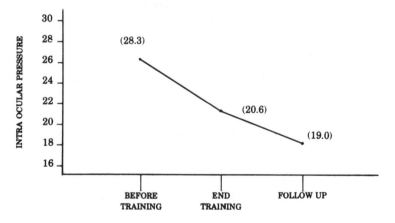

Figure 1. The average intra-ocular pressure (IOP), of the 10 successful trainees (out of the 19 who participated). Success was defined as a significant decrease in IOP or medication during and following the 10-week holistic training session. Average followup was 1.6 years.

through autonomic self-regulation, and maintained by a changed environment, these experiences are vital in maintaining, correcting and enhancing psychological and physical health.

Biofeedback and family therapy are part of the movement toward a more holistic kind of health care in which the patient/ client/participant will assume more responsibility for and power over, his/her own emotional and physical health. (We prefer and will use from here on the term "participant.") Both are learning experiences which provide tools for change, and therapeutic experiences which encourage and point the way to self-awareness. Both concern themselves deeply with homeostasis, and this commonality finally convinced us to fuse the two.

Elmer and Alyce Green emphasize the importance of homeostasis in their excellent book, *Beyond Biofeedback.* They define homeostasis as "the tendency of the organism to compensate for disturbance, to maintain stability. Homeostatic mechanisms govern the heart, for instance, to prevent it from going too fast or too slow" (Green & Green, 1977). It is also homeostasis which acts to prevent a family member from changing behavior or a family from accepting a "former patient as a whole member." The family can consciously or unconsciously help or hinder a member's movement to emotional and physical health. Even further, one member's illness may be necessary to a family's current homeostatic balance. For instance, a teenage girl may continually act up in school to keep her parents focused on her, rather than confronting the underlying emptiness of their relationship.

We felt that in order to mobilize homeostasis on the side of health, we wanted to work simultaneously with the individual's biological balance and the family's homeostatic system. When working with a participant who was to learn self-regulation skills, we would also see the family and enlist their cooperation and participation in the patient's new learning regime. They would help with home practice, recognize positive change, develop a healthier home environment, and practice relaxation exercises of their own. Sometimes establishing this supportive network involved altering the family system to make room for change. We found that the relaxation exercises helped to reduce stress and conflict within the family.

The basic premise from which we are working is that all emotional stress affects the body, and bodily tension affects health, both emotional and physical. In other words, it is our belief that mind and body are one, and for every thought there is a corresponding body activity. Try the following exercise and experience the connection for yourself.

Sit quietly and comfortably, be sure your belt is loose, close your eyes. Spend a minute or so to allow yourself to become relaxed. Now imagine a lemon, visualize it, notice the Sunkist lettering on the side, notice the water droplets glistening on the outside of the yellow skin. Notice its two chubby ends. Now imagine your favorite kitchen knife, and cut the lemon in half. Notice the inside, the white rind, the membranes containing the pulp and the juice. Notice the droplets of juice. Now take one of the lemon halves in your hand. Squeeze it and collect the juice in a glass. Notice the plopping of the pits and the sprinkling of the lemon droplets onto your hand. Notice how much you tightened the arm and shoulder as you squeeze the lemon half. Put this lemon half away, and now squeze the other lemon half. After having squeezed the second lemon half, take the glass with the lemon juice, bring it to your lips. Notice the cool glass against the lips and gently tip the glass. Taste and swallow the lemon juice.

Now observe how the visualization affected you. Did you smell the lemon? Did you taste it? Did you swallow it? Did you notice the increase in saliva? Did you notice a puckering of the mouth? Observe how a thought about a lemon induces the physiological change. Hence one needs to be very careful what one thinks—it will have an effect. If you read over this exercise, go back and have someone else read it to you and observe the effects.

Working from the belief that mind and body are one and continuing to experiment with ways to integrate and expand our approaches led to further learning. As we evaluated and re-evaluated our clinical and educational experiences, another set of criteria for a holistic model began to emerge.

These criteria covered a mixture of pragmatics and attitudes. Most had to do with consciousness, either ours or the participants'. All pointed to the importance of a totality of experience for the participants and toward the integration of what was being learned in the practitioner's office into daily life.

It became clear to us that people who benefited most from their decision to change were those who were willing to examine all areas of their life for places to reduce stress, practice their new skills, and increase their self-awareness. What continued to be exciting to us was the growing assurance that what we were learning would hold true for most of the healing arts and was applicable for self-growth and change for anyone.

Read the following as a practitioner in the field of holistic health care or as someone about to embark on a journey for self-change:

1. *What we communicate by word, act, and attitude, and our setting, will affect our potential for change.* Everything, from our choice of words to the type of room in which we practice, communicates something. There is no way to avoid communicating. Silence is an important message. When a friend passes without looking at us or speaking to us, we assume he is angry with us. When a doctor avoids answering a question about our health, we assume the worst.

Notice that when you walk into a bright yellow room filled with sunshine, your spirits rise. If the practitioner who greets you shakes your hand and leads you and your family into a comfortable room saying, "What have you all come to learn today?" you will feel that you are about to learn something. Look around your house or office. What does it say to someone who visits? Be aware of what your message is. Negative messages have serious consequences. Consciously choose a congruent message of positive change.

2. *What we believe is important.* Of all the many things we communicate, the most essential is our belief. What we believe affects our self-image. It affects our actions. It affects our health and our capacity for self-healing. For example, in a recent UCLA study, Schweiger and Parducci (1978) reported

that two-thirds of the subjects studied reported mild head-aches when they were told that the experiment, which in-volved passing an electrical current through their heads, might cause a headache. In fact, no electricity was used.

Again and again we observed that if the practitioner be-lieved that the participant could change the temperature of his hand and conveyed that by choice of words, tone, and attitude, the participant was much more likely to succeed than if any negativity was present. Further, when someone does raise his own hand temperature and the equipment feeds back that information, his belief in his ability to change suc-cessfully is heightened.

3. *Perceive yourself and your client as a whole.* When work-ing with a participant, always perceive the person as a whole and not as a pathology. Perceive the cancer patient as a person who has cancer, and not as a cancer with a person attached to it. By perceiving the person as a whole, we encourage growth of the whole person. By focusing on the pathology, we en-courage the unhealthy parts of a person. If we do not perceive the participant as a whole, we can never do justice to his/her growth because we have set arbitrary limits on what can be achieved. Being labelled without the wholeness feels demean-ing and reduces our individuality.

4. *The practitioner needs to be self-experienced.* When a practitioner is teaching or sharing skills and concepts based upon self-experience, there is a strong congruence between belief and action. The self-experience is the basis of the verbal and non-verbal cues by which the practitioner knowingly or unconsciously communicates to the participant that what is being taught and shared has meaning. After one has the self-experience there is no doubt that what is being taught is possible to achieve. If the practitioner can achieve it, anyone can. The research data observed in biofeedback training demonstrates that practitioners who can themselves warm their hands or have other control over their automatic body functions have a higher success rate in teaching others this skill than those who cannot themselves change their physiology (Peper, Ancoli & Quinn 1979). The practitioner must be

134   *Erik Peper and Casi Kushel*

an example in action of his teachings.

5. *Every part is connected to every other part, and every part in the system affects every other part.* This is analogous to physics where light behaves both as a particle and a wave. We are all part of the system—the participant, his family, the therapist, the co-therapist. In a network, they are all interconnected and have an effect on each other. There is no such thing as an independent observer. The moment one observes, it affects the system. Here our premises match those of physics—when one observes a particle, one affects it.

6. *Consider the whole setting.* Participants are encouraged to change their life patterns to optimize health by following and incorporating 12 Rules of Health. The Rules of Health (see Table 1), are derived from the observations of Belloc and Breslow (1972), who observed in the 7000 individuals they studied that those who followed six or more rules lived an average of eleven years longer than those who observed 0-3 rules. Pragmatically this means that when we are teaching clients to relax, and they drink twenty cups of coffee a day, we strongly encourage them to reduce their coffee intake.

TABLE 1
12 Steps to Health
1. Three meals a day, must include breakfast.
2. No sugar, refined flour, processed foods, or salt.
3. No smoking, no coffee.
4. Little or no alcohol.
5. Keep weight within 10% of ideal.
6. Exercise regularly (aerobics and stretches).
7. Relax regularly.
8. Seven or eight hours sleep.
9. Faith in self.
10. Resolve anger and fear daily.
11. Encourage a social support system.
12. Daily Skin Quotient (4 hugs a day).

7. *Teaching competence is the basis of change.* This means teaching the skills in such a manner that the participant cannot fail. The experience of a success affects the person's belief and will affect future progress, so that the feeling of learned

competence translates to other aspects of his life. For example, when a person observes he can warm his hands six degrees Fahrenheit, this shifts the possibility of success to an experience of success. One of our migraine subjects illustrated this in her report of how she warmed her hands: "I imagine my hands warming. I feel them warming. I imagine hot soup going down my arm. (And as the biofeedback equipment would indicate, she was successful), I am proud of myself because I have warmed my hands" (Peper & Grossman, 1979).

8. *Develop and support a positive self-image.* To change, it is helpful to be able to accept and like oneself. Often someone who has suffered a stroke feels angry and dislikes the limb that is "crippled." He is disgusted with that part of himself. "My arm is dead," might be what he is telling himself. To perceive oneself as whole, to own the limb again and accept it with love is the beginning of recovery.

An exercise we found useful in this case was to have a woman gently massage her arm, attending to all the sensations, while maintaining an image of herself as whole, and the arms a part of that wholeness.

9. *Encourage learning without judgment.* To develop self-awareness necessary for change, it is beneficial to allow all learning experiences to occur without judgment. For the stroke patient, this means feeling the tingling sensations in the arm without labeling those feelings as signs of illness. This "attending to the process" encourages accepting an experience without measuring it or anticipating the outcome. This allowed the stroke patient to feel sensation in her arm without negating it by saying, "but I still can't move it like I used to." In a systems view, this could mean learning about your mate's dreams and wishes without deciding whether they were "acceptable" or "silly," but simply listening to your partner to know him/her better.

10. *Acknowledge all changes, however slight.* Every change leads to the possibility of another change. Each change should be appreciated as progress.

11. *Reframe experience positively.* This "the glass is half full

instead of half empty" attitude allows us to use illness as a learning experience, an opportunity to grow. A family fight can be translated as an opportunity to learn new ways to handle anger and learn conflict resolution. Pain is a signal: the body's way of saying that it needs your attention.

Our internal language and thought are changeable. When we change our internal dialogue, we often change our experience. For example, one of our depressed participants looked with trepidation, fear and worry about noise. He was to move next to a railroad track, and was worried with the fear that he could not go to sleep. When he learned to reframe his internal dialogue from, "I hate this noise," to "I look forward to the noise as it will remind me to practice the relaxation exercise," he did not notice the noise.

12. *New skills must be practiced at home.* Learning is an ongoing process and should not be limited to the practitioner's office. Skills should be integrated into all areas of life. A family learning to improve its communication skills can practice making statements which begin with "I feel" or "I think" as a way of taking home the learning that "owning" one's statements helps eliminate blame from family interaction. The stroke patient may do twenty minutes of exercise every night. Further, it is necessary to be aware that the same patient may do those exercises and then "forget" them until the next practice session. Although it may be difficult to use the affected limb, for example, while opening a door or while eating, this facilitates both learning the necessary dexterity and the attitude of "I can do it." Practicing at home also implies the involvement of the patient's family. Their support (not sympathy or interference), becomes crucial. They become part of the patient's support network by not opening that door or offering to feed the patient.

13. *Fear of failure leads to failure.* Often our fears are our prophecies. Negative anticipation creates tension and increases the potential for failure. Often stroke patients faced with relearning to walk fear that they will fall. Then they tense their muscles, pull up their knee slightly, and are unable to maintain balance. They fall. A young mother believes

that if she asks her husband to help with the baby, he will become angry and refuse. She waits until she is tired and resentful and then blurts out that he never helps and she doesn't need him anyway. He doesn't offer to help.

There are no failures necessary. The stroke patient can be taught how to fall without injury and learn that falling is part of the road to successful walking. The wife can learn to ask in a positive and assertive way which assumes that her husband will share the baby's care.

14. *Be present oriented.* Consciously stay in the present. Experience and be aware of what is happening now. There is much to learn from the past, but change takes place in the present. The family that constantly rehashes old grudges is less likely to feel the potential for or even recognize new behavior in the present.

Since we found home practice such an important component for success, we have included the following exercises for use in your home. They are based on a combination of self-relaxation techniques and family therapy techniques, and they are designed to increase individual self-awareness, relaxation and stress reduction and better communications between family members. As you are doing these exercises, develop your own biofeedback system. Relax. Focus and listen to the sounds and rhythms of your body. What do you feel? Now enlarge the process and listen to the other members of your family. How does their experience affect you? How do you affect them? Keep in mind the preceding constructs and the rules for good health as you do these exercises.

We hope you will learn more about yourself and the people you share your life with as you do these exercises.

RELAXATION EXERCISE

This exercise focuses upon discriminating the sensations of tension and letting go (relaxation). When doing this, or any of the other exercises, always listen to the signals of the body. If one gets uncomfortable, stop the exercise and *do not* continue. .

The first step in learning relaxation is to optimize the

conditions for learning. Therefore:

1. Give yourself enough time, about thirty minutes uninterrupted. Take the phone off the hook and ask other family
members not to interrupt.

2. Be sure you are comfortable. If you need to urinate, do
that first. Sit or lie down in a comfortable position. Be sure
your belt is loose, your glasses are off, and the room is not too
cold or too hot.

Have another family member guide you through this exercise. As you are now in a comfortable position, let your eyes
be closed. Let the jaw be loose. Slightly separate the lips, and
as you exhale, exhale through your mouth gently whispering
the sound, "HA." Now curl your toes toward your knees, and
hold. Observe the tension. Let go. Observe the relaxation.
Note the difference between the tense and the relaxed
sensations.

Now press your heels backward into the floor and observe
the tension in the back of the legs. Let go. Observe the relaxation. In case your attention wanders away from the sensations in the muscles to other thoughts or worries, do not follow
up those thoughts; just gently bring your attention back to the
sensations in your body.

Now press the ankles, knees and buttocks tightly together.
Pull in the anus toward the belly button. Hold and observe
the sensation of tension. Let go and observe the relaxation.
Observe how different the relaxation feels from the tension.

Now arch your back. Hold. Observe the tightness in your
back. Let go and observe the relaxation.

Now take a deep breath, hold and observe the tension in
the chest, neck, and shoulders. Let go and feel the relaxation spreading through the whole torso as the chest becomes
soft upon the exhalation. Note the change between holding
the breath and letting go. Repeat the breath, holding and
letting go.

Now lift your arms in front of you, and make a fist while
slightly flexing the arms. Hold and observe the sensations of
tension. Let go as the arms drop loosely down and observe
the relaxation spreading down the arms.

Now wrinkle your face, tighten your eyes, clench your jaw, hold. Let go and observe the relaxation. Let the brow be smooth, let the jaw be loose and the lips slightly parted. Let the upper lip soften. Let the cheeks droop and the eyes sink softly into their sockets.

Each time you breathe, exhale through your mouth. As you inhale, say to yourself, "I am." As you exhale, say "relaxed." As you exhale, imagine blowing air through your arms and legs. Gently continue for a few minutes. After a few minutes observe how you feel. Note how much more relaxed you feel than when you started.

Now flex your arms, take a deep breath, exhale, and open your eyes.

Practice keeping the relaxed feeling throughout the day.

TOUCH EXERCISE

Touch is an extension of our emotions and thoughts; what we think will affect what we feel and how we touch, and will affect how another person experiences the touch. The touch experience is a nonverbal transmission of the toucher's intention. Our sensitivity to touch can be enhanced with practice and if we receive feedback from the person we are touching.

Read through these three different ways to touch. Then do the different touching styles, in any order, without talking to your partner.

1. A grasping touch: Feel yourself being "needy and lonely." Touch the other person's shoulder with the intent to grasp and pull the person toward you, as if you are going into a store and grasping your partner to pull him/her with you.

2. Experimental-clinical touch: Imagine that you are a health professional who is inspecting a diseased part of the body. Touch the shoulder and inspect this tissue of the body in total isolation from the rest of the organism. Stay detached, only focus on the subpart of the body. What does it feel like?

3. Whole and loving touch: Think for a moment of a person (or animal), who automatically elicits love from you, such as

your grandchild, (or favorite pet). After thinking of the love object, shift and think of the person you are about to touch, imagine that you can feel the whole person, all his/her qualities, all the positive potentials where you touch. Although you are touching only at the shoulder, remember that this is an automatic extension and inclusion of the whole person.

Before doing each of the touch intentions, visualize and feel within you the attitude the touch is to transmit. When you feel the attitude, touch the person on the right shoulder with that intention for thirty seconds. After thirty seconds, stop. Relax for a moment and then shift to the next touch intention. After you have done the touching, repeat the exercise by having the other person do the touching. Afterward, share the experience. How did the different touches feel?

PASSIVE MOVEMENT EXERCISE

Put your hands on your lap. Sit in a comfortable chair. Then have another family member sit across from you. The family member gently lifts your non-dominant arm by holding the arm at the wrist, and moves it slowly around. The arm is moved very slowly and gently. Let your arm be totally supported by the other person. Inhibit any intentions of helping. Do not anticipate the movement. Just let your arm be moved passively. The more you can "give your arm" to the one who is moving your arm, the more relaxed it is. Allow this passive movement to continue for a few minutes.

After a few minutes, have the other person ask you a few questions as he continues to move your arm, such as "What do you like?"; "What did you do last night?"; "Do you like your grandparent?" Observe what happens to your arm. Does your arm tighten as you attempt to answer the questions? Can you keep your arm relaxed and being moved passively without helping or hindering? Do you stiffen up when questions are asked?

Go back to having your arm moved passively. After a few minutes, while your arm is moved passively, start writing with your dominant hand. What happens to your arm being moved as you start to write? When you tighten that arm, stop writing, let the arm go. Only write as long as your arm which is being moved stays relaxed. The moment the moved arm tightens up, stop. Have your partner give you feedback, e.g., "Stop now."

Observe how easily we tighten our other bodily parts while doing a task (misplaced efforts). Note also that with practice, and receiving feedback from another family member and our own arm, it is possible to inhibit the tightening. (The family member has become our feedback machine.)

After having observed the misplaced efforts, continue to observe the areas of the body you may tighten while doing a task, such as tightening the neck and shoulders while driving. Can you inhibit the tightening?

EXPLORING THE ADVANTAGES OF ILLNESS

Explore the advantages of illness and gain the advantages without being sick. Go back over, in your mind, a past illness. Then on a blank piece of paper describe the advantages of the illness. Responses can include such things as, "When I was ill I got caring and attention; I was relieved from my responsibilities; I did not need to work. It gave me time to reflect upon who I am and what are my goals."

Having identified the advantages of the past illness, look at your daily life and initiate a change so that you can attain one of those advantages, e.g., "I ask my spouse for a hug, as I found out that the advantage of my illness was attention. So now we give each other attention especially when we are well."

This exercise can also be done with the whole family. For instance, "What were the advantages to you when 'Mother was sick?' " An answer might be, "I experienced an increase in my autonomy since I learned to cook and how to nurture my mother."

BREATHING EXERCISE

Take a deep breath and hold it. Note the tensions in your body. Observe the shoulder, neck, throat, etc. Where is the tension and what does it feel like? Stand up, sit down. Did you hold your breath? If you held your breath, repeat your actions and continue to breathe.

The moment we are startled, we hold our breath. When we hold our breath, we often tighten up and our pain increases. Learning to exhale during any activity reduces the stress. For example, take a step into a cold shower. Note that we tend to hold our breath and anticipate the worst. This time, enter the water (a shower or a cold swimming pool), and exhale continuously. Observe how different this feels. Note the absence of fear or tensing if one exhales all the pain. Apply this to other activities.

MIRROR EXERCISE

Imagine that your partner is a total mirror image of yourself. In fact, each partner is the mirror image of the other. The purpose is to mirror each other in total synchrony, which means that the one who leads has the responsibility to move slowly enough so that the other person can follow the mirror movement completely. The person who follows has the responsibility to mirror as completely as possible the movement of the one who is leading.

The exercise involves balancing, yielding and asserting, leading and following, in synchrony, so that an outsider cannot discriminate who is leading and who is following. When the movements are out of synchrony, the dysrhythm is the feedback which shows the *non*-blending of yielding and assertion.

Stand up and face your partner about one foot apart. Imagine the mirror between you. Be silent, and keep eye contact. Arbitrarily decide who is A and who is B. Start by having A lead. After two minutes, switch and let B lead. Make the transition fluid so that an observer cannot tell when the transition has occurred. Be sure to stay relaxed, breathe easily, keep eye contact, be silent, and sense the movement.

After another two minutes, switch back again so that A leads. Continue switching back and forth at two minute intervals. Finally, both lead simultaneously for five minutes (or both simultaneously follow).

Now sit down. Share your feelings. How did the mirror

experience feel? In the dual leading or following, did the duality become unity? How accurate was your self-assessment and the assessment of your partner? How helpful was the dysrhythmic movement as a feedback signal? Did you notice an enhanced sensitivity to each other? Did you feel an awareness and attraction between your hands and your partner's? Were there sex role differences and if so, did they appear or disappear later in the exercise? How did your feelings of intimacy change? What have you learned about your own ability to yield and assert?

THE "I WANT" EXERCISE

This is a simple exercise which can be done by a couple or by a whole family. A timer is set for three minutes. Each person must quickly, without stopping to censor, start a sentence with "I want," and finish it with any thought that follows. The participants follow each other in sequence, not pausing to think or responding to the others' wishes. Keep this up for the entire three minutes. Are you surprised by what you said? Did you learn anything new about your partner or child? Could you listen to other family members' "I wants" without judging them or feeling responsible? Share your feelings about what you learned with each other.

The last two exercises embody an attitude of reverence toward oneself, one's family, and the universe. They are exercises in wholeness.

FAMILY MEDITATION

Just before eating, while the entire family is sitting around the dinner table, share a moment of peace. Join hands and feel the energy pass between you. Take turns leading a short invocation of appreciation of our connection to each other and to the universe. Imagine yourself and your family sitting beneath a golden shower of love. Imagine it touching each of you, uniting you and spreading out over your town and raining down on the world.

THE HEART EXERCISE

While sitting (or lying), quietly beside your partner, place a hand on your partner's chest over the heart. With gentle reverence, with love, listen to the heartbeat through your hands and feel both of you surrounded with and permeated by love.

BIBLIOGRAPHY

Belloc and Breslow. "The Relation of Physical Health Status and Health Practice." *Preventive Medicine,* Vol. 1 (1972): 409-21.

Green and Green. *Beyond Biofeedback.* New York: Delacorte, 1977.

Peper, Ancoli, and Quinn, eds. *Mind-Body Integration: Essential Readings in Biofeedback.* New York: Plenum, 1979, p. 466.

Peper and Grossman. "Thermal Biofeedback Training in Children with Headache." In Peper, et al. *Mind-Body Integration,* pp. 489-92.

Peper, Pelletier, and Tandy. "Biofeedback Training: Holistic and Transpersonal Frontiers." In Peper, et al. *Mind-Body Integration,* p. 161.

Peper, Robinson, Craig, and Jampolsky. See Peper, et al. *Mind-Body Integration,* p. 160.

Schweiger and Parducci. *Brain/Mind Bulletin,* Vol. 3, no. 23 (1978):1.

12

Biofeedback and Transformation

ELMER GREEN, Ph.D., AND ALYCE GREEN

By now almost everyone "knows" what biofeedback training is. And that familiarity poses a problem because it tends to create a mental stereotype which interferes with the kinds of transformation which must take place if patients, and others, are to benefit from psychophysiologic *self*-regulation training. In the general mind, and even in the minds of some biofeedback practitioners, biofeedback is thought of as a kind of machine-aided body training by means of which the physiology is brought under control. That naive partially-correct view is, unfortunately, also held by some psychologists and psychiatrists who are not themselves using biofeedback to help patients get minds, emotions, and bodies under control.

Biofeedback per se is merely the feedback to a person of some of his or her own biological information, usually by means of a visual indicator, or by a tone. The specific sensory mode of feedback, usually vision or hearing, can on occasion have an effect on the rate of learning, but the important feature in biofeedback training is not the sensory mode, but the content, the *information* which is fed back. And that information must reach the cortex and be understood in order for *self*-regulation to occur in the autonomic nervous system.

Biofeedback training means using the feedback information

in such a way that one develops control of the physiological process being monitored, whether it is a process of the "voluntary" nervous system (cranio-spinal) or of the so-called "involuntary" nervous system (autonomic). The particular "way" of using the information involves deep relaxation followed by visualization of what one wants the body, the emotions, or the mind, to do. Knowing how to help clients use the physiological information often determines whether a biofeedback practitioner will succeed or fail in helping clients get well.

But, the main responsibility for success in therapy belongs to the patient—and this brings up an important point. A few patients, when they begin to realize that the training may succeed, stop practicing. The implication is, that illness is, at times, consciously or unconsciously preferred to its alternative, namely, taking up the responsibilities and burdens of being well.

A crucial question is: How can sickness or health be related to a conscious, or unconscious, preference or attitude? The psychoneurological answers to questions about the relation of emotions to health have been discussed in considerable detail in other places (Green and Green, 1977, 1984); suffice it to summarize here by saying that during psychophysiologic self-regulation, the mind (or psyche, or self, whatever its genesis or definition) chooses and creates a visualization of desired physical, emotional, and mental behavior. This seems to involve the *cerebral cortex* (the "thinking brain"). When a specific visualization is repeatedly "held in mind" during deep relaxation, then the brain's *limbic system* (the so-called "emotional brain"), accepts the visualization as a program to be implemented. If, in addition to mental and emotional changes, the visualization includes specific overt changes in the so-called involuntary nervous system (the autonomic), the limbic system programs the *hypothalamus* (the so-called "mechanical brain") to bring about these changes, and they begin to be observed in the body. The biofeedback machine merely tells whether or not the visualization is being implemented correctly, inside the skin. It is an outside-the-skin "truth" detector.

There is no space to go into the striking confluence of data from neuroanatomy, electrophysiology, learning theory, ethology, perception research, and psychophysiology, which elaborate on the mechanisms referred to above, but it must be recognized that contrary to general opinion (though not contrary to informed opinion), there is no such thing as training the body. Certain neural reflex arcs are built into the body by genetics, but in regard to "training the body," there is only the training of the central nervous system (CNS). The body is a slave of the CNS (and its hypothalamically-controlled pituitary, the "master gland" of the body), and what we call training in self-regulation of the body is in reality training in self-regulation of the brain, by the mind, with volition.

Figure 1 gives in condensed form the major outline of this psychophysiological rationale. If we attach electrodes to the body, it is because the body is the reflector of the psyche, and when previously hidden physiological information is fed back to the cortex, the mind, or psyche, becomes aware of significantly correlated relationships in mind/emotion/body. The psyche thus learns to choose, to implement, and to modify. (when useful) the homeostatic levels of neurohumoral functioning.

By way of analogy, the hypothalamus controls the pituitary and the physical body in the same way that a thermostat controls a furnace. At the next higher neural level, the limbic system controls the hypothalamus just as our hand controls a thermostat. And at the highest neural level, our cortex learns to voluntarily control the limbic brain in the same way that the cortex learns to voluntarily control the hand—through feedback. Lastly, at some indeterminate level, the psyche controls the cortex through imagination, choice, and volition.

It is worth noting that every *skill* that has ever been learned by humans was learned through feedback. Learning to walk and to talk was possible because of feedback of some kind or other to the cortex. Walking and talking are not possible without feedback. Playing a violin (musically) is possible because of auditory feedback. It is not a possible skill for a deaf person. Driving a car is possible because of visual feedback. It is not possible for a blind person. In a similar manner, through instrumental feedback of autonomic processes (with which Nature did not originally endow us) we can learn to control blood flow and a number of other autonomic processes in various parts of the body. It is as easy, in our estimation, as learning to play a harmonica. But without a feedback device voluntary control of vascular behavior is not easy, even though yogis, through years of practice, have been able to demonstrate that it is possible (Green and Green, 1977).

Turning now to transformation: At any level transformation may be usefully defined as a self-induced (autogenic) movement toward greater health—physical, emotional, mental, or

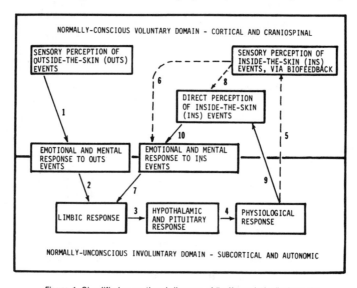

Figure 1. Simplified operational diagram of "self regulation" of psychophysiological events and processes: Sensory perception of OUTS events, stressful or otherwise (upper left box), leads to a physiological response along Arrows 1 to 4. If the physiological response is "picked up" and fed back (Arrow 5) to a person who attempts to control the "behavior" of the feedback device, then Arrows 6 and 7 come into being, resulting in a "new" limbic response. This response in turn makes a change in "signals" transmitted along Arrows 3 and 4, modifying the original physiological response. A cybernetic loop is thus completed and the dynamic equilibrium (homeostasis) of the system can be brought under voluntary control. Biofeedback practice, acting in the opposite way to drugs, increases a person's sensitivity to INS events and Arrow 8 develops, followed by the development of Arrows 9 and 10. External feedback is eventually unnecessary because direct perception of INS events becomes adequate for maintaining self-regulation skills. Physiological self-control through classical yoga develops along the route of Arrows 7-3-4-9-10-7, but, for control of specific physiological and psychosomatic problems, biofeedback training seems more efficient.

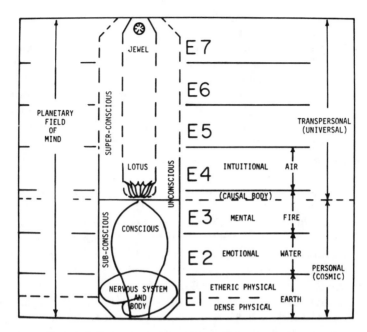

Figure 2. Symbolic interpretation of human substance and perceptual structure. Each line of the vertical cylindrical figure, which represents a human being, stands for at least three things: a boundary between different organizations of substance (different kinds of matter), a boundary between different kinds of possible perception and a boundary between different kinds of possible action.

spiritual—and in focussing on the transformational effects of biofeedback training, it is useful here to examine Figure 2. The first three levels up from the bottom of the diagram are shown as parts of the personal (cosmic) domain of consciousness, and the spiritual level is shown as the transpersonal (universal) domain of consciousness (Green and Green, 1971, 1977).

In working with patients we seldom make use of this diagram, or discuss the implications of transpersonal transformation, but on occasion it is useful to do so in order to break through an undesirable existential "plateau" which does not provide the happiness, satisfaction, or joy to which the client aspires. As will be seen in the examples below, however, on occasion patients get in touch with the deeper (higher) levels of being by contacting in themselves what seems to be the True Self (to use the Zen expression), and then they talk of spiritual feelings and insights.

Our purpose in including this diagram is to provide a context in which to talk of biofeedback and its relation to various levels of transformation. The diagram represents the Patanjali system of yoga in which everything in the cosmos consists of mind and its modifications (Taimni, 1967). This is the genesis of the idea of a "planetary field of mind," within which all bodies (organic and inorganic), and emotions, and thoughts, are forms of interrelated real substance. This diagram also represents (with appropriate translations of terminology) Aurobindo's concepts of mind, substance and states of consciousness (Aurobindo, 1955, 1958). It includes the Tibetan Buddhist hierarchy of substances and consciousness (Evans-Wentz, 1954, 1957, 1958), Blavatsky's theosophical postulates (Blavatsky, 1971), concepts from Barker's *The Mahatma Letters to A.P. Sinnett* (Barker, 1923), Bailey's detailed review of states of consciousness (Bailey, 1934), Hall's outlines of metaphysical thought down the ages (Hall, 1952), and Assagioli's and Wilber's modern syntheses (Assagioli, 1971; Wilber, 1980, 1981, 1983). Parallels can also be found in Sufi teachings of Islam, in the Kaballah of Judaism, in the American Indian Medicine tradition and in many shamanistic traditions and symbols from around the world.

The idea of specific energies of body/emotions/mind/spirit, symbolized in Figure 2, is obviously not new. But what *is* new is the fact that the above-referenced existentially-based concepts of substance, mind, spirit and their manifestations in nature are beginning to be found scientifically tenable (worthy of postulate, hypothesis and testing) by modern biologists, physicists, electrical and electronic engineers and members of other "hard science" disciplines (to name a few, Capra, 1975; Goodwin, 1983; Jahn, 1982; McConnell, 1977; Phillips, 1984; Puthoff and Targ, 1979 and Sheldrake, 1981).

If the question is now raised, what does this have to do with biofeedback, the answer is: If the above hypotheses of body/emotion/mind/spirit are correct, and the various energies and substances are in reality a continuum, then biofeedback-aided psychophysiologic training can "open" the normally-closed body/emotions door in the brain which leads to awareness of normally-unconscious processes in the spectrum of being.

Aurobindo referred to the idea of a continuum neatly when he suggested that if we are embarrassed by the word *spirit,* then the thing to do is not use it. Instead think of spirit as the subtlest form of matter. On the other hand, he said, if we are not embarrassed by that word, then we can refer to "matter" as the densest form of spirit.

Many people having psychosomatic disorders are seemingly stuck in a self-perpetuating emotions/body feedback loop, and cannot find their mental conceptual way to a higher level of control. Their "left cortex" is experientially deprived. In yogic theory, however, there is a useful idea which has a bearing on this problem. According to Patanjali, all the body is in the mind, though not all the mind is in the body. In this theory, every cell of the body is a cell of the mind, and from that point of view it is conceivable, for instance, that white blood cells will take orders when properly instructed (as in cancer control through visualization). Using this ideas as a heuristic hypothesis, some patients are able to break a limiting mental/ emotional existential barrier and move toward genuine psychophysiologic self regulation.

In this short space it is not possible to go into additional detail of the cortico-limbic rationale which explains *how* biofeedback training is used to lead patients and clients to the "inner door" of awareness. A full exegesis is in our chapter in the *Handbook of Altered States of Consciousness* (Wolman and Ullman, 1984). Instead of focussing on methodology, it is useful to discuss examples from our practice, which we call Psychophysiologic Therapy (rather than Biofeedback Training) because so many aspects of body/emotions/mind/spirit are involved beyond simple machine-aided knowledge of what is happening in the body.

We should remember, however, that knowledge and direct awareness of the body is of unique importance whatever our philosophical orientation. The body is our great "holographic" screen of consciousness (conscious and unconscious). In it are revealed many hidden aspects of the psyche. It is not useful to think of the body as inferior to the other parts of the psyche.

It is, rather, their "playground," their learning ground, and as such is indispensable. This is implied in the Patanjali-derived psychophysiological principle-cum-volition, which we paraphrase as: "Every change in the physiological state is accompanied by an appropriate change in the mental-emotional state, conscious or unconscious; and conversely, every change in the mental-emotional state, conscious or unconscious, is accompanied by an appropriate change in the physiological state." When coupled with *volition*, which is as yet of indeterminate origin, this principle allows a process called "psychophysiologic self regulation," to occur (Green, Green, and Walters, 1970).

Turning now to specific examples, three of the following six cases focus on three-level transformation, physical/emotional/mental, what might be called "personal psychosynthesis" (Assagioli, 1969), and the other three are concerned with four-level transformation, physical/emotional/mental/spiritual, called "transpersonal psychosynthesis" by Assagioli.

Briefly put, the procedures and techniques we use (biofeedback training, autogenic phrases, diaphragmatic breathing, mind-stilling breathing, guided and unguided imagery), are aimed at helping the patient achieve (1) *awareness* of body, emotions and mind, and (2) deep *quieting* of body, emotions and mind. Then, in that quietness, the patient visualizes what is wanted. With these concepts in mind, consider the following cases:

(1) There is the simple but joyous realization, "*I am a person*," of the older woman who has been so busy being a wife and mother that she has forgotten her own personhood, who, in the process of biofeedback-aided psychophysiologic therapy for healing her illness, discovers herself and blossoms out in many new directions.

(2) There is the satisfaction and pride of the young businessman, married and with a family, who, having heard that he would not be considered for a certain promotion because of his high blood pressure, took the hypertension training course, succeeded in achieving normo-tensive blood pressure—without drugs—and received his promotion

(Green, Green, and Norris, 1979). But he reported something else of perhaps greater importance to him—the greater happiness of himself, his wife and children and the changed atmosphere of his home because of the changes that occurred in him in the process of self-regulation therapy.

(3) An older man with hypertension, a psychiatrist, also achieved freedom from drugs and maintained normal blood pressure. At termination of training he said, "I have become childlike—not childish, mind you, but childlike. I notice things again. The flower garden of my neighbors—I didn't even know they had a flower garden. I was always in a hurry. When I drove somewhere I never noticed what was on the way. I just drove there and did my business. Now I notice things—you know—I had forgotten that Kansas has birds. I had forgotten that birds sing in Kansas."

(4) The following are some of the written reports of a woman who came to psychophysiologic therapy for the treatment of a serious case of ulcerative colitis, from which she had suffered for some years.

> Gratitude to have this time. Thought of the gifts I have received, learning to relax and to take quiet times without feeling guilty. New friendships with such beautiful loving people. A closer relationship with David, my husband. Freedom from the terrible colitis attacks and from the medications. A new way of feeling—a feeling of joy in living.

Another time she wrote,

> A beautiful visualization of rays of light. I could picture David's presence, experiencing these things with me. I had a strong feeling of our oneness, our love, our friendship.

Of another experience:

> For a brief moment I startled myself. In my mind's eye I was seeing myself face to face (it was so real, like looking in a mirror). I was seeing myself rested, with a cheerful smile. It made me realize that the weariness I am feeling is just temporary.

Again.

> For the first time I was able to empty my mind and just be

quiet, totally, in my mind and in my body. I experienced a
time of no thoughts, just being—a healing time.

In a recent report she wrote,

I read some pages of the journal I keep sporadically. I found it
hard to believe the depth of my depression just a few months
ago, a depression brought on by extreme weariness and living
with so much pain for so long. In one of the entries I had written,
'... I believe joy is not be found in this life. I pray each day that
I may find an inner sense of peace to help me live until the joy
of the next life becomes a reality.'

Then she added,

But each day now, even with continuing stressful things, I
awake and thank God for the joy of this life. What a wonder-
fully different way to begin this new year. It's so good to laugh
again, to enjoy going to a party and dancing all night as we did
Saturday night, to look forward to *living.* It's hard for me to
read those pages and acknowledge that I was the one who
wrote them.

(5) Then there was the bright, active, eighty-two year old
woman who came to our Biofeedback and Psychophysiology
Center from New York City for a week of intensive biofeedback-aided therapy, following an operation for cancer of the
breast. She had refused the chemotherapy and radiation treatment offered to her, having nursed her husband through a
slow and unhappy death while he was on such a schedule. In
her letter asking if she might come, she told us the following:
In the late 1970s she had experienced a slow, steady deterioration of her eyesight due to arteriosclerosis. Finally she was
told she must be prepared for blindness. "With the aid of your
book," she wrote, "I figured out what to do: since the problem
was caused by arteriosclerosis I had to get my heart to send
blood up and through clogged arteries. Every day I visualized
this procedure, combined with meditation." Because there
was no further deterioration she was able to find an ophthal-
mologist who was willing to remove cataracts from her eyes
(such an operation had been thought useless before). She
continued her daily visualizations and her doctor and his staff
"think it quite an achievement that I have so much vision ... I

marveled at this fall's beauty of foliage, seen only as a blur for years." Now she wished to learn ways of living and visualizing that would strengthen her immune system.

Not surprisingly, considering the above, she learned our techniques easily and well. She returned to New York. Her task now is surveillance. She visualizes light as a broad beam moving internally from her toes to her head, lighting dark corners. She "feels" each area of her body respond "as if answering a roll call." She described "an especially elevated mood—trance-like (with my consent and pleasure), removed from the ordinary, but very aware, seeing the lymphocytes spinning and dancing as they perform their task of protecting my body."

She restated her goals. (1) Physical well-being, improvement in my body and my life. (2) One looks for the further step of what one calls soul, something more spiritual—"to get in touch with the Essence of me." In further reports she used such expressions as, "transcendental mood," "spiritual awareness," "spiritual elevation," and "I am talking to my noumenon, I believe."

(6) Some patients move even more fully toward a transpersonal orientation. The following is the story of a patient with an inoperable lung cancer. It is a longer story so we will give her a name, Laura. We had treated her some years before, and she had successfully healed a recurring bleeding ulcer. Now she had an inoperable lung cancer and asked if we would work with her again. She was undergoing heavy chemotherapy and radiation treatment but the prognosis was not good. She was a woman approaching sixty, living alone and with few friends. Her only child, a son, had left her in anger years before because of her alcoholism and because she was cruel when she had been drinking. Though she had conquered that problem, he would not forgive her, nor allow her to see the grandchildren. She was not sure she wanted to put forth the effort to live.

An intelligent and artistic person, Laura progressed rapidly and her feelings and thoughts became more positive. She remembered that she had always wanted to shape things out of clay and she ordered a potter's wheel. She had done some painting before this illness and she ordered a new set of paints.

During a session, while in deep relaxation (a state similar to the theta brainwave state), she said she was seeing "the face of that seductive young man, that shadowy figure wearing a black cape, that I call death." He was standing at the end of a stone passageway beckoning her to come, as he had beckoned many times before, when she was under the influence of alcohol. She had responded three times in those days, attempting suicide. Now, however, she told him she would not respond. She mentioned her interest in painting and pottery. He continued to smile cynically. "You know only about death," she said. "There are so many things I want to do—and oh so many things I want to read—way into my old age."

There was a moment of silence, then, "Oh, he's gone . . . he threw down his cape and left when I said 'way into my old age.' " She felt this symbolized her intention to live, and the figure never appeared in her imagery again.

Laura had a wonderful gift of fantasy. She had seen "Star Wars" and been enchanted with the robot called C3PO. So she visualized her own robot, and called him Robie ("o" as in Rover). He was the captain, the clever and faithful leader of an army of R2D2 robots (her white blood cells) that went to battle any time of night or day to destroy the cancer cells. She was very courageous and very diligent in her practice of all aspects of the training and after two months her x-rays showed that the cancer was reduced in size.

Three weeks later she reported, "The immune system is right on target. For each x-ray the growth decreases and I know it will be gone in a month." And so it was. One of her physicians wrote, "It was truly amazing to watch so large and vicious a tumor simply melt away without a trace in the course of a few short weeks."

Her intensive chemotherapy and radiation treatments were continued, however, and Laura grew thinner and thinner, and more tired, too tired to do the many things she had planned to do. She found it difficult to eat, and we searched for foods that would stimulate her appetite, but with little success. It seemed that her body could not assimilate what she did eat. She grew very thin. This was of concern because we know her immunological system was greatly weakened, and her strength was failing.

Laura continued to have significant hypnagogic imagery. She saw an old battlefield of the Civil War. It symbolized for her the long battle with her internalized mother, but she said, "Now there is peace... the war is over." She had images of the potter's wheel. "I'm looking down at a spinning ball of clay on the wheel, telling myself I have the power in my being to center it and make it grow into a bowl." Then she added, "I seem to be internalizing my desires toward clay. Hopefully I will find the right position for centering." Another time, "I had the strange sensation of being very small and at the vortex of the clay pot I was throwing on the wheel. Just a tiny me." And again, "I was aware of being in the vortex of a turning pot on the wheel. It was as if I were looking down and within."

She also had recurring images of Greece, so often and so familiar, though she had never been there, that she wondered if she had lived in that country in some former life. Often she would be sitting on a high rock, looking down into a green valley, "a sheltered and beautiful place of peace and color. I was going down to live there. It was good and clean and ordered. I hope I can go down the somewhat rocky road into this peaceful valley." And about six weeks later, "I saw myself beginning the journey down the mountain path into my green valley. There is much luggage I have left at the pass. I am carrying only what I need."

Laura's physical condition had worsened as the weeks went by, even though the cancer was gone, and she grew afraid. She had handled chemotherapy and radiation without nausea and without fear in the beginning, but now she felt they were destroying her. She knew her white blood cell count was very low.

Dr. Carl Simonton has said, "Some cancer treatments are so potent, in fact, that patients fear the side effects... as much as the treatment itself," (Simonton, Simonton, and Creighton, 1978). I asked one of Laura's physicians if her fears were justified, if the treatment could destroy her, and he answered that it was possible. I could not reveal this conversation to

Laura but suggested that she confer with her doctors, attend carefully to what they said, and then make her decision, for it was her body and her life that were at stake. She refused further chemotherapy and radiation treatment.

Laura grew more cheerful and positive after she had stopped chemotherapy and radiation. Her appetite revived slightly, but she did not gain weight. She was put in the hospital, "to gain ten pounds." But it did not happen. She grew depressed with the hospital milieu and was allowed to go home. We had two therapy sessions in her home. She seemed very frail. Two weeks later she was in the hospital again. It had been decided that she should have another body scan. Her lungs were still clear, but now there was cancer in her liver.

The questions about life and death previously discussed in relation to her lung cancer had to be discussed again. Laura could not decide at first whether, in her depleted condition, she wanted to "go to battle." (It would be difficult to describe how emaciated she was.) Finally her answer was not to battle, that she and Robie just could not get activated again, that she felt she was ready to be released from her tired body. She knew that whatever her choice, we would continue to work with her, helping in any way we could to make her more comfortable. She asked that she be helped to die with dignity.

Laura remained in the hospital. She was not heavily medicated, and although she seemed to sleep a great deal she was lucid when she wanted to be. Her attorney came. He brought her son to see her. They wept together and made their peace. Her will was made. Laura was proud that in spite of pain and lack of energy she was able to do these things with dignity and clarity. Our last times together were spent quietly meditating on and moving toward the Light.

Patients can be helped to realize that just as it is possible to direct the course of living more intentionally, so it is possible to direct the course of dying more intentionally. To have the ability to call on elements of self-mastery, pain control, and peace of mind in terminal illness is a valuable asset for every human. Death is an experience which we all will share, and dying with dignity is a part of living with dignity.

In pondering the significance of various events and transformations in the above cases, it seems clear that life cannot be arbitrarily divided into packets labeled physical, emotional, mental, and spiritual. All aspects of our natures are present all the time, whether we think of them, are conscious of them, or not. An interesting comment in this regard was made in one of Alice Ann Bailey's remarkable books, *Esoteric Healing* (Bailey, 1953). Namely, all human personality problems, whether thought to be physical, emotional, or mental, "are due to the improper flow of soul energy" through the chakra systems of the physical, emotional, and mental "bodies" of the individual. The traditional mechanism, or channel, for this energy flow into the personal self is shown in Figure 2 at the top of the "bowling pin" labeled "conscious." The channel is called the antakarana in India, and the Lotus being is the "soul." It is interesting that this channel, which supposedly distributes energy throughout the personality, has been experientially (existentially) identified with the Tao (the Way), the Path (as in *Light on The Path*), the way of sacrifice, the tunnel of second birth, Jacob's Ladder, the crown (of the head) chakra, the top of the tower (as described in Carl Jung's *Memories, Dreams, and Reflections,* 1963; and in Franz Kafka's *The Castle,* 1954).

A few of our patients who knew very little of such things sometimes got vivid hypnagogic imagery during biofeedback sessions in which they clearly see how the personal is related to the transpersonal and what they must do to integrate the seemingly separate aspects of their being (Green and Green, 1984).

It was recognition of this need for personal and transpersonal integration in modern life that led Aurobindo to say that the day of nirvana was gone. What is needed in this modern world is transformation, he said, not escape. The change must be invoked by the mind and orchestrated by each person's Lotus self and eventually reflected in mind, emotions, and body (Aurobindo, 1954). He put the three aspects of personality in that order because he said that all intentional transformation starts with the *idea* of change. To that idea we add our emotion, and finally, the "vital energy" (the "prana," of India and Tibet) is reflexively activated.

It begins to modify and regenerate the cellular structure of the body.

It is not easy (and often not necessary) to discuss this with patients, however, and we do not try to abruptly change their idea that they have simply a body problem (especially in those cases where there is an obvious body problem). Instead, we explain the mind-body rationale as clearly as possible, wire them up and begin psychophysiologic training. As they go along it soon becomes clear that their emotions rule the body, and finally they realize (through visualization training) that the mind can rule the emotions and thus can also rule the body. As they come to this realization experientially, they often begin to think of their Self, and their need to become conscious of its integrative power and to let that force change their orientation toward life.

To some extent, we see movement in the transpersonal direction in all of our successful clients, even if their only goal is to get rid of a stomach ulcer, or to conquer hypertension and rid themselves of the oft poisonous side effects of medications. But whether we say much about transpersonal meanings and values depends on whether or not they get, from within themselves, transpersonal information which they wish to discuss. Like Ira Progoff, the Jungian therapist and creator of Dialogue House (Progoff, 1970; 1980), we do not attempt to interpret the meaning of a patient's imagery, even when the meaning seems obvious. If patients ask our opinion, we try to turn the questions back for them to answer. It is generally assumed by therapists in our Biofeedback and Psychophysiology Center that the best analyst for each person is his or her own True Self.

BIBLIOGRAPHY

Assagioli, R. *Psychosynthesis.* New York: Hobbs, Dorman, 1965; Viking, 1971.

Assagioli, R. Symbols of Transpersonal Experience. *J. Transpersonal Psych.* 1 (1969): 33-45.

Aurobindo. *The Synthesis of Yoga.* Pondicherry, India: Sri Aurobindo Press, 1955. Also, Institute for Evolutionary Research, 200 Park Avenue, New York City.

Aurobindo. *The Life Divine.* Pondicherry, India: Sri Aurobindo Press, 1951.

Bailey, A.B. *A Treatise on White Magic.* New York: Lucis Publishing Co., 1934.

Bailey, A.B. *Esoteric Healing.* New York: Lucis Publishing Co., 1953 (Vol. 4 of *A Treatise on the Seven Rays*).

Barker, A.T. (ed). *The Mahatma Letters to A.P. Sinnett.* London: Rider and Company, 1923.

Blavatsky, H.P. *The Secret Doctrine: The Synthesis of Science, Religion and Philosophy.* Wheaton: The Theosophical Publishing House, 1971 (first edition, 1888).

Capra, F. *The Tao of Physics.* Boulder: Shambhala Press, 1975.

Evans-Wentz, W.Y. *The Tibetan Book of the Dead.* London: Oxford, 1927. New York: Oxford University Press, 1958.

Evans-Wentz, W.Y. *The Tibetan Book of the Great Liberation.* New York: Oxford University Press, 1954.

Evans-Wentz, W.Y. *Tibetan Yoga and Secret Doctrines.* New York: Oxford University Press, 1958.

Goodwin, B.C. New Concepts of Order in Biology. In *The Nature of Reality.* Rotterdam: Studium Generale (Erasmus University), 1983.

Green, E.E., Green, A.M., and Walters, E.D. Self-Regulation of Internal States. *Progress of Cybernetics: Proceedings of the International Congress of Cybernetics* (E. Rose, ed.). London: Gordon & Breach, 1970.

Green, E.E., and Green, A.M. On the Meaning of Transpersonal: Some Metaphysical Perspectives. *J. Transpersonal Psych.* 3 (1971): 27-46.

Green, E.E., and Green, A.M. *Beyond Biofeedback.* New York: Delacorte, 1977.

Green, E.E., Green, A.M., and Norris, P. Preliminary Observations on a New Non-Drug Method for Control of Hypertension. *J. So. Carolina Med. Assn.* 75 (1979): 575-582.

Green, E.E., and Green, A.M. Biofeedback and States of Consciousness. Ch. in *Handbook of Altered States of Consciousness.* Wolman and Ullman (eds.). New York: Van Nostrand Reinhold Co., 1984.

Hall, M. *The Secret Teachings of All Ages.* 10th Ed. Los Angeles: Philosophical Research Press, 1952 (first edition, 1928).

Jahn, R. The Persistent Paradox of Psychic Phenomena: An Engineering Paradox. *Proc. of the IEEE.* 70 (1982).

Jung, C.G. *Memories, Dreams, and Reflections.* New York: Pantheon, 1963.

Kafka, F. *The Castle.* New York: Knopf, 1954.

McConnell, R.A. The Resolution of Conflicting Beliefs about the ESP Evidence. *J. of Parapsychology.* 41 (1977): 198-213.

Phillips, P. Psychokinesis and Fraud. Paper presented at the Fifteenth Annual Council Grove Conference. Voluntary Controls Program, The Menninger Foundation, April (1984).

Progoff, I. *Depth Psychology and Modern Man.* New York: Dialogue House Library, 1970.

Progoff, I. *The Practice of Process Meditation.* New York: Dialogue House Library, 1980.

Puthoff, H.E., Targ, R., and May, E.C. Experimental Psi Research: Implications for Physics. Paper presented at the 145th National Meeting of the AAAS. Houston: January (1979).

Sheldrake, R. *A New Science of Life.* London: Blond & Briggs, 1981.

Simonton, O.C., Matthews-Simonton, S., and Creighton, J. *Getting Well Again.* Los Angeles: J.P. Tarcher, 1978.

Taimni, I.K. *The Science of Yoga.* Wheaton: Theosophical Publishing House, 1967.

Wilber, K. *The Atman Project.* Wheaton: Theosophical Publishing House, 1980.

Wilber, K. *Up From Eden.* New York: Doubleday, 1981.

Wilber, K. *A Sociable God: A Brief Introduction to Transcendental Sociology.* New York: McGraw-Hill, 1983.

Wolman, B., and Ullman, M. (eds.). *Handbook of Altered States of Consciousness.* New York: Van Nostrand Reinhold Co., 1984.

IV

Broader Perspectives on Healing the Psyche

Are we whole and complete in the now, or are we in the process of growth and unfoldment? Can awareness in the present moment reveal our basic wholeness, or are we being moved toward wholeness by unconscious influences? The psychotherapists with papers in this section suggest different answers to these questions.

Welwood defines wholeness as an inherent quality of our nature that we can experience as a sense of aliveness and as an open, receptive, wakeful quality of mind. Walsh describes the development of sensitivity to internal states so that one increasingly differentiates states of consciousness, as prescribed by many systems of meditation. Both of these authors stress awareness in the here and now.

Haddick considers karma, the chain of cause and effect working out through time. But rather than being bound by its links, he suggests that we can achieve resolution by "touching bottom" in the ground of our being. Progoff points to a depth process beneath the surface of consciousness, carrying us ahead. He stresses the importance of letting an illness articulate its message and absorbing its meaning into our life. These two authors perceive us as being in a state of continuous growth.

Whether focusing on the moment or on a process of unfoldment, all these therapists envision a context in which our transient feelings and desires are transcended by higher or deeper levels of consciousness. Though they discuss a wide variety of techniques and types of treatment, they all relate therapy to meditative practices and insights.

13

Rediscovering Basic Wholeness

JOHN WELWOOD, Ph.D.

The fragmentation of modern life has given rise to a widespread concern with rediscovering wholeness in human experience. Yet the term "holistic" has already become overused and faddish, so that one might begin to wonder whether wholeness is just another passing fashion or another way to sell new panaceas. What then is the natural wholeness in human experience, and how can we rediscover it in the midst of an increasingly chaotic and rootless culture?

Wholeness is actually the fundamental nature of a healthy organism. The terms "wholeness," "healthiness," "wholesomeness," and "sanity" can be roughly equated. Wholeness is not something that we achieve, but is rather an inherent quality of our very nature, whether or not we seek it out. This *basic wholeness* is a fundamentally open, receptive, wakeful quality of mind which every person can get in touch with. This basically healthy state of mind may seem to be something we have to strive for, given the fact of our common confusion, aggression, and suffering. Yet it is a mistake to think that wholeness lies in some future moment, or that it is to be found in the opposite direction from our everyday life struggles. In fact, our basic wholeness may be rediscovered in the present moment if we lean into the pain and confusion of our lives,

165

rather than seeking after some utopian ideal of wholeness.

The idealistic view imagines that wholeness is something we can achieve by "getting our lives together." We feel fragmented, so we seek completeness by trying to figure out what it is we seem to be missing and going in search of that piece. "Maybe if I did some bodywork I would be more whole, maybe if I lived in the country, maybe if I found a new lover . . ." This distorted view imagines that wholeness is a personal creation that results from putting together various parts of our lives. But true wholeness is never a summation. It is a state of internal integrity that exists as the *very nature* of any organic system, from a cell to a tissue to a whole person. The parts of any whole are each of them also whole in themselves. They can cooperate and make up larger wholes because of their wholeness, not because they lack it.

THE EXPERIENCE OF BASIC WHOLENESS

How is it that we already experience our natural wholeness? It can be felt in our basic sense of aliveness, which is present not just in joyful moments but as the ground of the ordinary moments of every day. This sense of simple aliveness underlies all our actions, thoughts, and feelings. It is a sense of affirmation, of wanting to embrace life and face what is, even in the midst of suffering and disaster. In this aliveness is an intuition of the genuine heroism involved in being human. It is an unarguable sense that life is wholesome, despite all the ups and downs, the good and the bad. It contains a basic receptivity and openness of mind that also manifests as tenderness and gentleness. It is said in the Buddhist scriptures that even a ferocious beast of prey displays its buddha nature when it raises its young. Similarly, even in the steely eyes of a hardened criminal one can still glimpse moments of softness, which can never quite be hidden. Even the most hard-hearted person occasionally feels a love of life, a tenderness and gentleness, a longing to live in a full and rich way.

There are many different theories for why we lose touch with this basic wholeness and healthiness and fall into confusion, wandering through the thickets of our self-imposed torments. In the simplest possible terms, human nature is open and fluid, not fixed, solid, predefined. Each person has the opportunity, freedom, and responsibility to realize this open nature in his or her life. But because we are so open to begin with, we also are subject to both uncertainty and pain. Having to find our way on our own makes us quite vulnerable in a sense, and it is precisely this tenderness that we are trying to escape. Perhaps we do not want to be so sensitive, so easily hurt. As Sartre points out,[1] uncertainty about our identity makes us anxious, so we want to pretend we can attain the solid definition of a tree or a rock. We would like to grow tough skins, become invulnerable. But this desire to grow a thick skin is what blinds us to our innate wholeness. The way back to discovering this wholeness, then, lies in the direction of learning to remain open and vulnerable, learning to live with the tenderness and pain, so that we do not have to stiffen up.

However, this softness and openness which is our nature is not to be equated with weakness. Our basic wholeness embraces all the polarities of life that we conceptualize as irreconcilable opposites. Thus the other side of our basic wholeness is remarkable strength, fortitude, and wakefulness. We do not need to figure out how to put softness and strength together, to make an amalgam out of them. Rather, it is a question of discovering the strength that lies in gentleness, and the resiliency at the heart of strength. The Taoists have always illustrated the all-embracing character of this invulnerable vulnerability through the image of water. Water is extremely vulnerable and soft: it does not resist the touch and can be molded into any shape. Yet, for attacking what is hard and resistant, nothing equals or surpasses it. Water can turn the hardest of rocks into sand. As Lao Tzu pointed out, "the principle that what is yielding conquers what is resistant is known to everyone."[2] Suppleness and tenderness are a sign of life, while a hardening which cuts off one's responsiveness is the mark of rigor mortis.

Thus the search for wholeness does not require collecting a wide range of experiences or looking for answers outside oneself. For, as the *Tao Teh Ching* points out:

> Without going out-of-doors, one can know all he needs to know.
> Without even looking out of his window, one can grasp the
> nature of everything.
> Without going beyond his own nature, one can achieve ulti-
> mate wisdom.[3]

Lao Tzu is not making a case for introversion particularly, but
is suggesting that wholeness can be found within this open
sensitivity that is the essence of human awareness.

Confusion and pain could not arise if we were not basically
tender beings. Because our nature is not fixed, solid, secure,
we can be open to every moment in a new way. Yet this openness also causes us to question our nature, to wonder who we
are, what we should do, how we might proceed. And because
our skins are sensitive and soft, we feel pain. But if we realize
that the way to ourselves is not away from pain and confusion,
then we can look more deeply into them and perhaps find our
basic healthiness intact even in our wildest states of mind.

WHOLENESS AND FEELINGS

It is often thought that aliveness can be equated with feelings.
Yet discovering the basic sense of aliveness in which lies our
sanity and our health is actually more than what some psychologists have called "getting in touch with one's feelings."
Feelings and emotions do express this aliveness,[4] but aliveness is always more than particular feelings and emotions. Our
sense of aliveness is unconditional; it does not depend on
feeling good or bad. It is a very global sense of openness and
presence, which becomes folded into specific feelings and
emotions, just as water is a universal element enfolded in all
living tissues. Normally we deal with our feelings— either sup-
pressing them or indulging in them— without looking through
the forms they take to see how they are expressions of this
more basic aliveness, tenderness, and sensitivity.

If we look closely at our experience, we may find that we
have an intuitive sense of the difference between basic aliveness and specific feelings. If we let ourselves sense our
existence right now as a whole, what it is like to be alive at this
moment, we may discover an awareness of this aliveness that

is pure and simple, without any images or story lines about who we are or what we are doing. If we sit with this sense of aliveness for a few moments without trying to delineate any particular thoughts or feelings, we may at first, if only briefly, notice an awareness of undivided wholeness, a sense of being here which is alive, awake, and open to whatever arises, beyond the many things going on around or inside us. Or we may sense this undivided wholeness as a way of not being here in our usual way, as a kind of hole in our ordinary concerns, a momentary sense of open space without any personal anchors or reference points. This experience may be very global, not clearly defined, and fleeting.

Soon after such glimpses of basic aliveness, we generally find ourselves back in our ordinary self-centered concerns. As we focus on *particular* concerns, we are moving into the level of feeling. Feelings always involve a concrete bodily sense. If you focus on this bodily sense, you may not know yet *what* you feel, but you are now having a particular experience, whereas when you feel your aliveness, you have a hard time pinpointing it exactly. Feelings can be located as centered in certain parts of the body, but our basic awareness is too all-encompassing to pin down anywhere. Like the earth, it surrounds us on all sides, whereas a feeling is something that grows out of the basic ground of this aliveness. Moreover, bodily feelings often imply certain meanings, *felt* meanings which can be verbally articulated. You may express a feeling, for instance as "tension—I am feeling tense." As you focus further on this feeling, you can say more about it: "Well actually, I am not just tense, I'm impatient." This impatience might be further specified, as, for example, "wishing my life would settle down." As you continue to articulate a felt bodily sense, you unfold a number of meanings which seem to be enfolded or implicit in it.[5] Often when we feel stuck in a feeling, it dominates our attention and behavior, if only in a covert, background way. The process of unfolding a feeling is one way of releasing oneself from this domination, which· is particularly useful in psychotherapy and related introspective methods.[6]

Feelings have their own kind of wholeness, although it is of

a different order than our basic wholeness. Each feeling contains many different felt meanings, all enfolded together as a
whole. In maintaining a continuous notion of our "self"—a
fixed set of assumptions about who we are—our basic aliveness becomes colored by particular felt meanings. These felt
meanings are compact expressions of how we see ourselves in
relation to particular situations, how we react to this or that
about our lives. Our feelings are thus a mixture of our aliveness and sensitivity with a number of implicit beliefs and
judgments about ourselves and the world. For example, if I
move into a new house and become angry and upset about the
traffic noise I discover in the street outside, my emotions are a
mix of my sensitivity with certain ideas I have about what I
expect and will tolerate from my environment. As Chogyam
Trungpa has put it:

> The emotions are composed of energy, which can be likened
> to water, and a dualistic thought process, which could be
> likened to pigment or paint. When energy and thought are
> mixed together they become the vivid and colorful emotions.[7]

In this sense, feelings are a more limited form of our aliveness.
Although their colorfulness may be fascinating, this fascina-
tion may soon lead to a freezing of our aliveness if we become
too self-absorbed in their convolutions. Yet, since feelings
contain aliveness as their core, they can also serve to point us
back to our basic wholeness.

PSYCHOTHERAPY AND MEDITATION

Once we decide to work with our feelings directly as a vehicle
of self-inquiry and self-knowledge, there are at least two different approaches we could take. The psychotherapeutic
mode of working with feelings is often concerned with unfolding their inner meanings. This process is like peeling an
onion, layer by layer. As one attends to one's bodily felt sense
and articulates meanings from it, one discovers how each feeling is bound up with other aspects of one's life—"Yes, I always
get tense like this when such and such happens." As one
unravels all these felt meanings, at some point one may feel a

release from the feeling's grip. It is as though one had reached the center of the onion. Psychotherapist Eugene Gendlin has called this moment a "felt shift."[8] By unraveling what all seems to be involved in one's feelings, one arrives back at the basic ground of one's aliveness, which is a moment of both release and freshness. However, in therapeutic introspection, the tendency is often to continue exploring other feelings rather than to rest in this sense of basic aliveness. The limitation of this approach is that it may result in a continual preoccupation with examining feelings, which can become an endless project and distract one from the more basic reality of one's innate wholeness, which underlies all of our feelings.

The practice of meditation suggest a different approach to working with feelings. During meditation practice, feelings are not viewed as being so important as they are in psychotherapy or introspective methods. They are "no big deal." They are respected as the forms of energy that they are, but when the meditator is practicing, he does not regard them as anything special. Nor does the meditator try to unfold the meanings that his feelings may contain. He does not put any further energy into the story lines and judgments that his feelings suggest. Rather, he acknowledges the feelings and returns to the disciplines of his practice. This approach to feelings respects them as forms of aliveness, not to be suppressed, but does not give them undue importance. Feelings are not an important focus in meditation because the practice is oriented more toward our ongoing sense of aliveness than toward the colorations of our passing concerns. How then might a meditative approach to feelings work in an everyday life situation to bring one back to this larger sense of aliveness and wholeness?

Instead of trying to discern the meanings of his feelings, someone involved in a regular meditation practice would be more likely to see his emotions as transient forms of energy, and would spend less time trying to unravel them. Whereas we ordinarily tend to feel most alive when we are feeling intense emotions, meditation practice allows one to realize a more ongoing sense of one's aliveness as always present, even in undramatic moments. A meditation practitioner might understand that his aliveness is an immediate connection with the world that is more basic than his particular feelings of the moment. By seeing how he locks himself into particular emotional reactions, he loosens his attachment to his feeling states. His feelings are less likely to freeze his energy, but more quickly thaw out, become transparent, dissolve back into the basic fluidity of his aliveness. He is thus less likely to lose his connection with the world or disrupt his life through preoccupation with the self-importance of how he feels. In this way he would remain grounded, in connection with the earth.

This does not mean, however, that our hypothetical seasoned meditator would ignore or suppress his feelings. On the contrary, to the extent that he is not caught up in figuring out all the meanings of his feelings, he could let himself experience the energy and aliveness in his feelings more directly, quite apart from the story lines they suggest. If he really lets himself feel his pain and confusion, purely as expressions of his openness, he may simultaneously get in touch with an extreme tenderness, a vulnerability to life, which reminds him that he is fully alive, awake, sensitive, and exposed to the world. He realizes that he can move beyond all his thoughts, fears, images, and habits, and directly feels this naked quality of his life. And this realization (which he seems to have to make over and over again) is a breakthrough which actually feels quite good. Having made contact with his own basic aliveness, he experiences a sense of relief and a renewed interest in the world around him. When he turns to face his demons, they turn out to be none other than forms of his own living energy. He feels his basic strength, healthiness, and resources, which lie in his ability to face his life directly, without fear or distraction.

Meditation thus provides a practice that allows a person to see how he continually wanders away from his basic aliveness and connectedness with the earth, obstructing his own energy through endless preoccupation with his own thoughts, fantasies, and feelings. The more a person contacts his basic wholeness, the more he becomes inspired to work further to uncover his hidden obstructions, which keep his energy scattered and his life fragmented. Meditation is also a way of working with and removing those obstructions. This is a gradual task, but the wholeness that comes more and more clearly into view is something that was always there, like the sun behind the clouds. Out of this dawning realization, we can begin to act in accordance with our basic nature, and to realize our native vision of the goodness and heroism of life, with our feet at the same time firmly planted on the earth.

REFERENCES

1. J.P. Sartre, *Being and Nothingness.* (New York: Philosophical Library, 1953).

2. Lao Tzu, *Tao Teh Ching.* Translated by Archie J. Bahm. (New York: Ungar, 1958), p. 67.

3. Ibid., p. 46.

4. For the purposes of this article, I am roughly equating feeling and emotion, although, technically speaking, they should be distinguished. For a more technical discussion of these issues, see J. Welwood, "Emotion as a Vehicle of Self-knowledge and Transformation," *Journal of Transpersonal Psychology,* 1979, 11, (2).

5. The process of unfolding feelings has been researched and developed into a series of concrete steps in the "focusing" method of Eugene Gendlin, to whom I am indebted for this understanding.

6. There is an interesting correspondence between the way in which meanings are enfolded or implicit in feelings and physicist David Bohm's theory of an implicate order in the universe. For an exploration of this parallel, see J. Welwood, "The Holographic Paradigm and the Structure of Experience," in *ReVision,* 1978, *1,* (3/4), 92-96. To be reprinted in J. Welwood (Ed.), *Consciousness and Cosmos: Holographic and Holistic Metaphors.* (Los Angeles: Center Publications, 1980). See also J. Welwood, "Self-knowledge as the Basis for an Integrative Psychology," in *Journal of Transpersonal Psychology,* 1979, *11,* (1), 23-40.

7. C. Trungpa, *Myth of Freedom.* (Boulder: Shambhala, 1976), p. 64.

8. E.T. Gendlin, *Focusing.* (New York: Everest House, 1979).

14

Psychotherapy as Perceptual Training

ROGER WALSH, M.D.

This discussion stems from reflections on a powerful psycho-therapeutic experience I was fortunate to undergo some years ago. These reflections have resulted in the conclusion that sufficiently sensitive and empathetic therapists can some-times cultivate their clients' perceptual sensitivity to internal states to levels far beyond those usually thought to represent the upper limits of normality.

My personal psychotherapy experiences have been described elsewhere.[1] However, the essential results of in-terest for this discussion were an introduction to the awareness of a previously almost unknown inner experiential world via introspective training. This training allowed me to observe and discriminate subjective experiences, thoughts, sensa-tions, emotions and images to a degree far beyond anything I had known previously. Two brief examples involve auto-symbolic imagery and synesthesia.

At one stage of therapy, I became aware of the frequent presence of faint, formerly subliminal, visual imagery which would continuously shift and change. At a later stage, I realized that these images often portrayed in an exquisitely multidimensional symbolic manner the nature of my ex-perience at that time and could thus provide information about previously subliminal states, emotions, desires, etc. Such images, I subsequently learned, are termed "autosymbolic" because of this capacity of symbolizing the self state.

Synesthesia (cross modality perception) also developed unexpectedly. I was by no means a perceptually sensitive person when I entered therapy; if anything I had a well-deserved reputation for the opposite. But within a few months, my sensitivity had increased to the point that I began to observe that stimuli frequently elicited accompanying responses in other sensory modalities, e.g. the experience of "seeing" or "feeling" music. It seems that this phenomenon is always subliminally available, but whether I observe it or not is a function of my sensitivity and attention. This phenomenon has become even clearer with meditation training[2] [3] and raises the interesting question of whether this supposedly rare phenomenon[4] may not in fact be common to us all. It is certainly recognized in Buddhist psychology.[5] I could offer other examples but these should be sufficient to suggest that a significant training in perceptual sensitivity and altered states of consciousness did occur.

Therapy is obviously a complex and over-determined process, and to separate out the effects of any one factor is difficult. However, what I wish to suggest is that this training occurred as a result of a particular type of therapist feedback and that these levels of sensitivity are potentially available to us all.

By subjective recollection and examination of transcripts, it seems that this training occurred through feedback by my therapist of very subtle subliminal (to me) cues which I was giving off at a level below my own sensory threshold but above his. In essence, I was hooked up to a biofeedback system, only in this case the feedback augmenter was a highly sensitive, trained, empathic human being capable of picking up subtle yet very complex multidimensional cues containing information regarding affects, defenses, thoughts and states of consciousness.

For example, my therapist would frequently feed back information about very subtle changes in the pitch, timbre, tone and general quality of my voice. In addition to giving this specific information about the stimulus attributes that he was picking up, he would also give information about the responses it elicited in him. These responses included, for example, his visual and auditory images, the nature, quality, and degree of his affective tone, body sensations and movements, muscle tensions, and arousal levels. In effect, he would feed back information about several dimensions of my behavior and his own experience. For example, "When you said that I felt myself tighten up and pull back from you and become a little bit anxious," and "Your voice changed in a way which felt like you distanced yourself from your experience," or "For a while there, you were right in your anger, but then it felt as though there was a sudden wave of anxiety which made you pull back and wall yourself off, and as you did it, your voice became higher, and your throat seemed to tighten."

The effects of this type of feedback seemed to show a developmental pattern. At first, I was unable to recognize the validity of the feedback, either with regard to the stimulus cues which he was picking up, e.g. vocal and body changes, or the underlying changes in, for example, affect. The next stage was that there was a recognition of a change in the cue but no awareness of any underlying state change. Then came a period when I was first aware that indeed something had changed inside me, but I could not be sure what it was, and after that there came a period in which I was aware that there had been a state change but could only label it in a gross fashion such as "becoming more tense." However, with increased training of this type, I was able to identify and discriminate not only the nature of the cue but also the specific affective and awareness changes, e.g., dissociation, repression of a feeling or thought, reduced sensitivity to my experience and an opening up to this experience. This discriminant sensitivity training bears a similarity to the self-training which has been suggested as one basis for meditation effects.[6] [8] [9]

What did this process demand from the therapist? Firstly, and obviously, it demanded an ability and willingness to model the perceptual processes being taught. It demanded a greater degree of perceptual sensitivity than I, the trainee, possessed, both to the cues that I was giving out and to inner experience.

It also demanded the ability from the therapist to recognize the nature of his own experience without becoming identified with it. That is, it would have been of little use if he had been aware of his own responses of anger, frustration, etc. but had become so identified with them that they controlled him rather than being able to respond to them consciously.

Since it is apparent that I was being trained to differentiate actual state of consciousness in addition to simple thoughts or affects, this raises the interesting question of the relevance of state dependent learning. It was apparent to me and has been well-recognized in psychotherapy that affect-free intellectual insight is not enough. It was clear that the times when interpretations were most effective were when I appeared to be reexperiencing the affect/state in which I had originally learned the problematic conditioning. Thus, mulling over a problem intellectually ad nauseam was frequently ineffective, whereas at other times, when I was actually reexperiencing the situation and state of consciousness, a single question, suggestion or interpretation was often sufficient to transform it. These experiences suggest that the phenomenon of state-dependent learning may play a more important role in psychotherapy than has previously been appreciated.[9 10 11]

What then are some of the general principles which can be derived from these observations? First, it is obvious that it is possible for a therapist to increase a client's perceptual sensitivity and the range of discriminable states of consciousness to levels well beyond what are now considered usual in this society. The potential for increasing such capacities finds support from various yogic-meditative disciplines and non-western psychologies. Perceptual-attentional training with resultant modifications of consciousness are central to many such systems and have led to their increasingly widespread recognition as "state-specific technologies."[10 11 12 13] Indeed, some systems such as Buddhist psychology contain sophisticated cartographies of meditative stages, perceptual and attentional changes and corresponding states of consciousness.[12 13 14 15] These millenia-old claims have recently found preliminary support from perceptual and psychophysiological empirical studies.[7 8 12]

This process is also consistent with "the principle of increasing subtlety."[12] [16] This principle suggests that greater degrees of psychological well-being are associated with increasing subtlety of psychological barriers and perception, and that appropriate psychotherapeutic tools and approaches are increasingly subtle and less interfering (more "taoistic").

The second principle is that the therapist's effectiveness in teaching such capacities is presumably a function of his or her own level of skill. This is an example of the adage that you can only teach what you are, or as Ram Dass[17] remarked, "You only get as high as your therapist." In this specific case, my therapist had done considerable work to develop his own skills to the extent he had,[18] which bears out another of Ram Dass' comments that one of the most important characteristics in a therapist is his/her continuing commitment to work on him/herself.

All of this suggests that at its upper reaches the introspective training and sensitivity which can occur in psychotherapy may partly overlap that which occurs in meditative-yogic practices. Experiences may occur which have usually been thought of as unusual or even as numinous, transcendent or "mystical."[19] [20] [21] [22] When such experiences are recognized as signs of growth they can be valuable therapeutic stepping stones,[21] and Carl Jung,[20] for example, claimed that "the approach to the numinous is the real therapy and inasmuch as you attain to the numinous experience you are released from the curse of pathology."

However, when, as sometimes happens, a therapist unfamiliar with such experiences mistakes them for regressive and even psychotic phenomena (e.g. regression to union with the breast,[23] narcissistic neurosis[23] or regression to intra-uterine stages),[24] then progress may be slowed or even reversed.[21] [25] [26] In its strongest form, this confusion represents an example of "the pre-trans fallacy": a confusion of pre-egoic and trans-egoic experiences.[26] This fallacy has long hindered understanding of transpersonal experiences and has led to unnecessary conflicts between those schools such as the Jungian, which accept them as legitimate phenomena *sue generis,* and those such as the Freudian, which tend to interpret them regressively.

In any event, it is apparent that psychotherapy which trains introspection sufficiently may not only help pathology and assist in a confrontation with existential issues, but may also provide at least a glimpse into realms of experience which have usually been the preserve of the meditative-yogic traditions.

One final important principle concerns modelling. The importance of this process has been recognized and acknowledged in the behavior modification literature.[27][28] Recent information on its potency suggests that other therapies may have underestimated its power. Certainly one of the most powerful influences for me was the example of another human being modelling a self-reliant and responsible seeking-within-himself for the subtle wisdom with which to guide us both, constantly aware of his own fallibility, but with ultimate faith in our ability to enhance our awareness, sensitivity and authenticity by continuously searching ourselves for them.

A therapy experience such as the one described here is an incredibly over-determined thing, dependent upon the support, wisdom, and love available in both the therapy environment and outside. I count myself very fortunate to have had as my therapist Jim Bugental who shared with me the wisdom derived from many years of intensive work on himself and with others. Frances Vaughan and my family have also provided continuous support and love in these and other explorations.

REFERENCES

1. R. Walsh. Reflections on Psychotherapy. *J. Transpers. Psychol.* 1976, 8:100-111.

2. R. Walsh. Initial Meditative Experiences: Part I. *J. Transpers. Psychol.* 1977, 9:151-192.

3. R. Walsh. Initial Meditative Experiences: Part II. *J. Transpers. Psychol.* 1978, 10:1-28.

4. L.E. Marks. On Colored-Hearing Synesthesia: Cross Modal Translations of Sensory Dimensions. *Psychol. Bull.* 1975, 82:303-331.

5. Narada. *A Manual of Abhidhamma* (Rangoon, Burma: Buddha Sasana Council, 1970).

6. G. Deatherage. Meditation as Discriminant Training: A Theoretical Note. *J. Transpers. Psychol.* 1975, 7:144-146.

7. D. Shapiro. *Meditation: Self Regulation Strategy and Altered State of Consciousness* (New York: Aldine, 1980).

8. D. Shapiro, and R. Walsh (eds). *Meditation: Ancient and Contemporary Perspectives* (New York: Aldine, 1984).

9. C. Tart. Scientific Foundations for the Study of Altered States of Consciousness. *J. Transpers. Psychol.* 1971, 3:93-124.

10. C. Tart. States of Consciousness and State Specific Sciences. *Science* 1972, 176:1203-1210.

11. C. Tart. *States of Consciousness* (New York: E.P. Dutton, 1975).

12. R. Walsh and F. Vaughan (eds). *Beyond Ego: Transpersonal Dimensions in Psychology* (Los Angeles: J.P. Tarcher, 1980).

13. R. Walsh and D.H. Shapiro (eds). *Beyond Health and Normality: Explorations of Exceptional Psychological Wellbeing* (New York: Van Nostrand Reinhold, 1983).

14. J. Goldstein. *The Experience of Insight* (Santa Cruz: Unity Press, 1976).

15. D. Goleman. *The Varieties of the Meditative Experience* (New York: E.P. Dutton, 1977).

16. R. Walsh, and F. Vaughan. Beyond the Ego: Towards Transpersonal Models of the Person and Psychotherapy. *J. Humanist. Psychol.* 1980, 20:5-32.

17. Ram Dass. *The Only Dance There Is* (New York: Anchor, 1974).

18. J. Bugental. *The Search for Existential Identity: Patient-Therapist Dialogue in Humanistic Psychotherapy* (San Francisco: Jossey Bass, 1976).

19. J. Bugental. *Psychotherapy and Process* (New York: Addison-Wesley, 1978).

20. C. Jung. (G. Adler, ed). *Letters* (Princeton: Princeton University Press, 1973).

21. F. Vaughan. In *Beyond Ego: Transpersonal Dimensions in Psychology,* R. Walsh and F. Vaughan (ed). (Los Angeles: J.P. Tarcher, 1980), pp. 182-189.

22. F. Vaughan. *Awakening Intuition* (New York: Anchor/Doubleday, 1979).

23. B. Lewin. *The Psychoanalysis of Elation* (New York: *Psychoanalytic Quarterly,* 1961).

24. F. Alexander. In O. Strunk (ed) *The Psychology of Religion* (New York: Abingdon, 1959), p. 59.

25. S. Grof. *Realms of the Human Unconscious: Observations from LSD Research* (New York: Viking Press, 1975).

26. K. Wilber. *Eye to Eye* (New York: Anchor/Doubleday, 1983).

27. A. Bandura. *Principles of Behavior Modification* (New York: Holt, Rinehart, and Winston, 1969).

28. A. Bandura. *Social Learning Theory* (New Jersey: Prentice-Hall, 1977).

15

Karma and Therapy

VERN HADDICK, Ph.D.

The concept of "obligatory scene" has long been employed in professional discussions of the arts. It has been used to point up the need in a novel, play, or musical composition to come to terms with the ultimate issue—to test and move it ahead toward resolution within the context of the given materials. The concept has provided a tool for describing what is exactly right about Lady Macbeth's "Sleepwalking scene," the final confrontation between Raskolnikov and Ilya Petrovitch in *Crime and Punishment,* and the climax in which reasserted order replaces the long-sustained tension in Beethoven's *Fifth Symphony.* The movement unfolding in all such well-developed compositions is toward meaningful encounter with the underlying principles of existence, and it demonstrates that persons who have undergone such profound confrontations can never be "just the same," either to themselves or others. Having passed through "obligatory scenes" in which the fundamental issues of their lives have been probed to the depths, Lady Macbeth, Raskolnikov, the full participant in a Beethoven symphony, have moved to new ground in their meetings with life and its significance.

If therapy is an art—as such practitioners as Rank, Assagioli, Progoff, Crampton, and Bendit have implied or stated—an art in which therapist helps client advance toward more meaningful encounter with life, an obligatory scene is a necessary part of the proceedings. This assumption was already made by Freud, who saw the work of psychoanalytic sessions as directed toward uncovering and ventilating a repressed memory and its emotional charge, so allowing the patient to win freedom from neurosis in living. A generation later Rank looked into the trans-rational depths of the psyche and saw the goal of therapy as relating the individual fully to his will, which when experienced both inwardly and outwardly brings the necessary sense of wholeness to a human being. In doing therapy Rank apparently oriented the sessions to helping the client "touch bottom," establish contact with the ground of being which lies beneath the striving, resisting subpersonalities found within every individual, and build a new life upon that foundation.

Assagioli and Crampton have written about a similar process in psychosynthesis, which has as its goal the integration of all dimensions of the individual personality and eventually relating them to a transpersonal, evolutionary process which is understood as moving from fragmentation toward inclusiveness and unification. Progoff's writings incorporate even more explicitly such perceptions that the raison d'etre of both psychology and therapy is to help along the human search for meaning in life. The thrust of Progoff's work, both as theoretician and therapist, has been to uncover ways that enable the modern person to experience and actualize the meaning of life through contacting inner resources for wisdom, and to activate his fundamentally spiritual nature. Thus again in the art of modern therapy the obligatory scene has been established as central in meaningful work with a human being who possesses both psychological depth and spiritual magnitude.

One of the most comprehensive views of the human being as uniting psychological richness and transpersonal significance is the perennial wisdom and its statement for the modern world by writers such as Blavatsky, Humphreys, Besant, Shearman, Bendit, and many others. Through the centuries theosophical writers have discussed the fundamental nature of the human being and the relationship of the human race to other dimensions of existence. Their statements about human nature and the conditions under which it flourishes provide the outline for a comprehensive understanding of the person's spiritual qualities. In light of modern depth psychology as set forth by Rank, Assagioli, Progoff, and others, such comprehensive knowledge of human relatedness to the universe, if made available to the individual through direct experience, can help him rediscover within himself resources and creativity of a magnitude he never dreamed he possessed.

Since, according to theosophical writers, each person is also connected meaningfully to many dimensions of the universe, individual transformation can contribute to the advancement of larger social units, and ultimately of the evolutionary process. A form of modern therapy which helps the individual experience and integrate into living the implications of human relatedness to all of the universe seems especially needed at the end of the twentieth century, when so many aspects of the person's relationship to his essential nature, society, and world are at a turning point. In that situation a broadly based theosophic therapy can have particular relevance, and in such therapy the issue of confronting the roots of all one's actions, of "facing one's karma," can provide the crucial focus.

KARMA

Blavatsky recognized the centrality of the concept of karma in a theosophical understanding of the universe when she wrote:

> We consider Karma to be the Ultimate Law of the Universe, the source, origin and fount of all other laws which exist throughout Nature. Karma is the unerring law which adjusts effect to cause, on the physical, mental and spiritual planes of being.[1]

Furthermore, she recognized, the concept of karma has been central in the perennial wisdom throughout the ages. The word derives from the ancient Sanskrit root *kri,* which means to do or make; therefore karma is "doing" or "making," or "action." Not action in the sense of individual behavior, alone, but also in the fundamental sense in which all action is one and harmonious, just as all life is coherent and purposeful. Accordingly, as Blavatsky wrote again:

> *Karma* is that unseen and unknown law which *adjusts wisely, intelligently and equitably* each effect to its cause, tracing the latter back to its producer. Though itself *unknowable*, its action is perceivable . . . Karma (is) that Law of readjustment which ever tends to restore disturbed equilibrium in the physical, and broken harmony in the moral world . . . Karma does not act in this or that particular way always; but . . . it always *does* act so as to restore Harmony and preserve the balance of equilibrium, in virtue of which the Universe exists.[2]

Thus the law of karma operates impartially and universally, within both nature and the human being. All things are innately seeking balance and harmony, and within the large cyclical pattern of the ordered universe the immutable law of karma works toward fulfilling that quest. As Humphreys pointed out, the operation of karmic law can be understood both exoterically and esoterically: in the one case as the law of causation, or the balance of cause and effect so that action and reaction are always equal and opposite; and in the other, from the spiritual point of view, as the law of moral retribution whereby not only does every cause have an effect, but the person who puts the cause in action ultimately reaps the effect of it.

In this way an individual, by properly understanding and applying the law of karma, may come to act free from the influence of personal desire and link himself to the harmonious movement of universal life, so achieving balance and harmony within his individual life when his actions participate in the movement of the comprehensive arrangement. On the other hand, if the individual breaks the law on which the harmony of nature depends, his act carries within itself a thrust which will seek to restore the cosmic balance. Therefore, when acting in ignorance or violation of the law of karma one may experience destiny as binding or ruling him; yet in reality he is entangled by causes set in motion by his own reactive behavior.[3] Blavatsky recognized these bipolar experiences of karma, too:

Those who believe in Karma have to believe in destiny, which, from birth to death, every man is weaving thread by thread around himself, as a spider does his cobweb... and this destiny is guided either by the heavenly voice of the invisible prototype outside of us, or by our more intimate astral, or inner man, who is but too often the evil genius of the embodied entity called man.[4]

At the individual level, as well as at the universal, the law of karma is the principle of adjustment, balance, restoration of equilibrium and harmony, in both physical and moral domains. It gives back to each person, or larger unit, the actual consequences of the act, adjusting each effect to its cause widely, intelligently, and equitably, thus working to reinstate the harmony of the Absolute throughout the processes of manifestation wherever disturbances occur.

Because no individual can live to himself but is inevitably caught up in relationships of family, group, nation, and humanity as a whole, the law of karma is perceived to operate at the collective level, also. Blavatsky again pointed out the connection in *The Key to Theosophy,* stating that the aggregate of individual karma within the group becomes the karma of the group itself, just as the sum of individual karma within a nation becomes that of the nation to which the individuals belong. Each person is tied to both the smaller cultural groups, into which he is born, and the larger national and racial groups of which he is a part. In one case as the other, according to wider applications of the law the individual's cumulative karma has placed him in the settings of which he is a part. Therefore nobody can stay outside of or run away from the karma of his group. The operation of "distributive karma" insures that the doings of the group involve all members of that group, whether they agree outwardly with the group operations or not; just as, again according to Blavatsky:

No man can rise superior to his individual failings, without lifting, be it ever so little, the whole body of which he is an integral part. In the same way, no one can sin, nor suffer the effects of sin, alone. In reality, there is no such thing as "separateness;" and the nearest approach to that selfish state, which the laws of life permit, is in the intent and motive.[5]

Another facet of the universal law of karma is that cyclical ebb and flow of nature, or periodicity, or, as Blavatsky wrote:

> [There is] regular alternation of ebb and flow in the tide of human progress. The great kingdoms and empires of the world, after reaching the culmination of their greatness, descend again, in accordance with the same law by which they ascended; till, having reached the lowest point, humanity reasserts itself and mounts up once more, the height of its attainment being, by this law of ascending progression of cycles, somewhat higher than the point from which it had before descended.[6]

That rhythmic pulsation is rooted in the source of life itself; therefore the cyclical pattern, through a long series of events and experiences, seeks to restore ultimate balance, equilibrium, and reunion with the primal Reality that is the origin of all life and movement.

KARMA IN MODERN DEPTH PSYCHOLOGY

Rank, Assagioli, Crampton, Progoff, and Bendit have all recognized, in one way or another, such bipolar and cyclical processes in human life, as well as the possibility of using the law of cosmic balance to rise above past conditioning and initiate new courses of action in the living present. Implicit in their work is an understanding of the human need to participate in the long process of attaining an ultimate destiny; and in fact all five depth psychologists have made use of aspects of the law of karma to help clients reclaim their intrinsic freedom and thus face the future as more capable builders of their own fate.

Rank, the earliest of these practitioners, reached such a position after many years of cultural studies, close attention to the dynamic growth of his personal and professional life, and involvement in the development and transformation of many clients' lives. He came to see clearly that the basic issue in human experience is to find a tangible way to relate to unfolding existence. This "will to immortality" has been satisfied in various degrees through different social arrangements, conceptual systems, and ritual enactments; but behind all solutions stands the need to convince oneself that bodily death is not the end of the human story.

On the other hand Rank also perceived that the drive toward union in order to achieve immortality runs counter to another need, the urge to follow a unique path of individual self-unfoldment. Thus he had to recognize and take into account the bipolarities and pulsating rhythms which the perennial wisdom had long described as a key element of universal life. He came to understand that union and separation, merging and re-emergence, constitute the rhythm of life. Since each is part of a continuous process, one demands the other; the series of life, death, and rebirth is the pulse-beat of existence, and freely chosen recognition of all three factors is the most satisfactory attitude to take toward such a life process. That attitude, expressed on the verge of the Second World War, was ahead of its time, as Rank recognized in *Beyond Psychology:*

> I have realized more and more that, because of the inherent nature of the human being, man has always lived beyond psychology, in other words, irrationally. If we can grasp this paradoxical fact and accept it as the basis of our own living, then we shall be able to discover new values in place of the old ones which seem to be crumbling before our very eyes—vital human values, not mere psychological interpretations pre-determined by our preferred ideologies.[7]

In his work as a therapist Rank sought to allow such an attitude to develop in his clients "by supporting the individual striving for self-realization." He saw this striving as expression of the will, the "autonomous organizing force in the individual which . . . constitutes the creative expression of the total personality."[8] Thus in Rank's usage the word "will" resembles the theosophical view of the orderly, dynamic flow of cosmic and individual unfoldment. Carrying, as it does, the implication of becoming consciously cocreator with the trans-rational, with nature, it parallels the theosophical way of "mastering karma" by reorienting oneself to the flow of cosmic processes, which become increasingly unitive without destroying individuality.

Rank's system of psychotherapy, upon which he built such an understanding of life process and human nature, involved work to balance the need for union and the need for creative self articulation in an integrated life style. He accordingly approached each client as a unique individual who needs to develop himself, rather than to be educated by another person. Furthermore, Rank assigned the client a central, responsible part in the therapy process as a means to encourage self-development and self-reliance. And throughout the relationship he placed emphasis on producing an emotional rather than just an intellectual experience, because he felt that mere rational knowledge was not an adequate foundation for creative living. As already noted, the obligatory scene in his work with clients often involved encounter with the basic facts of existence, or "touching bottom," as one patient described the experience. Such vital experience often brought the person a new sense of connection to life that extended beyond the present moment in all directions, thus producing a new freedom from the past conditioning which had contributed to his difficulties.

Psychosynthesis, as developed by Assagioli and Crampton, has drawn inspiration and conceptual understanding from modern theosophy, although Assagioli did not stress this fact during his lifetime. Like theosophy, it recognizes the presence of various energy structures and seeks to coordinate their functioning within the total personality. In a schema somewhat simplified from theosophy it also conceptualizes and works with a "personal self" and a "transpersonal or higher Self"; and it stresses activity of the will and spiritual transformation in the self-unfoldment process. Crampton wrote in her booklet, *Psychosynthesis: Some Key Aspects of Theory and Practice:*

> The psychosynthetic process can be considered as involving two stages which are successive but not rigidly separated: the personal psychosynthesis and the transpersonal psychosynthesis. In the personal psychosynthesis, the "I" serves as the integrating center around which the process takes place. During this stage, the subpersonalities and personality vehicles are harmonized and integrated so that the person becomes able to function effectively in the realms of work and personal relationships and develops a relatively well-integrated personality.

During the transpersonal psychosynthesis, the focus of personality integration gradually shifts from the "I" to the transpersonal Self. The "I" continues to collaborate in the process, but the transpersonal Self increasingly assumes a foreground role, becoming the new center around which integration takes place.[9]

Like Rank, Assagioli and Crampton work toward the synthesis of bipolarities into a higher, nonsuppressive unity; but, to a greater degree than Rank, they stress working intelligently with symbolic models of emergent personal development. In building a counterpoise to past conditioning they stress both the freedom to be gained through fresh choice in the present moment and intentional building of "good karma." Thus, again like Rank, while they recognize the chains that link past causes to present effects, they also emphasize proper application of the law that permits the individual to move forward toward a more balanced life through linking himself to the harmonious movement of the universal process. In both theoretical writings and the practice of therapy all three psychologists challenged directly the fatalistic belief that "the person is his past, and therefore its victim." Like other writers, they would agree with Chaudhuri that, "In point of truth, the law of cosmic balance is the most well-known vindication of the intrinsic freedom of man."[10] While the individual's situation at present is the outcome of actions performed in the past, he always has the built-in ability to rise above the past and initiate new courses of action through exercise of will, visualization, and other powers.

These and other themes reappear in the writings and therapeutic practices of Progoff. In *The Death and Rebirth of Psychology* he wrote of "vital experience" taking place at a psychic level deeper than rationality and resulting in a sense of connection to life that makes the "sense of immortality" become not merely continued individual existence, but "a sense of more-than-personal participation in everlasting life." Such transformative experience "opens a vision of man's life and of its transcendent significance that brings conviction on a level that psychological rationalizations cannot reach." Thus it changes the nature of life itself and allows the person to become a kind of individual he could not be before.[11] On the basis of this understanding that grew out of Rank's writings, Progoff developed the Intensive Journal method which he described in *At a Journal Workshop* and *The Practice of Process Meditation:*

> The *Intensive Journal* is specifically designed to provide an instrument and techniques by which persons can discover within themselves the resources they did not know they possessed. It is to enable them to draw the power of deep contact out of the actual experiences of their lives so that they can recognize their own identity and harmonize it with the larger identity of the universe as they experience it ... The effective principle operating in this is that, when a person is shown how to reconnect himself with the contents and the continuity of his life, the inner thread of movement by which his life has been unfolding reveals itself to him by itself. Given the opportunity, a life crystallizes out of its own nature, revealing its meaning and its goal.[12]

Thus Progoff's work centers around helping the client regain felt experience of the ebb and flow of his life, of the latency, growth, and ultimate flowering of seeds ever present within his nature. These themes, if pursued seriously and developed fully, lead back to the obligatory scene of immediate, dynamic, dramatic discovery of life's meaning.

Developing another theme from Rank's work, Progoff has also seen vividly the need for deep experience of the inevitable movement of one's life forward into the area of transpersonal, suprarational, more-than-conscious unity. Such movement is fostered by many exercises which involve "twilight imaging," "inner wisdom dialogues," "time-stretching," "dream extension," and "process meditation." The momentum is channeled toward a new encounter with "now, the open moment," in which the possibility of fresh choice and freedom resides.

The most relevant aspects of Progoff's message seem to be that life is always carrying the individual ahead to encounter new inner riches; stagnation and pathological conditions arise when the person, chiefly out of fear, blocks or divides that flow into segments and then denies the continuity.

Progoff reveals continuities and restores holistic functioning through a variety of dialogue methods which, again, share elements with the interpersonal relating that Rank saw as a key to psychotherapy, and the many "encounters" and "dialogues" which Assagioli and Crampton used in the practice of psychosynthesis. With all four therapists the present moment is important: "now" is the time when karma can be finally resolved; the flow of the past to the present need not totally determine the flow of present into the near future. The possibilities of the future exist now as potential realities, not just as anticipatory fantasies, and through the exercise of free choice and will they can be grown as fruits of present action.

Thus, in a larger sense, Rank, Assagioli, Crampton, and Progoff also agree that blockages to further self-unfoldment arise as resistance to the onward flow of experience, which constantly attempts to break down what has been outgrown in the past in order to allow new creation to take place. Overcoming such "stuckness" involves making fresh "encounters of the spirit"; gaining new contacts, new breakthroughs in the process of symbolic unfoldment, which can then be related back from the obligatory scene to the activities of daily life. By such means karma can be faced and resolved into dharma, one's highest duty or calling.

TOWARD A "KARMA-THERAPY"

One likely place to start applying the broad understanding of karma in a practice of therapy is suggested by Shearman in *Modern Theosophy:*

> The theosophical account of the universe . . . tells (the individual) that the whole universe is ultimately his own choice, and that, if he wants to know why he chose thus, he must search into his own innermost nature and know himself and not hope for an answer in words from some external authority.[13]

This situation holds because:

> Through our ultimate oneness with the Universal Self . . . we choose every experience that comes to us, however adverse it may seem to be from the limited point of view of some separate

portion of our constitution, such as mind or body or the whole personality... The more an individual clings to the particular and identifies himself with his personality and the cravings of his personality, the less is he free... But if he gives himself to the Universal Reality, lets life live itself through him, surrenders to God, lives his life from nearer the center, then he becomes free and is capable not merely of reaction but of action. Freedom comes from within and is expressed as actions initiated from within.[14]

Bendit has done some exciting work toward translating such a conceptual orientation into a practical program for self-unfoldment, which in *Self Knowledge: a Yoga for the West* he defined as:

the deployment in actuality of [one's] latent potentials both of action and of perception. Yet in its essence its success depends on the elimination of the personal ego as a factor in one's apprehension of life. This ego is ... an outgrowth from the animal aspects of the mind, and so is filled with desires, memories, associations which get between us and things as they really are.[15]

The goal of therapy following such a model would be to help the individual perceive and act from a position of understanding "things as they really are."

Bendit's compact book developed a framework for thinking about the shape of a self-realization program, whether carried on alone or in conjunction with a therapist. Four levels of fresh perception are involved. The first is "catharsis," or making uncensored contact with what one thinks and feels; this, in itself, may lead toward some new integration. The second is the creative work of "active imagination," or use of the image-making power of the mind to take a further step toward reality. One approaches a problem not merely face-to-face, but also by allowing some image or symbol of it to appear, speaking with the image and listening for answers. Through such work a wider gestalt may be perceived and allowed to influence future action. The third level of fresh perception may become that of "passive alertness," of "stepping back" to the position of the transpersonal self which watches and understands the encounters and dialogues in which one participates. This objective attitude represents yet another move closer to the reality of things, uncolored by desires, fears, or prejudices. The fourth level is that which approaches, insofar as possible, seeing things from the position of universality. Shearman describes the view from here:

> Since the one Supreme Self is the ultimate very Self in each of us, everything that happens to us [is] our own choice. Through our unity, our identity with the one Life which ensouls the whole universe, we have chosen all the laws of that universe and have accepted them in our innermost being, including such frictions as they may involve for us. And the laws of the universe necessarily imply friction since they are laws of limitation and hence of incompleteness.[16]

Holding such a framework in the back of his mind as he works with a client, the therapist can gain a sense of the sequence of experiences which may be useful to others' full development. Of course the therapist cannot provide clients with the experiences merely by educating them in the model. At each level he will need to translate concepts into immediate terms by using approaches and techniques already known to modern depth psychology, or devised by himself in moments of need.

The following exercise is included as a beginning example of what such translation must involve. It works with a program for self-realization, or encountering karma, as outlined by Bendit. Under special circumstances it might be appropriate to use as an actual experience in a therapy session; but perhaps more often it will serve merely as a map for the sessions which the therapist can consult from time to time as he helps clients pass over the ground toward their eventual "obligatory scenes."

1. Catharsis stage of making contact with what one thinks and feels:

   a. Sit comfortably, with feet flat on the floor, and close the eyes. Become aware of the breath passing inward and outward. Take a few breaths, and as you exhale each time, say the word "relax" to yourself.

   b. Concentrate the attention on your face. Become aware

of any tension in the face. Make a mental picture of the tension in the face; then mentally picture the tension relaxing, so that the face becomes comfortable as you exhale and say "relax" to it.

c. Proceed in this manner to relax the other parts of the body.

d. Next proceed in this same manner to relax the thought process.

e. And the process of the feelings.

f. Experience the body, thought process, and feelings process as a unit now, all comfortable and relaxed.

g. Has that unity anything new to tell you about yourself?

2. Active imagination stage:

a. Now see yourself—as the unity of comfortable, relaxed, alert body, feelings and mind—in a natural setting that is attractive, warm, and serene. You are in a sunny meadow which you are going to walk slowly across to climb the gentle incline to the top of a hill on the other side. As you make the crossing during the next few minutes and climb the hill, review in backward-sequence the chief events of your life, from coming here just now, to what you did earlier in the day, to what you did yesterday—and so back to the time of your birth, or near it.

b. In the review as you get back near the time of your birth, you approach the top of the hill. Up there, ahead of you, you become aware of a bluish-white glow, which moves forward to meet you. There is nothing threatening about it or about the experience.

c. As the glow comes near you see that it is actually a person or some friendly being. You become aware of the details of its appearance, and you realize it is your Wise Person. There in the sunlight on the top of the hill you stand face-to-face with the Wise Person, who begins to speak to you about the purpose of your life, the reason for which you were born. Take some time to allow the discussion to proceed as far as it can; get in contact fully with the message which the Wise Person shares with you.

d. What new understanding has come about from encounter with the Wise Person on this peaceful hilltop?

3. Transpersonal self stage:

a. When the dialogue with the Wise Person has run its course, you turn aside and start to descend the hill. Alert to what you have learned, you begin to accept its meaning for your life. You begin to realize that the pattern of events in your life may have its origin in a realm beyond the scope of personal choice, as you previously understood choice. As you walk slowly back to the meadow you review the chief events of your life in chronological order, beginning with your birth and coming down to the present. As you do so, you observe how the purpose of your life, as the Wise Person spoke about it, has been expressing itself in your life.

b. In what ways can you participate more fully with that purpose? Will you choose to do so?

c. When the experience has completed itself, breathe deeply several times to relax your body, mind, and feelings again; then slowly open your eyes and record or share with another person what you have gained from the exercise.

Use of such an approach toward meaningful encounter with the underlying principles of one's existence—of all existence —may take us another step nearer to the fifth act "obligatory scene," which so many wise men and women—artists, perennial philosophers, and depth psychologists—have declared is the goal of self-realization.

REFERENCES

1. H.P. Blavatsky, *The Key to Theosophy; an Abridgement,* ed. Joy Mills (Wheaton, Ill.: Theosophical Publishing House, 1972), p. 121.

2. Blavatsky, *The Key to Theosophy*, pp. 121-22, 124. Emphasis in the original.

3. Christmas Humphreys, *Karma and Rebirth* (London, Eng.: John Murray, 1943, repr. 1952).

4. H.P. Blavatsky, *The Secret Doctrine: the Synthesis of Science, Religion and Philosophy* (Pasadena, Calif.: Theosophical University Press, 1974), I, p. 639; II, p. 364.

5. Blavatsky, *The Key to Theosophy*, p. 123.

6. H.P. Blavatsky, *Isis Unveiled: a Master-Key to the Mysteries of Ancient Science and Theology* (Pasadena, Calif.: Theosophical University Press, 1976), p. 34.

7. Otto Rank, *Beyond Psychology* (New York: Dover, 1958), p. 14.

8. Rank, *Beyond Psychology*, p. 50.

9. Martha Crampton, *Psychosynthesis: Some Key Aspects of Theory and Practice* (Montreal: Canadian Institute of Psychosynthesis, 1977), p. 13.

10. Haridas Chaudhuri, *The Evolution of Integral Consciousness* (Wheaton, Ill.: Theosophical Publishing House, 1977), p. 49.

11. Ira Progoff, *The Death and Rebirth of Psychology* (New York: McGraw-Hill, 1973), pp. 250-51.

12. Ira Progoff, *At a Journal Workshop* (New York: Dialogue House Library, 1975), p. 10. Progoff, *The Practice of Process Meditation* (New York: Dialogue House Library, 1980).

13. Shearman, *Modern Theosophy*, p. 82.

14. Shearman, *Modern Theosophy*, pp. 146-47.

15. Laurence Bendit, *Self Knowledge, a Yoga for the West* (Wheaton, Ill.: Theosophical Publishing House, 1967), p. 37.

16. Shearman, *Modern Theosophy*, p. 134.

16

Finding the Message of Illness

IRA PROGOFF, Ph.D.

The development of resources and techniques for use in physical healing has been one of the major achievements of science in Western civilization. Especially in medical aspects, those in the healing arts have greatly expanded the possibilities of human life in recent generations with respect both to the understanding that medical concepts give people and the extensions of the life-span that its practices have brought.

Nonetheless, there is considerable restiveness with regard to the medical arts. There are substantial concerns about the impact and implications that its continued successes will have on other aspects and directions of human existence. While we gratefully accept the benefits of the medical arts, especially as a means of controlling the physical and emotional problems that accompany modern civilization, there is a perceptible unease about what the eventual effects will be for human experience as a whole. These concerns lead to fundamental questions about the future role of the healing arts in modern civilization. It may be that we require an approach to human experience that makes possible a step beyond the present conception of healing.

One reason that the questions about the medical arts were

bound to arise is that the medical sciences have been built on a base of materialist philosophy and, in the momentum of their technical progress, little attention has been given to the other aspects of life. Some of the developments that have taken place in the medical arts, however, as well as awarenesses that have arisen in other areas of modern thought, give us the understanding now with which we can open new approaches to meaning in human life.

It is important for us to bear in mind that the healing arts are fundamentally creative arts, and that the human beings who practice them are artists. Eventually this observation gives us a significant lead in appreciating and understanding the individuality of those persons who work within one or another branch of the healing arts. It can also help us extend the work of the healing arts.

To begin, we note a fundamental principle in the study of creativity: that every human activity, to the degree that it is creative, is an art. We see the significance of this when we consider that the essence of an act of creativity is that it brings something new into existence. It creates something that was not there before. In certain circumstances the "something" that is created may be altogether new, in the sense that it had no existence at all in that form before the act of creativity took place. Examples of that type of creativity are the making of a sculpture, the writing of a novel, the conception of a research project, the founding of a business enterprise. In other circumstances the something new that is created may be an addition to what is already in existence. It may be the solution to an unresolved problem, the improvement of something that required a significant further development. It may be the healing of an illness.

In either case, the creativity that takes place is an act of art in two main senses: firstly, because it expresses the special capacity and knowledge of the artist with respect to that particular subject matter; and secondly, because the artist proceeds in a self-directed way toward achieving the purpose of the work as fully and as well as is possible. These are the two primary functional aspects of art: that it draws upon a special, personally developed, often intuitive knowledge of its subject; and that it applies this knowledge to meet the person's individual criteria of quality. These self-established criteria are one main indication of the artist in any area of creative activity. We can identify the artist-persons because these are the persons who seek to do more than merely carry out a task that is given to them. As persons their urge is to develop their work into its optimally possible form within the range of their individual vision.

In the continuity of history some areas of art accumulate combinations of specialized technical knowledge that are drawn from several segments of society. This gives them a multiple resource for the information and concepts which they can use as well as for the diverse contexts in which their work can be conducted. Since these areas of knowledge contain several orientations and types of subject matter, they are generally referred to in a plural form as the "arts." In this way we have among others in modern society the architectural arts, the literary arts, the industrial arts, and the broad area of the healing arts.

The healing arts draw upon several areas of expertise, sometimes of special talent, as they approach the two main areas of human illness: the physical and the emotional. The many differences among the healing arts reflect the varied cultural history of the human species, especially in the recent centuries that have preceded the modern era. The differences tend to be based on a diversity of philosophical or cosmic outlooks which become the starting point for a variety of conceptions and techniques. On the practical level, however, whatever the differences among the various healing arts may be, there is unity in the fact that they are always directed toward improving the condition of a human being where that condition is perceived as having fallen into a state requiring repair. Sometimes there are errors in that perception and in the remedies that are prescribed, but there is general agreement as to the underlying goal and the subject matter of the healing arts.

In the case of the medical arts, which are a particular form of the healing arts, the specialized knowledge that is drawn upon as a primary source is that of the sciences of biology and chemistry. As one fruit of modern scientific method these have developed a technical knowledge and professional disciplines based on the materialist view of nature that has dominated Western civilization in recent centuries. Many of the other forms of the healing arts proceed from a quite different foundation as they apply the arcane principles of non-Western cultures, the ancient Chinese, the Hindu or the American Indian. There is considerable social significance in the fact that in recent years, despite the impressive successes of the medical arts, there has been a growing number of attempts to develop healing approaches that begin at a non-Western starting point and proceed with a non-medical orientation.

These have developed some significant systems of thought as well as business enterprises, but it would be a mistake to view the medical and non-medical approaches as alternatives to each other. They need not be seen as being in a competitive relationship. Rather, the fact that the modern medical approach to healing is not universally accepted despite its many achievements should be a sign to us that, beyond the needs for which the medical arts have developed forms of treatment, there are additional human needs that reach out for help in a healing context. It may be that it is because these needs remain unsolved, despite, and perhaps beyond the great contributions that the medical arts have made, that non-medical approaches to healing continue to attract large numbers of appreciative participants. There is apparently something in the modern human being that is reaching out for help and asking to be healed. Those of us who are concerned about the future of civilization will not ignore this request, but consider the needs of which it is a token.

It is probable that the source of the problem is not a limitation to be found in the medical arts alone but that it reflects a limitation in the current conception of the healing arts as a whole. It leads us to the question of what healing is and what the process of healing should achieve for the person who is its subject.

In general it is correct to say that when we experience an illness, whether we feel it to be primarily physical or emotional, our main desire is to rid ourselves of its effects as quickly as we can. Another way to say this is that we wish to be healed of the illness with as little bother as possible. Healing in this context is primarily a means of eliminating something. In earlier centuries and in simpler societies than ours, the task of healing was undertaken by means of special incantations, by rituals and prayers, and by focusing the energy and power of the individual who was felt to have healing qualities on the person who was ill. This was the vitalistic form of healing. It undertook to use what were perceived as being spiritual agencies in order to bring about a healing result that could be recognized on the physical level. Essentially these shamanistic approaches proceeded in terms of a cause-and-effect view of the world, but within the context of the symbols and images in which they believed. This vitalistic view of reality could often achieve healings for reasons that depth psychology is now able to appreciate but which it understands in another context of experience.

Many persons in the modern era who practice psychic seership as a means of diagnosis and healing utilize comparable principles, although in most cases not as naively as the people in primitive cultures. Historically there were two main reasons why the vitalistic approach was eventually replaced. One was that its rate of success in healing was not great enough for survival in the long run. There were too many aspects of illness that the vitalistic point of view was not able to comprehend, and these made it too vulnerable to failure. The second reason was that during the early centuries of the rationalist era in Europe the increasing successes of the inductive methods of science in understanding the material world led to many insights in the areas of biology and chemistry. These proved to be highly useful in overcoming the illnesses that accompanied the growth of European commerce and the increasing concentration of population in the towns. The benefits of medical healing were increasingly accepted in the material world while the techniques of the vitalistic approaches were steadily replaced. This trend has continued, and in recent years the advancements in technology that modern industry continues to develop have made it possible for the medical arts to contribute many remarkable techniques with which to heal physical illnesses.

There are substantial differences between the vitalistic and the materialist medical approaches to healing, both in the resources they can draw upon and what they can accomplish in the healing of human beings. We must take note, however, not only of an underlying sameness in the goals of their work but also in the view of causality on which they rely to achieve their healing effects. Both direct their attention to the physical condition with which an individual is afflicted, and both seek to heal the illness by intervening with some factor or force external to the person that their special knowledge or ability enables them to apply. Whatever factors and techniques they use, they view as in a "cause-and-effect" relationship. Whatever treatment or ritual they apply, they consider it a "cause" that will have a healing "effect."

There is considerable variation in the effectiveness of these treatments, whether from a vitalistic or from a materialistic medical point of view. It is essential, however, that we take note of the sequence of events that is set into motion when healing is effectively carried out. We observe then that when healing is successfully achieved by forces external to the integral process of the person's life—whether by modern medicine or by non-medical procedures—the net effect is to release the individual from the task of finding the personal significance of the illness. The person is healed of the illness, i.e., is rid of it, and is thus set free to proceed with the conduct of life as it was taking place before the illness came. It may be, as is often the case, that the fact that the illness occurred in the first place is a message to the person with respect to the conduct of life. The illness may be seeking to call attention to particular aspects of the life or to the conduct of the life as a whole. As long as the illness continues to be present in some form, there is reason to think about it seriously and some of its implications for the conduct of life may be recognized. Once the illness is healed, however, the message it was carrying tends to be neutralized and forgotten. It is pushed aside by other concerns since the illness is no longer pressing for attention.

In this regard we must note as a fundamental fact of human existence that each of the events of our life carries a message for some other aspect of our life. One effect of this is that the human life span becomes an opportunity for continuing education, an opportunity that grows larger as the possibilities of longevity increase with the advances of medical technology. Each event in a life carries with it an additional truth which, when it is recognized and understood, can be applied in the next phase of our life-experience. The reason for this lies in the nature of the depth processes that move in a human life beneath the surface of consciousness. These processes are multiple in a human existence, for they carry the continuity of a person's inner relationships, to other persons, to work activities, body conditions, cultural loyalties and religious experiences. They are separate parts that come together in varied interconnections to form the integrated unity of a human life. These many mini-processes, which comprise the unitary process of an individual life, are separate from each other; but what happens in one often has a message for another. It is important that these messages be communicated and recognized, although the communication can take place only on an interior level and within the person.

The messages that are carried by the mini-processes within a person often contain the kind of truths that can be called "life wisdom." Sometimes they are brought to us by studies and meditations that deepen our individual consciousness with inner experiences. Often they are carried by the events of our outer experience in the world, including changes in the condition of our body. Some of these events are markedly unpleasant, especially when they take the form of physical illness, emotional illness, or combinations of the two. Whether they are pleasant or not, they carry the seed of an additional understanding, a "life wisdom" that enlarges the inner education and development of a person. We observe, however, as a fact of experience that if the healing takes place too quickly or is too effectively achieved by an external intervention, nothing new will be learned. These two factors, the speed of healing and healing by external interventions that eliminate the physical expressions of an illness, are important to consider.

In pre-medical types of healing, where belief in the symbols often seems to be a major factor, the effective healing of an illness is often interpreted to be a reason to increase one's faith in the religion, or in the particular means that were used. When medical healing, or variations of it, are successful, there is a similar effect. It renews the faith in materialist philosophy and in the particular pharmaceuticals, the form of surgery, special foods, vitamins, body manipulations, or whatever factors were brought to bear. If the healing was achieved in the vitalist tradition—perhaps in a modern form of it by the focusing of psychic energies or other shamanistic type practices—the result is comparable. By either approach, whether the healing arts are carried out from a materialist or from a vitalist point of view, when their interventions are successful the person is set free to forget about the illness and to ignore the issues and whatever guidance for the life, whatever reconsiderations for living the illness may have been carrying. The principle seems to be that if a healing is brought about primarily by factors that are external to the inner process of the person's life, the conduct of life that preceded the illness can be resumed without change and with impunity. But then no message, no new wisdom of life, has been learned. The pain of the illness has been experienced, but we can truly say that the pain was in vain since it led to no new awareness.

While rapid healings are very much to be desired, we must bear in mind the counter-effects that occur when healings are achieved too quickly or easily by the intervention of methods or physical factors that are external to the inner process of a person's life. The too-rapid healing of an illness by factors external to the person will very likely mean that the person learned nothing from it for the further conduct and development of life. This will be so whether the healing has been brought about by materialist or vitalist means.

We come thus to the question of whether we have to avoid the rapid healing of illnesses in order to have time to learn the messages they are carrying for us. Not at all. We may allow ourselves to be healed as quickly as possible, provided that we understand the difference between an illness being healed by the intervention of factors that are external to our personal inner process, and an illness that has been healed because its message has been absorbed into the consciousness of our life as a whole, where its message can be incorporated into our future conduct. In the former case, the intervention by external factors is something that is done to us in the name of helping us. From this point of view the net effect of the healing is the same whether it is done in vitalist terms or in materialist terms. We are objects of it, patients more than persons. If, however, the illness is taken into our inner process and is allowed to tell us its reason for being, we can absorb its message into our life. At that point the physical illness may no longer be necessary, since its message for the conduct of life has been received. The illness will then be free to leave on its own. It will often do that, departing as mysteriously and with as little explanation as it came.

When it leaves as though of its own volition, the illness nonetheless leaves behind itself further responsibilities which the person must fulfill. If these are not carried out, the illness will need to return. The next time it will likely be in another, stronger form. The most important responsibility that is left behind for the person is the task of finding and comprehending the message for the future conduct of the life that the illness was carrying. Doing this may have a number of aspects as it relates to the several small processes, the Mini-Processes, that are present in the depth of the person. In addition, there are often more objective aspects that must be considered and acted upon. Sometimes, while the illness is delivering its message, there are physical side-effects that develop, and these may remain after the message has been recognized. Once the message of the illness has been received, however, these can be treated in whatever objective physical terms are indicated by the current state of the medical arts. It may also be that the message carried by the illness reached deep into the underlying levels of consciousness in the person's life. In that case, further interior explorations are necessary. One message and effect of the illness may be to set these in motion.

Sometimes the continuity of inner work leads to unexpected realizations. One may find, for example, that the illness is not to be eliminated, but in some form is to have a permanent

place in the person's life history. It may be that there now is a
new physical condition which the individual must absorb at
interior levels into the larger meaning that is unfolding in
the life.

There are a number of circumstances in which a physical
condition can have a more-than-transient role in a person's
life. It may be that the illness has a particular relation to the
way the person's life has been lived. In working to overcome
the illness, issues may be raised that reach beyond the physical
condition affecting the direction and the conduct of the life.
Sometimes in seeking to overcome a weakness, unexpected
strengths and new possibilities are developed. These unexpected developments may turn out to be a major aspect of the
message that the illness was carrying. Sometimes a person's
illness becomes a permanent part of the life simply because
no means of healing it is found. Not being able to eliminate the
physical condition, the person may be forced to draw on the
native ingenuity of life to find a means of living with it. Sometimes, in fact, the relation with a physical condition develops
so strongly that it leads to new circumstances and new meanings that could not have been envisioned at the beginning.
Then, unexpectedly, the illness becomes a constructive element in the life, in large part because it was not healed.

Something of a larger significance is involved here, however, for it shows us where to look when we are seeking the
meaning of an illness. There are the events of the past that
led to the illness or that established a fertile ground in which
the illness could occur. These may be the visible sources of
the illness, but they are not its meaning. The analytic style of
thinking that is customary in the modern rationalist era looks
for the meaning of events in their apparent causes, that is, in
the events that preceded them. There is another aspect to
meaning, however, that is more fundamental. We find this
in the observation that the meaning of a life is not present at
its beginning, but that it forms itself and discloses itself as the
events of the life unfold. Out of the raw material of happen-
ings and circumstances the direction of a life takes shape, and
thus each life moves toward its unpredictable outcome.

It is one thing to identify the meaning of an illness by

analyzing the "causes" and proximate sources from which it seems to have come. It is something other to enter into a relationship with the illness by which the illness is able to articulate its message for the life. The relationship of dialogue is one of the important possibilities that the *Intensive Journal* method makes available. It is underlain by the approach to meaning in human existence that it derives from holistic depth psychology.

In this conception, meaning is not to be found in the "causes" that lie in the past, nor in the determinants, the specified possibilities, that are contained in the seed of each organism. Rather, meaning emerges out of the movement of events as a human life unfolds. Meaning is an *extra* that emerges sometimes in the course of a human existence. It is not present at the beginning of a life, nor is it contained in the seed as an inevitable potential of growth. But there is the possibility that meaning will emerge as an extra, as an additional *plus,* in the course of a human existence, much as beauty and truth may emerge as extras that carry the unexpected meaning of an artwork. The artist can work with commitment and intention toward achieving beauty and truth, but no artist can be sure in advance that beauty and truth will make their appearance in a given piece of work. Nonetheless the possibility is always there that beauty and truth will become present, that they will happen. And if they do, that will be the meaning of the artwork.

So it is with meaning in a human life. We cannot plan for it. But we know that it can never happen unless we do the groundwork and thus open the possibility that it can come to pass some time in the future unexpectedly. We never know in advance when meaning will take shape and be embodied in a life and become the emergent of that life as an artwork.

The essence of the *Intensive Journal* method is that it approaches a human life as an artwork from which meaning may potentially emerge at some point. Its principles are drawn from holistic depth psychology, especially the perception that each life is unique both in its content and in its potential for meaning. At a Journal Workshop it is apparent that this principle of individual uniqueness is not an abstraction for it is quickly made concrete as the Journal exercises are carried out. One of the early exercises at a Journal Workshop is the listing of Steppingstones, a dozen brief statements marking off the events in an individual's life that are felt to be personally significant. These are spontaneously recalled and briefly recorded in the quiet atmosphere of a Journal Workshop. The first Steppingstone is common to everyone. We begin by completing the statement, "I was born . . ." The second Steppingstone completes the phrase, "And then . . ." And the same for each successive Steppingstone that follows in the life. The dozen or so Steppingstones that comprise the list recapitulate the movement of the life from birth to the present moment when the listing of Steppingstones is being made. While the first Steppingstone is the same for everyone and there are similarities among some of the Steppingstones that follow, each list is different from every other list. No two are the same. This expresses the fact that each individual human existence is unique, as are the possibilities for meaning in its experiences.

A second principle that the *Intensive Journal* process derives from holistic depth psychology is that an individual human being is to be approached not as a case history possessing pathologies but as a life history that contains potential for meaning in the events of the life. Directing our attention to the life history of a person becomes particularly important when we seek to find the message that an illness is carrying. The first step is to establish the context of the life as a whole. We do this with the Journal exercises that enable us to work with the Steppingstones. Having established the context of the life, and having made contact with some of its contents, we have access to the material in the life to which we can apply the Journal Feedback method. Working within the Journal structure in order to maintain the framework and continuity of our life as a whole, we use the active, non-analytic techniques to feed back to ourselves in order that we can add to the various perceptions and entries that we have made in the Journal sections. Thus we direct our attention to the aspects of our life that now seem particularly significant to us, and we amplify the contents of our earlier entries. The experiences in our life that relate to our illnesses and to the condition of our body in general come to the fore in the Journal section called *Dialogue with the Body.* Here we use the self-expanding procedures of Journal Feedback as our means of drawing out for our personal perception the implications of the events and contents of our physical life.

As human beings our lives have a physical body at their base. These bodies do not contain meaning in themselves. Because of their intimate relation to us, however, our bodies are organs of experience by which meaning can enter our lives. When our bodies become ill or are injured, they need to be healed. To achieve this healing, or fixing, of the body there are many techniques that are available to the healing arts. Some of these techniques have a vitalistic source. Others, especially those that are more widely used in the modern era, are derived from materialist medical practice. The essence of healing however does not lie in the efficiency with which the body and its parts can be restored to strength. It lies in the meaning that is added to the life of the person who suffers the illness or the injury. This meaning is not something that can be given to the person from the outside, for example, as a belief can be stated and recommended, or as a treatment of the body can be given from the outside. This added meaning can come only by means of an experience that takes place within the person as an individual finds interiorly the message carried by an illness, absorbs it into consciousness and allows it in its own timing to disclose its meaning for the life.

V

Human Fields and the Energetics of Healing

The authors of the pieces in this section share a perspective in which an individual is seen as a local concentration of energy within a larger field. Furthermore, in this view several inter-penetrating fields at different levels are focalized within the individual, so that we are each a system of interacting energy fields. Our emotions, thoughts, and actions can be seen as ener-getic patterns of flow or blockage, and disease results from dis-harmony in these patterns. This model is consistent with yoga philosophy and other religious traditions, and some scientists take it seriously, finding that it fits data from the study of psychosomatic medicine and other areas.

Krieger and Kunz discuss Therapeutic Touch, a practice somewhat akin to the laying-on of hands, as an energy exchange between the healer and the patient which influences the energy flow and patterns in the field. They hold that this is accom-plished by drawing on a universal healing power, which can penetrate the fields at all levels to help restore order and harmony in them. But for a lasting effect, often the patient must learn to change and de-energize harmful emotional and mental patterns (Kunz and Pepper, Kunz).

Before treating a patient, a healer transcends the orientation of the personal ego by centering, thereby opening to finer energies at higher levels within his or her own fields. These have the potentiality not only of integrating one within, but also, when focused by the healer's intentionality, of touching the patient at this level of wholeness (Kunz, Krieger). Healing others strengthens this aspect of the self and, like meditation, is a vehicle for self-transformation. Both practices can connect one with the spiritual ground of being in which all things are unified (Macrae).

17

Fields and Their Clinical Implications

DORA KUNZ AND ERIK PEPER

Part I

A dualistic material perspective is the common assumption underlying much of Western psychology; namely, we are physically and mentally apart and separated from each other. This article proposes that an energetic perspective, in which individuals are interconnected and are local concentrations within a larger field, is a more accurate description, or working hypothesis of reality. In fact, when one describes interpersonal (emotional) interactions between people such as "he gives me a lift" or "I feel drained," the language reflects this dynamic, energetic perspective. Underlying this model is the assumption that the energies interchanged in ordinary human interactions are modulated in (via) a universal field which permeates all matter. Such a model can be used to generate useful clinical interventions.

Every individual living organism can be described both as a physical entity and as a system of energy fields that are constantly interacting with the environment, which includes all other organisms. These fields (like all those known to science) permeate space. Each individual is a localization (concentration) of energy within these universal fields. Moreover, these individual local fields interact with one another, being part of one whole, dynamic, and interdependent system.

The perspective that each of us is interconnected offers a holistic model of how human beings affect each other. We propose that it furnishes a description of (as well as a mechanism by which) such disparate phenomena as placebo and experimental bias affect the outcome of research studies; how bedside manner affects the health of the patient; how some schizophrenics sense our strengths and our insecurities; how we may become exhilarated and/or drained by other people with or without verbal contact.

An energetic approach to human interaction may explain how individuals unknowingly affect each other; it offers us the possibility of developing strategies to influence and change these interactions. In fact, the application of such a perspective may have outcomes that change our perception of human relationships, since every thought or emotion is an energy that may affect the energy field of others. These interactions can be positive, negative (draining), or neutral and are illustrated in the following examples: a person in a group becomes angry or hostile and immediately arouses a similar emotion in the other group members; a disturbed patient is soothed when a nurse quietly places her hand on his shoulder; a discussant becomes exhilarated during a lively discussion; a nurse becomes tired and drained after seeing one patient while calm and relaxed after treating another.

These experiential observations describe an energy exchange which is common to all human interactions whether they be thoughts, emotions, or physical actions. These energies radiate out from the body into space in wavelike patterns of motion that slowly attenuate and dissipate. At a distance they sink back and merge into the universal field.

Each thought, action, and emotion can thus be seen as an energetic pattern with distinct characteristics—a pattern which we may unconsciously radiate or deliberately direct at another person. In fact, illness and health have characteristic patterns of energy flow within each individual. Such dynamic patterns may be likened to the ripple formation caused when a pebble is dropped into water. The amplitude of the wave which is generated depends upon the force of the impact when the pebble hits the water. Similarly, the intensity and duration of the human energetic patterns are modulated by the degree of concentration (focus), or intentions provided by the emotion, thought, or action. At times, one is unaware of the action. For example, one may feel little emotional response when he/she is engaged with an intellectual problem. Even though unperceived, changes are always taking place and this can be perceived as a field phenomenon.

In describing the principle characteristics of the individual within the larger universal field, it is important to remember that such a description is only a static representation of a dynamic process. It is like a still photograph of a falling rock which, by freezing the motion of its descent in mid-air, might deceive us into thinking that the rock is floating in space. In the same way, any static description of the energy fields needs to be seen as a momentary, artificial arrest of the continuous motion which characterizes any field.

These fields are local concentrations within a universal field. This focus of energy is what we experience as *ourselves*. The different fields of an individual can be perceived in terms of sub-categories related to specific functions. Somewhat analogous is the way white light can be perceived as a composite of all the colors, yet can be separated into its component spectral colors with the use of a prism.

The fields which constitute a person include, among others, the electro-magnetic, the strong and weak nuclear (of the physical body), and in addition, consist of:

1. The vital field, which is closely associated with the body and is often referred to as the etheric.
2. The emotional field, often called the aura, which is made up of feelings. (Individuals can project this field.)
3. The mental field, which is the embodiment of our thinking and incorporates our visual images as well as our concepts and ideas.
4. The intuitional field, which is characterized by order, creativity, and compassion. (This field is a source of healing.)

ENERGY FLOW IN THE FIELDS

The human field is much like a musical symphony. The musical
dynamic is expressed in terms of inner consistency and
harmonic relationships, no matter how dissonant the individual elements appear. Within the field, energies continuously circulate and flow outward and, sometimes, inward.
The basic physical energy or vitality comes from what is called
prana in Eastern philosophy. Prana enters the body through
the vital counterpart of the spleen (not the actual organ,
which in fact may be missing or damaged) and is modulated
and distributed by a field mechanism known as a chakra
(wheel), which might be called an energy "transformer." The
solar plexus chakra transforms this prana into the vital energy
which is so important to the physical body. The level of vital
energy depends on how much energy flows through the
spleen chakra, how it is processed in the solar plexus chakra,
and the rate by which it flows outward and is distributed
throughout the body.

This process can be illustrated in Fig. 1 by the water hose
analogy.

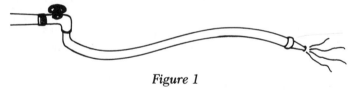

Figure 1

In this illustration, the open intake of the hose at the left
represents the point of entry of prana at the spleen chakra,
while the valve represents the solar plexus chakra. When the
flow of water passes freely through the hose, without meeting
any obstructions at the intake, middle, or end, a state of health
ensues. Any obstruction which hinders the flow constitutes a
pathological condition. A state of lower vital energy in an
individual is usually related to a constriction in the solar
plexus chakra, which inhibits the flow of prana and/or leads
to the depletion of the vital energy through excessive tension.
Lowered vital energy is often the precursor of pathology.

Lowered energy may be experienced as a highly nervous

state in which the "driving energy" disturbs the organizational balance of the individual and often results in a state of exhaustion. The physical symptoms associated with this lowered energy may range from irritability and exhaustion to tightness in the abdomen, to difficulty in initiating even the simplest actions, which can feel overwhelming. The psychological symptoms include depression, a sense of withdrawal, immobilization, discouragement and hyper-nervousness.

Ironically, individuals tend to be unaware that their energy level is changing or dropping until a threshold is reached and the previously named symptoms come into the foreground. Awareness is masked by various factors, such as one's attention being too involved in one's work or by being emotionally driven. In either case the exhaustion may set the stage for future illness, unless the process is reversed and the flow of energy is replenished. Ironically, when one's energy is low one tends to search for stimulants to "pep up." The result is often addiction, such as alcoholism: however, "pepping up" is not the solution for energy depletion. To enhance the vital field, we must allow ourselves to relax. The process of relaxation increases the flow of prana through the solar plexus, thereby increasing our reserves of vital energy, a process in which we expend less vital energy.

DETAILED DESCRIPTION OF THE VITAL, EMOTIONAL, MENTAL AND INTUITIONAL FIELDS

The Vital Field: The physical body is surrounded and permeated by the vital (etheric) field, which attenuates at about one to six inches from the body or two inches on the average. This field is an intrinsic part of the body itself; every cell is part of the vital field and contributes to its overall rhythm.

When the vital field is healthy, there is within it a natural autonomous rhythm. It is only when pathology occurs that dysrhythmic patterns and other accompanying changes appear. The whole etheric system can be thought of as analogous to the functioning of the heart. If the heart is dissected, each small part will seem to have its own autorhythmicity, but when the heart is healthy, the pacemaker establishes a unified overall rhythm.

In the same way, each organ in the body has its corresponding energetic rhythm in the etheric field. Between the spheres of the various organs the different rhythms interact, as if a transfer function were occurring. When the body is whole and healthy these rhythms transfer easily from organ to organ. However, with pathology, the rhythms as well as the energy levels are changed. For example, the residue of a surgical appendectomy can be perceived in the field. The physical tissues which are now adjacent to each other have an altered energy transfer function which was previously modulated by the appendix. In physics this is called impedance matching or mismatching. Each adjacent tissue is "impedance matched," which means that the energy can easily flow through all the tissue. Surgery or illness changes the impedance matching, so that the energy is to some degree dissipated rather than transferred.

It is only through field interactions that one can become aware of a field. In order to experience the vital field, we must be in close contact with another person so that the two fields can meet and interact. By exercising the powers of awareness, one can become sensitive to the presence of another person's field. For example, gently rub your hands together, then stop and very slowly separate the hands while feeling and listening to the sensations in the hands. Imagine that the hands are connected even though they are actually separated in space. Note the feelings, such as tingling, electrical connection, or magnetic drawing. Now gently place your hands over your partner's hand without touching and listen or feel for the sensations as shown in Fig. 2.

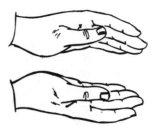

Figure 2

This intention of sensing for the field establishes a resonance between the fields of different persons. In this instance, the fields interact and resonate together in order for awareness to occur—the observer and the observed are always interacting. A detailed teaching strategy for learning this energy sensitivity for healing, known as therapeutic touch, has been developed and described by Dolores Krieger in her book *The Therapeutic Touch.*[1]

The Emotional Field: Interpenetrating both the physical body and its vital field is the emotional field. This field is wider in scope, extending about eighteen to forty-eight inches beyond the body. Thoughts or intentions can enlarge its normal ovoid shape to express the strong feelings projected by the person—elasticity is one of its major characteristics as illustrated in Fig. 3.

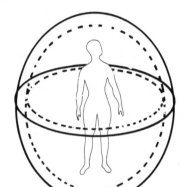

Figure 3

Through thoughts and intention, the individual emotional field can be stretched to considerable distances, such as ten to fifteen feet. As it projects out, and if another emotional field is there, it tends to interpenetrate the other's emotional field and thereby affect the other person's feelings. This interaction is illustrated in Fig. 4.

1. D. Krieger, *The Therapeutic Touch: How to Use Your Hands to Help or Heal* (Englewood Cliffs, N.J.: Prentice Hall, 1979). Additional information can be found in M.D. Borelli and P. Heidt, *Therapeutic Touch* (New York: Springer, 1981).

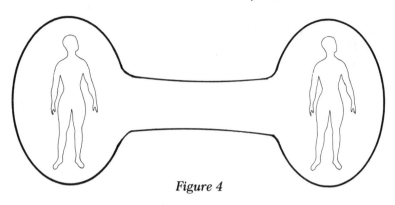

Figure 4

Such interactions frequently cascade and result in a domino effect, thereby affecting people at a distance. For example, actors or musicians may affect the emotional fields of people sitting in the front rows of a theater; these in turn affect others around them, and so forth, until the whole audience is influenced by the performance. The emotional field is more permeable and more easily affected by other people's emotional fields. Like bacteria and viruses, emotions are highly contagious, as is easily observed in mob hysteria.

The emotions enter the vital field through the chakras, such as the solar plexus, and thus affect the vitality and health of the physical body. The solar plexus, a focusing point or nexus, is where the vital and emotional energies most directly intermingle.

Feelings move through the emotional field freely, and their effects are almost instantaneous. For example, when a person's anger is aroused, that emotional energy either explodes from his field in all directions or is projected at a specific person like a bullet to a target. If there are other people present, this energy pattern of anger will interact with their fields, resonate with them, and amplify any similar feelings which they may have. The result is that anger may be aroused in another person even if he/she is unaware of it. Of course when there is little interaction among the people present, the original feeling of anger tends to attenuate and dissipate. However, if anyone responds at that time, the anger will escalate and more and more people will become affected. The process by which anger may trigger the similar feeling in others has an analog in physics. Most materials have a frequency which can be amplified with little or no energy if force is applied at the resonating frequency of the material—the standing wave gets larger and larger. If the force is applied at a non resonating frequency, a standing wave is not initiated.

One can nullify the effects of this interchange by recognizing the source of the anger and determining its irrelevance and unimportance. This process allows one to diffuse the situation rather than actively to attempt to control the energy of anger itself. Active control of the emotion, "I must not be angry!" tends to return the energy back to the angered person instead of allowing it to dissipate at the periphery of the field. This returned energy, if not dissipated, has long term, deleterious effects. It is more effective to recognize and to acknowledge the feeling in ourselves at the moment by saying, "I am angry and I know it." By singling out the reasons for one's anger, one can often smile at the ridiculous disproportion between the anger and the precipitating event. Similarly, if one can acknowledge to oneself the feeling of being hurt or unloved, one can transform the disharmonious energy pattern of anger to a smoothing pattern by thinking of something that restores the other person to his or her usual place in one's affections. In other words, the anger is recognized, dissipated, and transformed by the caring thoughts.

These factors affect the emotional field; each such perturbation affects the solar plexus chakra either positively or negatively and thereby influences the flow of prana into the various organs. The energy generally tends to radiate outward from the body in a continuous flow in healthy people. This energetic inflow and outflow is effected by what the person does. Relaxation tends to expand the field; meditation allows the field to expand in all directions and becomes more energized, balanced, and harmonized, while anxiety tends to constrict the field.

The Mental Field: The individual's mental field is part of a universal mental field and interpenetrates the emotional as well as other fields. The mental field can be described as representing one's intellectual functioning. It reveals one's ability to visualize and rationalize or conceptualize, to think clearly, and to synthesize or make meaning out of one's experiences. This process is more complex than described since categorization and rationalization are related to the emotional field; while conceptualization, synthesis, and creativity are associated with the intuitional field. The size and luminosity of this field relates to the way the intellect functions.

If a clear mental image is combined with emotional drive then the mental field can reach far out into space and/or extend itself to someone at a great distance. Athough usually smaller in size than the emotional field and highly localized, it is more intense. It has the ability to radiate out a very small portion of itself over long distances when directed by one's thoughts. For this field to reach out to others, it needs the impulse of a strong emotion such as love or anxiety. The emotional impulse is often triggered when there is need, such as fear or anxiety. This need allows the mental field to reach out and resonate with the mental field of another person.

The Intuitional Field: The intuitional field is omnipresent and, like the other fields, permeates the whole universe. The interconnections with this field deepen when there is a harmonious relationship between our emotional and mental fields, that is, when our emotions are at peace and our chattering mind is quiet. Even though the energy of this field permeates everything, one symbolizes it "as coming from above." This appears to be an actual experience, since the energy comes from above when one is centered and grounded. This is an experience in which we are *still within ourselves.* The action of this field can be likened to soft, beautiful background music that we cannot hear through the din of our daily lives. Yet the sounds are ever present and can be perceived clearly when the world is quiet. Hence people, if they train themselves to listen, can become aware of the music even when there are loud noises present.

The different qualities within each of the fields are similar to the spectrum of light, in which there are different vibratory frequencies or wave lengths, as well as densities and degrees of brilliance. This effect has often been described by clairvoyants, who already have enhanced perception. People who

have not developed this ability can enhance their awareness
of these fields by learning meditation, therapeutic touch for
healing, and other strategies.[2] With practice many therapeutic
touch practitioners can learn to discriminate and recognize
some of the characteristics in a patient's vital and emotional
field. For example, when practitioners gently attend to the
sensations and cues in their hands as they assess the patient's
field, they may sense a lack of energy or tingling. These sensations may indicate a physical or emotional disturbance. The
sensations in the hands are often similar to the feeling of the
warmth or coldness of an object at a slight distance. In addition, the emotional field can be sensed when the healer's
empathy deepens to the point that there is an impression of
the person's feelings and an intuition of that person's difficulty.

FIELDS AND THEIR INTERACTIONS

As mentioned previously, the four fields just described are
integral and have distinctive features. They are variations of
the whole human field, just as red, blue, and yellow are parts
of the spectrum of white light. The fields continuously interact with one another through the chakras and they are also
affected by the fields of others. It is this interpersonal interaction that keeps us alive.

To maintain a state of health, the energy in all the fields
must be incoming, outgoing, and freely flowing. A pathological
state takes over when the energy is blocked and/or constricted in any of the fields, causing the flow to falter or slow
down. Seen from this point of view, man is part of a dynamic
energy pattern—the interactions of which cease only at death.
This process is analogous to the dynamic interaction of wave
patterns in water which are in a state of incessant motion.

These interactions occur between people, in which one's
physical, vital, emotional, mental, and intuitional fields express the state of the organism. A change in any of our localized
fields affects our expression in the other fields, since we are
one whole. These categories are in turn interrelated, for

2. Krieger, *The Therapeutic Touch.*

when a field interacts with another field it changes and re-organizes itself. It is important to remember that this is a system's perspective. Within the human field perspective, every part is affected by and affects every other part.

Part II

For health, one needs to be aware of the energy level in the vital field and how to replenish it. Usually one does not realize the energy is diminishing until a state of exhaustion is reached. Ironically, the more exhausted one is, the more difficult it is to replenish and restore the energy supply. To avoid energy reduction, one can become aware of the initial cues such as a tightness in the throat, tension in the neck and shoulders, or constriction in the stomach area. Unfortunately, most people do not listen to these "faint" internal signals; our attention is directed outward by choice or circumstance.

To reverse this cycle of depletion what one needs in most cases is rest. Rest allows the flow of vital energy to be re-established; relaxation is the primary mechanism for this replenishment. The specific technique used to restore the energy depends upon the individual. The field perspective allows different strategies to be created. In all cases the practice would affect *all* fields since they are interactive. To enhance and restore the vital energy one or all of the following strategies can be used:

For the vital field: learn to relax.
1. Practice relaxing your body physically by tightening and letting go of different muscle groups.
2. Take short naps and enjoy the feeling of lying down or curling up even when sleep does not come easily, as in cases of exhaustion or overtiredness.
3. Take a number of deep breaths so that when you exhale the abdomen tightens and flattens, and when you inhale

We thank John Kunz and Michelle Moran for their incisive comments and critique during the preparation of this manuscript.

the abdomen rounds and protrudes—this increases the oxygen supply.

For the emotional field: let go of the emotion.
1. Let go of negative feelings about yourself or another person.
2. Shift to a positive feeling about someone else.
3. Go out to others with positive emotions, and interact with positive energetic people whenever possible.

For the mental field: stop worrying.
1. Let go of "fixed ideas," stop ruminating; let go of the conflict or problem for now, knowing that a solution may appear tomorrow when you are in a more relaxed state.
2. Distract yourself by thinking or reading about something else; take up a hobby; listen to music; play a game; do a puzzle or watch TV.
3. Act now; do the task instead of procrastinating.

For the intuitional field.
1. Become still or centered, and then connect through meditation to the intuitional field to achieve a sense of peace and harmony.
2. When healing, allow the healing energy to flow outward through you while thinking of the harmonizing force as flowing through yourself to the patient (healee)—thereby encouraging the patient's sense of wholeness.

Generally, our interactive connection with others occurs through our feelings which depend upon the degree of caring—one's sympathy, empathy, and compassion. The stronger the intent, the more effectively the healing energy can be transmitted. If one is too personally involved in the outcome, then the healer's own energy may be drained. To avoid being drained, perceive yourself as the conduit through which the healing energy flows.

By staying relaxed and allowing the outward-going flow to pass through, one can simultaneously transmit healing as well as enhance one's intake of prana. The relaxation and healing process also stimulate the solar plexus chakra through which the vital energy flows. The actual interchange of energy with another person occurs through a resonance in which the healing energy is the catalyst to trigger and enhance the self-healing potential within the person.

An analogy to this healing process can be found in physics. If one connects two identical vessels together, each of which contains water at a different height, the siphoning process will allow the water level in the two containers to be at the same height. Similarly this would occur to the energy field of persons doing healing if they were not connected to the intuitional field. Their energy level would be drained by the patient. However as long as the healer is a channel, through which the healing energy flows, he/she does not use his/her own energy. The healer's level of energy during this syphon process is continuously replenished as is illustrated in Figure 5.

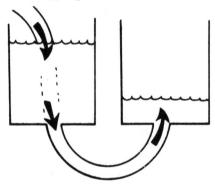

Figure 5

To avoid being drained, the healer can do the following: First, try to feel a connection with the intuitive—this would strengthen one's own vitality. Second, just stop the treatment. During healing, the healer's emotional field, propelled by compassion and the intent to heal, interacts with the patient's field and allows an exchange of energy to occur. The flow lasts as long as the healer maintains the open connection with the inituitive and healing field. The flow ceases when the healing feels completed.

THE PROCESS OF HEALING

In all healing, the healer needs to be relaxed and not personally concerned about the outcome; such concern would produce anxiety which reduces the energy flow and is inimical to the healing process. The healer needs to have the intent to heal while simultaneously being detached about the outcome, as he/she is only the channel. Specifically, anxiety affects the exchange of prana by inhibiting the healer's connection to the intuitive and healing field. In such a case, the needs of the patient could drain the healer's own energy. The more healers desire success (anxiety for performance) the less likely will they be successful. It is the *intent* of the healer which facilitates the healing energy exchange. This intent—to be an effective channel—facilitates the channelling which is also facilitated by the patient's feelings of trust and acceptance.

The less empathy that exists between healer and patient, the less likely it is that an interaction—a successful exchange of healing energy—can be established. Another block to successful healing can occur when patients are totally preoccupied with their own problems and have no desire to change. To facilitate the healing process, the patient should be open-minded and relaxed. Often the first step is to reduce the patient's tension and anxiety so that the pain may be alleviated and the vital energy enhanced and restored. The patient feels better when the low energy levels have been regenerated. If the emotional and mental fields are actively engaged, then it is more likely that the pathology can be affected.

The more the healer can channel the healing energy, the more likely it is that the patient will improve. To facilitate the healing process, the healer may use the following steps:

1. Cultivate an attitude of trust and non-judgmental acceptance before and during any interaction. This may encourage relaxation in the other person as well as reduce hostility.
2. Relax, and become still within. This will enhance your own energy flow and make you more aware of your connection with the healing energy.
3. Focus on the intent to heal. This focus will allow a direct connection with the healing field and also will enable one to be aware of and direct the flow of the healing energy.

4. Think of the patient as whole and not fragmented. These thoughts expand the emotional field which, in turn, energizes the patient's vital energy and, therefore, permits a physical healing or reduction of pain to take place.
5. Send healing energy steadily and continuously, so that the patient is flooded and permeated with this energy.
6. Discontinue the healing when you experience that the patient has absorbed all he/she can for the moment or when there is no more flow of energy.

At the same time as the healing, the patient can facilitate the process through a deep inner willingness to get well and a genuine openness to the experience. These attitudes permit the energy to enter deeply. On the other hand, if the patient is emotionally closed to the experience or rejects it mentally, his/her field is more self-contained and the energy will reach no deeper than the edge or surface of that field. In this case the energy is blocked and attenuated—little healing will take place. The patient can also facilitate the healing process by techniques such as relaxation and visualization. Visualization enhances self-healing and is used as an adjunctive technique in the treatment of cancer and other illnesses. The self-healing can be facilitated when the patient develops:

1. Self-acceptance of the physical condition. This reduces the anxiety or fear triggered by the illness, thereby allowing an increased flow of prana.
2. Acknowledgment that the physical body is not the whole person. This means an experiential awareness that one's body is an instrument, and that life is more than physical existence. This permits an open connection with the intuitive and healing field from which one can draw energy.
3. Conviction that one can affect one's body by thinking of oneself as a functioning whole being at all levels.

The healing process is modulated by an inner self-confidence, that is, a sense of self-identity. Self-confidence is related to an unconscious sense of wholeness; in addition, when the power of will is evoked the healing energy is released through all the fields. This can be enhanced by visualizing wholeness. This sense of wholeness needs to be experienced at "the roots of one's being." Yet one is often plagued by doubts and mistrust of one's wholeness and existential identity. Patients as well as healers can become aware of this sense of inner wholeness by:

1. Training and practicing self-healing imagery, through which the ability to sense one's wholeness is enhanced. Many years of prayer and meditation have enabled some people to draw upon this resource during stress.
2. Imagining and remembering a time when one felt whole. After reaching a state of inner quietude, he/she can go back to a time when everything seemed to go wrong, and yet he/she somehow felt all together, strong and whole. Using this memory can reactivate the sense of wholeness.

Although it may be possible to mobilize self-healing, often patients do not have the energy or the will necessary for the task. A common cause underlying this lack of energy and will is depression, a condition which has many aspects and interactions.

ENERGETIC TREATMENT PERSPECTIVE OF DEPRESSION

Depression is the most energetic and contagious process of the emotions. In a depressed state the mental and emotional fields affect, and are affected by, one's own fields as well as those of other people. In depression, the energy intake as well as the energy outflow is reduced—which decreases the interactions with other people.

Dynamics

A lowering of the vital energy level may trigger a slight depression. When this energy is lowered by anxiety, or an excessive expenditure of energy through forced concentration, the lowered energy may allow negative (sad) images or thoughts to rise to the foreground of the mental field. When these negative thoughts are given attention, the energy inflow is reduced even more. Slight depression may be alleviated by regenerating the energy, such as through a new social interaction or a good sleep.

On the other hand, if people habitually experience the sense of not succeeding or reaching their expectations, that is, if they feel in their "heart of hearts" that they are not good enough, a chronic depression may occur. Such people may do their best, but the best will never fulfill their expectations, so that they continually have a sense of failure. Every time this happens, there is an emotional sense of rejection which the intellect interprets negatively.

Emotionally, such people have the experience, "I am not doing well"; mentally they say to themselves, "I cannot do it," while interactionally they say to others, "I should be doing it well." These negative inner feelings reduce the flow of energy by slowing down the solar plexus chakra. This slowing down often affects the physical body and results in minor or major gastrointestinal distress. When this process is repeated over and over again, the depressed person feels incapable of doing anything. The energy level is lowered and becomes more enclosed and/or inwardly turned, instead of flowing outward as in normal interactions. The individual thinks mainly about himself. As the mental field closes inward on the negative self, less and less energy is exchanged and the field is more and more blocked. To reduce this blockage in the field and thereby break up the depression, any one of the following strategies can be used:

Increase the vital energy.
1. Rest and allow the low energy to regenerate.
2. Do physical exercise which will enhance the energy level.

Expand the emotional field.
1. Help other people in a way that allows the emotional field to expand and exchange with others.
2. Get a pet, such as a dog or cat, who will demand caring and attention from you. Giving out caring expands the emotional field and decreases the depression.

Mobilize the mental field.
1. Acknowledge that you are depressed; however, do not ruminate on it.
2. Acknowledge, even while depressed, that this depression is a passing thing. Tomorrow will be different.

3. Inhibit the energy drain by not anticipating difficulties, which leads to resentment and a decrease in energy.

Connect to the intuitional field.
1. See yourself as part of the universal whole.
2. Allow the healing energy to flow through you and mobilize you.

As mentioned before, depression is both pervasive and contagious. Thus when one is depressed, those in close contact with him or her may feel a lowering of energy and want to get away from the depression. Strangers would automatically move away, and this would give them space to relax, take a deep breath and revitalize their energy.

However, if people are trapped in the situation and cannot or choose not to move away, such as when they are married or work closely together, then the interaction is even more insidious and mutually reinforcing. In such cases, the partner may feel drained, irritated, and bored by the depressed person. Often the partner will react negatively to the depressed person, since he or she does not see the depression any longer as an illness but as a personal affront. This in turn reacts on the depressed person, and a runaway feedback system is generated which tends to aggravate the pathology rather than enhance health.

This dynamic interaction inhibits the partner's ability to help. The paradox in the interchange is that the moment the depressed person becomes nasty or reacts negatively, an emotional link is established which may allow a health mobilizing energetic exchange. The channel of energy exchange is opened, since the depressed person probably expects an antagonistic response to his nastiness. If instead of severing the connection with a negative response, the partner could at that moment send a calm and loving energy, it would revitalize the depressed person.

In order to facilitate healing of depression, whether in a life partner or a client, one needs first to protect oneself from the potentially draining dynamic interaction. The different energy fields offer alternative strategies to enhance self-protection against being drained and to facilitate healing.

On the etheric level.
1. Protect yourself from being too drained. Monitor your own energy level and when you feel it decreasing, do something about it, such as taking a deep breath.
2. Take short breaks; under stressful conditions, one needs to regenerate one's energy approximately every two hours.

On the mental level.
1. Perceive the depressed person as sick, so that if he or she is nasty you do not take it personally.
2. Focus your mind on something positive or cheerful.

On the emotional level.
1. Be calm.
2. Do not exhibit too much cheeriness since the depressed person will oppose, resist, and resent those positive feelings.

On the intuitive and healing level.
1. Send out waves of good will.
2. Connect to the intuitive and healing energy and let yourself be a channel.

Regardless of the state of health, human beings are always interacting, and thus it is possible to channel energy to another person. Our individual fields are interconnected and any perturbation in the field, although it tends to attenuate with distance, affects others. The energetic field perspective as described in this chapter appears to be a useful hypothesis. The hypothesis allows us to create useful pragmatic self-growth and clinical interventions to mobilize our own health and healing in patients. The interventions presented are based upon a monistic, non-dualistic perspective, in which interactions (positive and negative) always occur—to be alive means we are interacting with ourselves and with each other.

Part III

Anger and How it Affects Human Interactions

An ability to be energetically outgoing (altruistic) and compassionate is the well-spring of health. Even though love and anger are both "outgoing" energies, love tends to radiate a sense of quietness, peace, and tranquility by which the energetic connection between people is opened. Anger is more likely to close and shut out the other person because the recipient tends to respond in the same way and thus a barrier is formed. In each case this implies that there is some form of energy outflow from the person to the target, and this energy impulse may and can affect another person regardless of verbal or non-verbal cues.

By becoming aware of the effects of those outgoing energies, health professionals, who are in constant contact with hostility, may learn ways to prevent burnout, exhaustion, and frustration as well as experience peace, tranquility, and an enhanced therapeutic effectiveness.

To be able to control and understand these energetic exchanges is a challenge. The more emotionally involved one is, the more difficult it is to be objective. Strong emotional attachments tend to override the experience of the present, so that past images and future anticipations influence the interaction. For example, when people talk to each other, their communication becomes less effective if they try to conceal their feelings. Their openness is affected by their previous experiences of disappointment, non-support, or non-caring. Each person brings to the interchange conditioned expectancies, images, and emotions which may affect the future course of communication.

In dealing with energies in this way, we adopt a view which we shall call the "energetic perspective." It assumes that thoughts and emotions are not only contained within the individual, but are also radiated outward. Further, it holds that each individual is a localization in an energy field which permeates space and which interconnects with and affects others. Thus this makes it clear that we interact with one another because we are part of one whole, dynamic, and interdependent system.

We thank Michelle Moran for her incisive comments and critique during the preparation of this manuscript.

If one realizes that one interacts with and affects others all the time, what can one do to foster health and growth not only in oneself but also in others? Before offering possible strategies, we will describe first the mechanism by which negative effects such as anger, resentment, biases, and expectancies affect another person; then we will consider strategies to reduce the impact of anger and resentment.

HOW EMOTIONS SUCH AS LOVE AND ANGER AFFECT US

How do love, anger and resentment affect our energy exchange? Often love is not freely given; it may be conditioned by the fact that one unknowingly expects love to be returned in a certain measure. This may bring about some unconscious latent hostility and stop the free flowing energy as one begins to focus on oneself. On the other hand, sending out love without centering on oneself may affect the receiver by opening him or her to more spiritual influences. By encouraging a more altruistic, outgoing pattern, one will bring about an enhanced empathy and allow a free-flowing exchange between two people. Ironically, anger has the same strong outward-going flow as love, except that when it reaches a target it energizes the other person's hostility and inhibits the establishment of a relationship. Anger tends to be reflected and returned to the sender, so that a mutual antagonism is developed. The impact of anger is unconsciously perceived

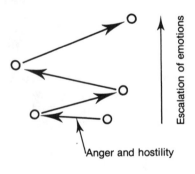

Figure 6

or felt by the sensitive recipient as if one has been violently hit by a disruptive, fragmented energy in the emotional field, which the recipient automatically rejects. Usually it is returned with hostility to the sender unless one can become quiet and allow the energy of anger to dissipate and attenuate. In this dynamic process, the recipient of anger often "shuts down" and thus communications become almost nil. In most cases a person will return anger with anger so that the spiral of anger, resentment, and antagonism builds. The result is an escalating runaway feedback system as is illustrated in figure 6.

POSSIBLE SIDE EFFECTS OF ANGER

Although the emotional charge associated with anger may be directed at the person with whom one is angry, it is also experienced by others in the immediate vicinity. Even without words the energy patterns associated with anger radiate outward and affect others in the immediate environment, as is illustrated in figure 7.

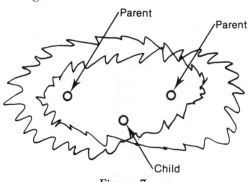

Figure 7

It is through this process that parents may unconsciously hurt their children. For example, if spouses are angry with each other, their children are often in the middle and are energetically assaulted by the emotional exchange between the adults. It is as if the parents release arrows at each other which might injure their children, who are caught in the cross fire. The child thus becomes a casualty. He may throw a temper tantrum, cry, withdraw, or appear to act irrationally because his feelings have become fragmented. Children are often quite sensitive and have less ability to reject negative energies.

It is not understood why some children and adults can more easily reject anger than others; however, some children appear to be born with a greater sensitivity than others. Those who are more sensitive are most easily fragmented by waves of anger. Since children cannot discriminate sufficiently to understand that often the anger is not aimed at them, they experience the assault personally and assume that they are at fault—a process which diminishes their self-confidence.

Most of our emotional interactions are usually of short duration and the effects are transient. But if we repeat this same interaction and at the same time are not aware of this emotional upset when it occurs, it can make one's shoulders tight or one's solar plexus constricted. When this emotional reaction becomes habitual, it may lead to gastrointestinal disturbances. Another result is a decrease in energy intake which may lead to chronic exhaustion and susceptibility to illness.

HOW NEGATIVE EXPECTANCY
AFFECTS THE THERAPEUTIC ENCOUNTER

These concepts about energies can be applied in therapeutic situations. To enhance the therapeutic encounter, the therapist must not carry with him negative expectancies about his client nor bring with him the feelings, emotions, and biases associated with the previous session. Whenever one anticipates difficulty, one tends to tighten up and become exhausted, which is one of the contributing factors leading to burnout. In addition, there is a high probability that the client will unconsciously experience the projected negative feelings and reject the proposed therapeutic intervention. This unconscious reaction is most likely triggered by the negative energy outflow associated with the therapist's thoughts, images, and expectancies. A momentary thought such as "I hope this person isn't going to be angry," "I wish the session were over" or "I do not think she wants to get better" is unconscious negative imagery. Patients and clients react to this automatically. At times it seems as if they are literally telepathic and fulfill the projected expectancy. This projection, incidentally, is probably the mechanism by which experimental bias affects the research outcome.

Negative prejudging tends to initiate anxiety and/or automatic rejection by the client, since it tends to resonate in the client's field with similar unconsciously held beliefs, thoughts, or images about himself. Instead of decreasing internal doubts, his internal negative self-images are activated so that his sense of self-esteem and self-confidence is lessened. A similar process occurs if one is too anxious for a successful outcome, such as therapists wish for their clients or parents for their children. In those cases, the clients or the children experience pressure to perform, which may slow down their learning of new skills. Moreover, it may enhance their anxiety or fear that they will be rejected if they do not achieve the therapist's or parent's goals.

STRATEGIES TO ENHANCE
THE THERAPEUTIC ENCOUNTER

To avoid the effect of negative projection, it helps to be quiet and still the mind and feelings for a moment before any difficult upcoming interview. During this momentary pause, conditioned biases are at a low point so that there are fewer negative anticipations. This non-judgmental attitude is essential in the therapeutic encounter.

Yet how does one let go—how does one allow the mind and emotions to become neutral? It is probably easier, instead of actively trying to make the mind blank, to be quiet and visualize a unifying scene which symbolizes an inner sense of wholeness, such as a tree or a mountain. This momentary shift of attention in which one identifies with a quality of wholeness and unity is called "centering." In the process of shifting one's awareness toward this more unifying experience, one may develop an awareness of the chattering of one's mind and of a pattern in which one continuously ruminates. The therapist or parent may now consciously shift from a negative to a positive feeling about the client or child, as this would bring about an enhanced empathy and allow a free-flowing exchange of energy between the two people. We postulate that regardless of who one is, within each one of us there is a human potential, or "Buddha Nature." If we keep this in mind, each exchange of positive energies can stimulate this potential, to a small extent, in the person confronting us.

These skills are easier to practice in a therapeutic setting, since one tends to be less personally involved with the client than with friends or close family members. Yet, even if they are friends or close family members, one can adopt a similar attitude, in which for a moment one visualizes them as whole and not as fragmented by emotional disturbances or disease patterns.

STRATEGIES TO REDUCE
THE IMPACT AND EXPRESSION OF ANGER

Continued resentment and anger may often lead to some sort of illness. Therefore, it is important not to identify automatically with a person who is angry, but to be conscious of one's own rising anger in response to his. Even if one's own anger is already rising, one can for a moment shift one's attention and visualize someone with whom one has a loving relationship, and let that love flow out even briefly; then one can face his own anger as well as the other person's hostility. This shift of attention allows us to become more aware of the causes of anger and of our ability to diminish our own hostile responses. In short, it gives one a better perspective of the pattern of the interaction. It is possible that this process may, after a while, allow a more positive outflowing of soothing, calm thoughts to be sent towards the person with whom one is angry. Although this appears, at first, an impossible task, an attempt to implement this strategy will develop one's awareness and slowly shift the automatically hostile response to a more neutral, soothing response.

Even though one may be aware that one is reacting with anger, hostility, and resentment, so often one chooses not to change, since not reacting negatively to another's negative emotion is frequently interpreted in our culture to mean that one has become weak or has given in to the other person. Nevertheless, by deliberately choosing the positive response, one develops an active method of changing one's automatic behavior.

The following strategy is often helpful in reducing the feeling of resentment:

1. Sit quietly and allow yourself to relax. Take a few slow breaths and each time you exhale feel yourself gently sinking into the chair. With each exhalation feel the force of gravity pulling on you allowing you to relax more and more.
2. Think of someone you love or imagine a very quiet place in nature such as a waterfall, a large tree or a mountain. Experience the tranquility and peace. When you imagine the scene from nature, see, hear, feel, taste, and smell it in your imagination.
3. Imagine the person or event which you resent about twenty feet in front of you. Hold this image without effort while you continue to breathe easily and relax your whole body. If you tighten up in response to the image, let go of the image.
4. Now, again imagine either a person whom you love or a peaceful place in nature. Let these feelings of love and peacefulness fill you and wash out any traces of resentment.
5. Once again, repeat the visualization of the person or event for which you felt resentment and follow this with imagining either a person whom you love or a peaceful place in nature. Repeat this once or twice.
6. Hold the feeling of caring, love, or peacefulness and allow this to flow outward to the person or event for which you feel resentment.

Practicing these interventions takes time. However, by becoming aware of the effects of the strong emotional feelings, one may be able to intervene, reduce tensions, and optimize human relationships.

From a field perspective one can summarize these interventions as follows:

For the vital field: Learn to become relaxed.

For the emotional field: Learn to calm and center yourself before reacting to anger. Do this instead of reacting with hostility or defensiveness (shutting down) to another person's anger.

For the mental field: Focus on your intent to be willing to change your perspective—do you *want* to be angry? Even though you feel that the anger is "justified" from a "realistic" or conventional point of view, are you willing to give it up?

For the intuitional field: Become centered, project and perceive a sense of wholeness in the other person and in yourself.

Part IV
Depression from the Energetic Perspective:
Etiological Underpinnings

Depression is the most common of all the emotion disorders. It tends to be pervasive, and to permeate and surround the person like a grey cloud. Regardless of how depression is described, the truly depressed person experiences a *lack of energy and vitality* in which even a simple daily task feels like a chore. The person does not seem to have the will to carry on. This often produces feelings of guilt. In the depths of depression, everything feels so overwhelming that the person feels it difficult to mobilize his faculties. Even going to work seems to require a great effort of will. Consequently, there is no satisfaction in the successful performance of any task. The following example is typical of people who are depressed: "This morning I wanted to go running, but it felt like too much effort . . . Should I or should I not run . . . Finally, I just kept sitting there while the clock ticked away . . . I just do not feel like doing anything . . . It all seems futile . . . Nothing is humorous . . . What is wrong with me . . .!"

This paper focuses on the process of depression from the energetic field perspective and includes a description of the etiology of depression, the internal sensations of depression, the process of blocked will, and strategies to ameliorate, reverse and heal the depression. This paper is directed to the depressed person, his close friends and family members, health professionals and practitioners skilled in Therapeutic Touch.

Most, if not all, of us have experienced some sad feelings varying in intensity from the lack of joy, feeling low in vitality, to the momentary inability to act fully. In the deep states of depression, one experiences futility and a sense that nothing matters—that there is no hope for the future. Although a decrease of energy is a common quality of depression, there are many complex factors involved. The intensity varies from normal mood swings in which feelings dip and then recover in a few days to the crippling, immobilizing feelings in which people become totally incapable of caring for themselves and have to be hospitalized. These states can be categorized into normal depression, chronic depression, immobilizing depression and manic depression.

Normal Depression: Normal mood changes occur in everyone whose emotions go up and down over the course of a few days. In this case the sense of sadness slowly diminishes because the inherent thrust of health within the system takes over and allows the person to feel better. Usually, the temporary depressive feelings tend to be related to an event. In other words, the person is reacting to an outside event or an internal reaction such as being criticized by his supervisor or being disappointed about coming in fifth instead of first in his athletic competition. Such occurrences may trigger in the person a sense of disappointment and a mild depression. However, the healthy individual's basic self-esteem and self-confidence is not threatened.

Chronic Depression: Mood changes in this state occur more frequently; also, the person's self-image is threatened by depression. Each new cycle of this state of mind activates previous memories of past painful episodes and triggers internal patterns of self-doubt. Consequently, derogatory comments from others are not as easily rejected because they resonate with an already pre-existing doubt and belief of incompetency—of not being good enough—a process which erodes self-confidence. Often in these cases, the frustration may result in bleak depressive episodes from which it is difficult to recover, and it may also trigger physical symptoms such as indigestion and ulcers. Family support, Therapeutic Touch, or pharmacological and psychological interventions may help to quicken recovery.

Immobilizing Depression: This category describes a situation in which episodic, or chronic depressive episodes become so severe as to immobilize the person to such an extent that he may have to be hospitalized. During this phase, the chronic depressive patterns of thoughts and feelings become so overriding that often life appears meaningless. The person feels that the past, present and especially the future hold no hope. This induces a feeling of hopelessness and consequently the person may even contemplate suicide. Ironically, the most dangerous time for the depressed person is right after he has passed through the deepest part of the depression. During the upswing, his energy is increased so that he could literally act on his self-destructive impulses.

Manic-Depression: Periodic alternations of apparent boundless and excessive energy and actions with consequent corresponding periods of severe withdrawal and depression characterize this disorder. During the manic phase, the person does not dare to slow down for he fears that the moment he relaxes a painful change of thought and mood may occur. Paradoxically, the expenditure of excessive energy may lead to an overall energy depletion which can result in the ensuing depressive phase. An analogous situation is often seen in young children, who get so "revved up" that their hyperactivity masks their exhaustion. From this perspective, energetic interventions are difficult to initiate during the downward depressive cycle. Instead, the aim is to reduce the amplitude of the manic swing. Sadly, if the person does not learn over a period of time to decrease the manic phase, his system becomes energetically damaged and the depressive phase predominates.

Aside from the intensity of the feeling tones, the major difference among the above categories is the rapidity with which one can regain vitality and can reject and not identify with the depressive memories. Regardless of the intensity of the depressive moods, common to all is *the lowering of vitality and a corresponding drop in energy* which may lead to a loss of initiative and a blocking of or decreased accessibility to the power of the will.

THE ENERGETIC DYNAMICS OF DEPRESSION

From an energetic perspective, the solar plexus is a center where emotions and vitality get distributed throughout the body, and thus it may become a nexus for psychosomatic problems. The solar plexus is not an anatomical structure but a focus and center through which the person's vital energy circulates. In Eastern metaphysical systems it is one of a number of chakras.

The flow of energy in this particular center slows down when a person becomes depressed. This may lead to gastro-intestinal distress as well as to a sense of constant fatigue. The fatigue and exhaustion are the result of the slowing down of the solar plexus. Ironically, as the whole system is energetical-ly recharging at a slower rate, the person simultaneously is expending more energy through his turbulent feelings. More-over, if a person with low vitality and a constant sense of fatigue performs his task with no sense of personal accomplish-ment, it may result in resentment and frustration. This is likely to make one feel tense, especially around the shoulders, and it may produce headaches. Again energy expenditure may be increased and energy intake lowered. This psycho-physiological process often affects the breathing pattern and the person consequently breathes shallowly. In time, the whole body will tend to take on a depressive posture. The shoulders will sag and collapse down and forward, thereby reducing the level of vitality even more. Breathing becomes limited to the mid-lower chest. This shallow breathing con-tributes to the chronic low energy since less *prana* (universal energy) flows through the system (See Kunz and Peper, 1982, 1983a and 1983b for a detailed description of the energetic system). In addition to lowered vitality, one of the first indi-cations of the onset of depression is an uncomfortable feeling around the area of the heart. This discomfort is often ac-companied by a restriction in the outward flow of one's feelings. It is associated with one of the centers of consciousness, the heart chakra, which is the center of the outflow of emotion. Thus, the solar plexus and the heart centers are both involved when deep depression occurs.

THE FIELD EFFECT OF DEPRESSION

Often, when one reaches a certain stage of depression one gets a feeling of not wanting to move as any task seems to require a great effort. Ironically, this lack of activity induces more depression. The depressive field permeates the environment and further re-resonates (retriggers) the depressive pattern within the person. If one becomes attached to and feels secure in one particular room during this mood, his environment (i.e. the room) would, from this perspective, become pervaded with negative thought. Consequently, he continuously lives in a grey emotional atmosphere. *This field interpenetrates the room and lingers even when he is not there.* In time, the field fades out, dissipates and attenuates in his absence. If there is little or no attachment to the environment, the residual field dissipates within a short time after the person leaves. This is an important observation because even if a person may leave his room, the lingering depression field in the room can resonate with the person's depressive undercurrent and thus reactivate his feelings of depression when he returns.

This reactivation is analogous to hitting a tuning fork which then vibrates at its assigned frequency and generates the tone we hear. If a similar tuning fork is brought quickly into the environment the sound waves will cause it to vibrate at the same frequency. This resonance will only occur if the tuning fork has the same harmonic frequency as the original tuning fork. If it is not in the same harmonic range then the sound will not cause it to resonate.

The field model predicts that the depressive field would resonate the depressive qualities in anyone who entered the field. To repeat, if one is vulnerable to depression, the previous depressive field would cause the depressive undercurrents in one to resonate. This in some cases could trigger a drop in energy and a possible depression. This model extends beyond the cognitive behaviorist's model of depression in which either internal or external conditioned stimuli trigger the conditioned depressive response. From this perspective one major intervention one can use is to move the person to a different environment. Obviously, this physical act of changing mobilizes the depressed person, which tends to increase his energy as well as initiate hope. Sometimes, even cleaning and painting the room can symbolically dissipate the lingering depressive field. From this field perspective, it is important for people not to reinfect themselves with their own or others' depressive fields. To move to a totally different environment where the residual field does not resonate with depression is often helpful.

THE ETIOLOGY AND PROCESS OF DEPRESSION

Childhood Patterns Which May Foster Depression: Some children seem to be born with a lower than average energy level, and this is often combined with a sensitivity to the emotions of others. For example, when the child's energy field is hit by his parents' emotional energy, such as anger, he may shrink and try to protect himself from the pain.

In this shrinking, the child withdraws and constricts his emotional energy field. It is not necessary for the anger or resentment of the parents to be directed at the child. The violent emotions radiate outward and away from the arguing parents and can reach anyone in the vicinity as is shown in Figure 8. The child shrinks away from pain induced by the

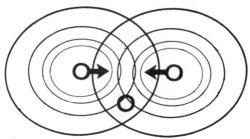

Figure 8. The anger directed by the parents to each other unknowingly assaults the child.

energetic assault at the emotional level, and his or her solar plexus slows down. This shrinking may be the first step toward a feeling of isolation, a drop in vitality, and may be the start of a habit-forming depression. As the child experiences the energetic emotional impact, he simultaneously experiences an undefined fear and discomfort—it is a feeling of being hurt. One way to avoid the pain is to withdraw into one's own world; namely the child isolates himself from others to prevent being hurt. This process induces a sense of uncertainty, and if this becomes a repetitive pattern it may weaken not only the ability to respond to others but also the ability to reject this battering emotional energy. Consequently, the energetic system is less resilient.

Often the earliest signs of depressive precursors in young children ages five to six are apathy, social isolation (not making contact with others) and withdrawal as well as crying without an obvious cause. The child tends to be by himself. As some children grow older, they may develop more self-awareness and learn to no longer identify with the emotions of others. Often this development does not take place and the child's self-confidence is undermined. Many times these children are brought up in a family where one of the parents appears highly critical of the child. As a result, he feels unloved by one of his parents. This issue is highly complex, since often the parent does love the child. However, the child does not perceive the love. For example, for years one child continued to resent his parents for sending him to boarding school. The child experienced being sent away to school as a total rejection. Even as an adult he continued the resentment which eventually evolved into a chronic depression. Ironically, the parents sacrificed everything to send him to a private school so that he would not become involved with drugs. However, they did not share their reasons with him. Some children react to such an event with a sense of worthlessness—partially activated by their perception that they are unlovable while, for others, this experience mobilizes their energy. They may respond by saying to themselves: "I'll show you." However, to take this latter stance, the child needs an *abundance of energy.*

The sensitivity to others becomes exaggerated during and

immediately after puberty. During this period, the teenager is searching for meaning and self-identity. At the same time, he is concerned with the judgment of others. As the adolescent is highly concerned whether he is liked by his friends, he often doubts his self-worth and this doubt reduces his self-confidence. A depression can be triggered or deepened by comments of others or by his own negative interpretations of other people's comments, especially when the depressive person believes that there is some truth to those comments. The comments resonate with the pre-existing depressive patterns and trigger more doubt. Consequently, the potentially depressed person has difficulty in dissociating himself from the comments. He finds it difficult to say: "Hey, what they are saying is their opinion and is not an intrinsic truth about my whole character."

The undercurrent of all depression is lack of self-confidence. Being depressed often produces a guilty feeling. The guilt undermines self-confidence and reduces energy even further. This runaway feedback system facilitates a downward slide. As a person experiences the physiological sensation of lowered energy and isolation, he tends to become increasingly self-centered in the sense that his mind and energies become more and more turned in upon himself. On the other hand, a healthy person may momentarily feel let down but is less personally attached, less ego-involved. When he finishes a task, he says to himself, "I have done my best," and he then goes on to his next task. The depressive person, on the other hand, constantly wonders: "Did I do well enough?"

In summary, chronic depression originating in childhood generally involves the following constellation of factors:

1. Absence of support. The child does not experience supportive love from at least one of the parents. This does not mean that the parent does not love the child; it is, rather, the child's own experiential perspective. Supportive love implies that the parent genuinely feels love for the child and acceptance of his interests and capacities as well as sets boundaries.

2. Lowered energy level. The child experiences a lowered

level of vitality either due to a natural predisposition or an habitual constriction and withdrawal of his energies in the face of emotional or physical assaults.

3. Battered emotional field. The child's field is repeatedly disturbed by emotional or physical abuse.
4. Lowered self-confidence. The child experiences either chronic criticism or a sense that he can never measure up to the standards of one or both parents.

Depression Triggered by Trauma: It is not unusual for a depression to occur after a person experiences a significant loss. This loss can take many forms, such as the death of a spouse, the loss of a job or a sequence of stressful events, such as moving or the insecurity of a new job, or any number of smaller disappointments. The sequence of events triggers a sense of insecurity which can express a lack of self-confidence. For example, a chronic traumatic depression was triggered in one person when a long and close relationship was terminated. The traumatic loss was a devastating experience, since she continuously relived it and, furthermore, interpreted the experience to mean that she could never have another close relationship. Whenever she thought of her past, she re-experienced her sense of failure, and it triggered the belief that she was unable to have a meaningful relationship in the future.

The processes involved in a traumatic depression are very complex. For some it may be the feeling that nothing in their world is meaningful and that they are powerless to change their circumstances or themselves. For example, a fifty year old man may suddenly find his job disappointing and less meaningful, thus triggering a depression. Due to his life-long concentration on his job, when he now desires to reach out to his family or friends, he is unable to do so. He feels cut off from ways to express his caring and love. The awareness that he cannot even share the love he feels, isolates and encapsulates him in his depression. Common to these cases is an inability to express one's self in a new area of endeavor. These people lack emotional communication with their family—they have for too long focused attention and will, albeit cheerfully, externally on work.

Obviously people's reactions to a loss vary. It is the cognitive interpretations of the event which affect the emotional outcome. Depressed people tend to interpret events as failures and to perceive the future as hopeless; accordingly, they reduce their self-confidence. On the other hand, nondepressive people tend to interpret events less personally. For example, after the loss of her fourteen year long relationship, the woman could have been thankful for the lovely years together, or think of the new opportunities to meet and establish new relationships instead of blaming herself for her failure. However, for the person who reacts to the loss with depression, his or her thought pattern only perceives a deep sense of failure, a belief that never again is it possible to have what has been lost.

Although the previously described process appears most common, other situations, such as adolescent frustrations or first time life failures, may also contribute to depressive and self-destructive episodes. A young person may at times be overwhelmed by the tumultuous demands of adolescence especially if, as a child, he had abundant energy, a vivid imagination and an absence of behavioral boundaries set by the parents.

Having had no experience with boundaries, and thereby no training to take initiative after a rejection, the young person feels overwhelmed by the depressive feelings, and he later finds it hard to imagine that it may lift or that he can take responsibility for his depression and life. On the other hand, those who have had previous bouts with depression may remember that it will once again fade into the background. It is important for the depressed individual to be aware that vitality and health will recur, since this memory will facilitate the inherent thrust for health. A dramatic imagination accompanied by the absence of will may allow a teenager or young adult to experience his present and future as hopeless and even trigger a self-destructive episode; on the other hand, mobilizing health occurs as one takes responsibility for the depression.

The above is illustrated by the comments of a twenty-three year old woman who discussed her hospitalized bout with depression: "After a week in the hospital, I finally saw the pain on the faces of my family members, and I realized that the world did not cause the depression. It was my responsibility."

This woman was lucky. She had experienced supportive love as a child, but she had not learned how to deal with responsibility. In many ways her will had been unchallenged during the growing up phase of her adolescence and early adulthood. From this point of view, will is the individual's decision to consciously use his determination to change the circumstances or his state of mind.

THE ROLE OF WILL IN DEPRESSION

The blocked will, in the absehce of energy to do anything, is consistently one of the outstanding characteristics in severe depression. Yet, what is will and how does it relate to self-esteem and self-confidence?

Will is an intrinsic quality within each of us; it can mobilize one's mind and feelings and thereby integrate and activate the whole person. One aspect of will is determination, which may be expressed as stubbornness, and can become a deep-seated pattern; it again is a facet of becoming self-centered. This absorption turns the energies inward instead of to a healthy, outward flow.

The will involves conscious choice. If the will is mobilized, in most cases it means that one has objectively observed one's own situation and has had an insight which enables one to mobilize one's will to change. This involves conscious choice. Thus the mind and emotions both play a part in the solution. The will becomes blocked in depression because one gets locked in one's own feelings and thought. Consequently, a depressed person finds it too hard to change or find a way out although there is an undercurrent of wishing to change.

Will has the power to mobilize one's energy in crisis. When will is mobilized during a crisis, it can coalesce "one's whole being" to face the crisis. Crisis is an opportunity for growth and new direction; however, the mobilization and the continued expression of will require energy. When this energy is outwardly directed, it enables one to relate to others, which again enhances one's energy. Consequently, by using will to go outward the depressed person, whose previous focus was mainly on himself initiates the thrust toward health.

BIBLIOGRAPHY

Krieger, D. *Therapeutic Touch.* Englewood Cliffs, NJ: Prentice Hall, 1979.

Kunz, D. and E. Peper. Fields and Their Clinical Implications, Part I. *The American Theosophist,* 1982, 70, 11.

Kunz, D. and E. Peper. Fields and Their Clinical Implications, Part II. *The American Theosophist,* 1983a, 71, 1.

Kunz, D. and E. Peper. Fields and Their Clinical Implications, Part III, Anger and How it Affects Human Interactions. *The American Theosophist,* 1983b, 71, 6.

Margenau, H. *Physics and Philosophy.* Boston: Ridel Publishing Company, 1978, p. 373.

Part V

Depression from the Energetic Perspective:
Treatment Strategies

The treatment of depression is highly complex; treatment strategies depend upon the individual's age and general health and the cause and depth of his depression. Treatment procedures can be organized into the following strategies: what depressed people can do for themselves; what family and friends can do for the depressed family member; how family members can protect themselves so that they are less affected; what therapists can do for their patients and to prevent themselves from becoming drained and exhausted; and finally, how Therapeutic Touch strategies can be applied with depressed people. Treatment procedures, from the field or energetic perspective, are always interactive; any action affects the whole field and is contextually bound. (See Kunz

---

We wish to thank William Nicholson for his incisive comments during the preparation of this manuscript.

and Peper, 1982, 1983a, 1983b, 1984a.)

Although there may be many factors which facilitate or inhibit depression, this paper will focus on the processes, both in children and adults, which must be activated to abort, interrupt and redirect a depressive cycle. These are:

1. An enhancement of vital energy.
2. An increase in self-confidence.
3. A mobilization of will.
4. A redirection of the focus of emotional and intellectual energy, from withdrawing and shrinking to outgoingness.
5. A reframing of the perception of the present and future, from the absence of hope to the possibility of future hope.

Germane to any of these strategies is the fact that the therapist or family member continues to be relaxed and centered while helping the other person so that he or she does not get drained.

RELAXATION AND CENTERING

The helping process, namely reaching out without demanding, giving support without anxiety, projecting an inner peace and accepting the child or person as he is, usually involves relaxation and centering. The more a person or therapist is centered the less likely he will be exhausted or disappointed in his own therapeutic effectiveness. Centering increases the likelihood that he can positively affect the child or depressed person. Centering usually involves learning to rapidly become relaxed or quiet and for the moment put to the side one's own personal needs.

Learning physical and emotional relaxation is the first step for those who genuinely want to help others. The following techniques can be helpful in practicing and promoting this sense as a precursor for centering.

1. Relax by exhaling while whispering "HA," and then let a diaphragmatic breath come in. Then gently exhale again without effort. As the air goes out let your jaw go slack and feel your shoulders dropping. Again let the air come gently in as your abdomen expands. Repeat this process a few

times while mentally saying to yourself on the inhalation "I am" and on the exhalation, "Relaxed."

2. Think of a peaceful quiet place in nature. Visualize a place such as a waterfall or a tree which is, to you, a symbol of peace. For example, imagine yourself sitting against a tree. Feel the bark pressing into your back. Hear the whisper of the breeze rustling the leaves and listen to the chirping of the birds. See the green, peaceful meadow with its bubbling brook in front of you. Smell the mustiness of the moist earth, and feel the gentle warmth of the sun against your face and arms, and identify with this symbol of warmth and light.

Once one is relaxed, one can approach the most important step in learning to help others. This is the process which we call "centering." Since, from the energetic perspective, emotions are contagious, learning relaxation and centering is important. Centering involves, first of all, the intent to be quiet within. It is the focusing of one's energies and attention to a place of stillness within one. One is not reacting to outward circumstances, but one turns to one's own sense of wholeness and oneness for a moment. This leads to a sense of being integrated. It is the opposite of the experience of a fragmented or chattering mind. Slowly a sense of peace and integration is experienced. Often an intuitional insight can occur. With practice, centering can become part of a daily routine and, in times of crisis, the experience can prove even more meaningful. From this stage, one can reach out in a truly helpful way. One's intent is enhanced and clarified and so one is more likely to be effective in one's therapeutic encounter. Furthermore, because one is working from a center of strength and integration, one is less likely to be exhausted or disappointed by one's interaction.

TREATMENT OF CHILDREN

In the treatment of depressed children one must not only interrupt the depressive cycle, but also attempt to:

1. Increase the intrinsic low energy of the child,

2. Reduce the impact of the indirect emotional battering when other family members are upset or angry,
3. Encourage the child to go outward.

The exact healing strategy depends on the child and his or her social network. For example, some children have constitutionally low energy and a greater risk of developing depression because they are more sensitive in their interactions with other people's feelings, or emotional fields. Consequently, they seem less able to reject disturbances in the field around them. However, this risk is lower if they are brought up in a sensitive, loving family. The parents, through their supportive love and openness with each other, could facilitate the enhancement of the child's energy and prevent the occurrence of emotional assaults in the child's field. In addition, they could protect him from overexertion. These children tend to be unaware of *depleting* their own energy level, and periodic rest is important for them. Finally, the parents could enhance self-confidence in their child by encouraging him to achieve competence in an area which he likes and in which he has talent.

This supportive encouragement implies that the parent truly knows that the child can achieve the task. For example, if a child has natural musical talent and enjoys playing the piano, parents may set an achievable goal for the child. In such a case, the goal might be to have the child learn how to read music. This means that the child will have learned a concrete skill instead of dabbling. He thereby can experience an enhanced self-confidence through the pride of having learned to read music.

If a family is sensitive and supportive to the needs of the child, the likelihood of depression would be reduced. Ironically, it is often in those families where there is little awareness of others that depression and other illnesses may develop.

Sadly, when parents are battling with each other their emotions are contagious and affect others. We realize that it is very difficult to develop an awareness and control over one's emotional outbursts even though one may wish not to hurt others. Hopefully, the parents can learn to be aware and act consciously instead of reacting automatically, and thereby reduce the unintentionally negative-emotional-impact of their outbursts. For example, they could tell their child that they were going through a difficult time. This explanation would tend to trigger within the child a sense of caring for the adult and establish an open flow of communication, which would reassure him. It is important to open up the channel of communication. Another approach that parents, friends, or therapists can use is to surround the child with supportive love. This can be done by approaching the child indirectly. Just let your calming presence fill the room. Reach out only in response to the child's reaching out. If the child is receptive, touch tends to enhance the communication; however, it has the potential of amplifying within the child the emotions felt in the parent or therapist. It is critical that the adult is "quiet within" and is willing to reach out with a supportive love without demanding that the child must change. It is the act of reaching out and doing one's best which is important.

A therapist can work with a child by encouraging him for example to participate in play therapy while music is played. The supportive atmosphere enhanced by the rhythmic music tends to facilitate the child's outward movement and action. Regardless of the specific therapeutic intervention, the basic premise underlying the healing approach is an attitude that encourages the child to go gently outward and increase his social participation. The theme by which one facilitates an outward flow of energy is ACTION. The child needs to exchange with the environment. Approaches which encourage action and facilitate self-confidence usually involve the following components:

1. The awakening of curiosity within the child. For example, a child may be taken for a walk and encouraged to see how many different small animals can be found in the trees.
2. The development of competence. The sense of achievement implies that more competence is possible. For example the child may be encouraged to play with "lego blocks" and build a house.
3. The development of affiliation and concern for others. For example, the child may join a swim or ballet club.

In the awakening of curiosity, the development of competence and social affiliation, the child unconsciously reaches outward. In this outward expression his energy is enhanced and his self-confidence is increased.

Paradoxically, this reaching out can usually only be done indirectly by creating an atmosphere in which that quality is triggered. The moment one demands curiosity from the child one inhibits the process. The child is put in an unsolvable double bind. For example, if a mother asks her very obedient child to be less obedient, the child becomes stuck. In this case if the child obeys by becoming less obedient he is becoming more obedient.

TREATMENT OF ADULTS

Climbing out of the depths of depression takes courage, as the future and present still tend to look bleak. If the person has experienced a previous episode of depression he may be aware that his thoughts paint a distorted and negative picture, but he may still feel that he does not have the energy to struggle upward toward health since his will is blocked. Success in the prevention of depression is most likely achieved not during the darkest moment but at the onset phase. Once one is dragged down into the darkness of the lethargic, immobilizing phase, one has to let the cycle of depression ride its own course. Usually, even from the depths of this deepest stage, the underlying, life-promoting forces can slowly move one upward to functional health. However, a depressive undercurrent does persist, and it can overtake and pull the person into the depths of depression again and again.

Potentially the most successful opportunity to overcome depression occurs during the first prodromal phase—just as the undercurrent starts to take hold. It is during the onset of the first symptoms that the individual may be able to alter the course of the cycle. The first step in the treatment of depression is to mobilize one's own desire for well-being. This is critical since without the person's desire and willingness there is very little that can be done. Yet, even at this first stage, many people have already too little energy to mobilize the will. The therapist and family members must continuously remember that, at this moment, the person is *very low* in vitality. In addition, there may be a feeling of shame for being depressed— the person does not want other people to know. This masking of feelings again enhances his isolation.

The first onset signal of a depression is a sense of exhaustion and tiredness in which the individual lacks the vitality to accomplish his usual tasks. He experiences a reluctance to do things. It becomes hard for him to distinguish normal tiredness from the feeling of low energy that is the precursor of depression. The moment the person recognizes the drop in energy, it is imperative that he initiate strategies to enhance his energy.

Strategies which facilitate the expansion of energy focus on the enhancement of vital energy such as the shifting of attention from preoccupation with self to attention outside of one's self as well as flooding the person with energy through Therapeutic Touch. (Krieger, 1979)

Usually, vital energy can also be enhanced through rhythmic, physical exercise. At the onset of the energy drop, the person needs to go out and exercise, swimming, walking or running. It is at this point a spouse could be helpful by saying to the potentially depressed partner: "You look a bit tired; let's go for walk."

It is important that one acknowledge that one is tired or depressed. The person who says to himself: "I am depressed and falling into my depressive pattern" shows an awareness which marks the beginning of change. It is important to recognize this pattern, but it must be followed by action. The person can ask: "What can I do to stop the cycle and mobilize myself for health?" At every stage of the depression, it is essential that the person act and not just intellectualize. The internal intellectualization will tend to block the expression of will since the internal or introspective dialogue that asks: "Why? How did it happen to me?" or "What is the cause?" tends to inhibit action and increase self-blame. To repeat: *action is imperative in order to re-energize and direct one's attention outward.*

Imagery can faciliate this outgoing energy. At this early stage, the person is able to believe that the depressed feeling can be projected outward. The person can sit and imagine these feelings moving outward like waves on the ocean, as is illustrated in the following practice:

> Bring your hands to your chest; take a deep breath and, with the exhalation, push your hands away from your body. Metaphorically, this represents the outflow of the depressed feelings. The feelings are directed into the expansive sea and like the waves rhythmically flow away into the distant horizon.

Since the depressive field tends to reactivate the depressive components within the person, it is very important for the person to leave his environment. Again, this movement initiates some physical action and encourages the attention to be ever so slightly directed outward.

For the depressed person, it is at the time when a reactivation of depression may occur that he must *invoke* the will. The person must overcome the overwhelming inertia of depression and drag himself into physical activity. In the act of mobilizing himself, he strengthens his will and begins the first tiny step towards building, his self-confidence. After the person has been physically active, he follows this up with an activity that continues to draw his attention away from himself. These specific outgoing activities vary and can range from seeing an exciting movie, observing the plants and trees outside, reading a book or going to a folk dance. Yet underlying all this is the invocation of will. What are the ways which block and facilitate the invocation of will?

STRATEGIES TO MOBILIZE WILL

The process to self-mobilize will as a drive to initiate outgoing action can take many forms. Underlying it is a process which redirects the attention away from the negative preoccupation of self to external interests. As was cited earlier, mobilizing either curiosity, competence or social affiliation and concern is a way to initiate the outgoingness; however, for a chronically depressed person these are not enough. The person just does not have the energy to do anything. In adults, energizing will, despite the perspective of overwhelming hopelessness can include imagery of light or a sense of drawing upon a higher power to help go through the depression.

A number of depressed people have reported that when they were depressed the metaphorical darkness could be lifted if they could think of a light and/or a feeling of expansion in which they feel the space around them to be expanding. Light appears to be a positive symbolic image which contrasts with the bleakness of the depression. Some specific imagery practices which have been helpful are:

1. Become very quiet and centered. Especially helpful are pre-recorded guided relaxation practices which range from progressive relaxation to slow, diaphragmatic breathing to detailed imagery of soothing, quieting nature scenes.
2. Imagine a distant light which energizes you and feel the flow of this energy permeating through you and radiating outward; with each exhalation, feel the light expanding around you.
3. Think of a higher power from which you can draw support when you feel your own energy waning. Especially helpful are religious, spiritual and meditative symbols.

Although imagery is very helpful, breaking through the depressive isolation can often be directly or indirectly facilitated by allowing the depressed person to reach out or act in a physiologically different manner, as is illustrated in the following two strategies:

1. Give the depressed person a pet to take care of. The act of stroking a cat or dog allows one's emotional energy to go outward. If the person is less depressed, walking a dog twice daily is an even more effective antidepressant.
2. Have the person change his posture. Have him breathe deeply and thrust his shoulders backwards. Taking on a non-depressive posture tends, unconsciously, to trigger non-depressive behavior and an expansion of energy since, through imitation, one tends to become the acted-out image.

STRATEGIES FOR FAMILY MEMBERS

Family members of a depressed person are often resentful and angry at him because they may perceive him as simply "wallowing" in his depression without doing anything to alleviate it. For close family members, such as a spouse, the depression can be frustrating and contagious. To reduce the negative effect on the family, one can implement some of the following strategies:

1. Leave the house for a short while. This going away is not to escape but rather to "recharge one's own batteries." One cannot easily facilitate healing if one is drained.
2. Do not show sympathy. Do not talk about it, just let it be. As much as possible, be kind and compassionate. Use the centering strategies described before to nurture yourself.
3. Realize that, for the moment, the person is incapable of showing interest in others and this is not necessarily a hostile intent.
4. Project a feeling of support to the depressed person and then "do your own thing." Just let the person be since he cannot, for the time being, respond to a call or demand for responsible action.

CONTRIBUTIONS OF THE FIELD PERSPECTIVE TO THE UNDERSTANDING OF DEPRESSION

The field perspective of depression offers a number of unique contributions to the understanding and treatment of depression. The three most significant aspects not usually included in the more traditional psychological models are:

1. The observation that depression is preceded by a drop in energy. It is this drop which allows the depressive undercurrent—the habitual and conditioned depressive patterns —to come to the foreground. Consequently, one critical new intervention, which is suggested here to abort a depressive cycle, is to intervene at the beginning of the perceived drop in energy, before the depression can occur.
2. The view that an energetic field surrounds and affects all of us. This field can interact and resonate with another person's depressive field. If one has a depressive undercurrent, this resonance could trigger a drop in his level of energy and possibly lead to the onset of depression in him as well. Field perspective extends beyond verbal and nonverbal communications as modes to trigger depression. The energy model proposes that a depressive field can permeate one's environment and can resonate with and, thereby, trigger

the depressive cycle within one. It is important to note that this is a totally external independent stimulus; it is the fading field which may reactivate the depressive under-current.

3. The suggestion that the mobilization of will underlies the successful treatment of depression. From this perspective, the development of the will is a potential which is present in everyone to some degree. If one realizes this, one can use it with an intention to act. One should not act driven by one's feelings, but act in a search for meaning at a more impersonal level—a level where one experiences a sense of wholeness and the strength which goes with this sense. If will is aligned with one's mental faculties, one can make choices, and this can change one's attitude and reverse a depressive cycle.

From this perspective, will is also a form of energy, and so it can be a source of movement toward change and health. Emotions and thoughts about oneself make up one's self-image. This self-image can be very disturbed if one's conditioning in childhood was negative. If one builds a self-image of being a failure, this can be a cause for depression. One's view is often distorted because of preoccupation with oneself. This can block one's will and lead to inaction or wrong action. The use of will is one way of learning how to destroy one's negative self-image. "The principle of choice is at present an enigma. We call it will. But will is a supreme, a peak manifestation of human consciousness." (Margenau, 1978)

BIBLIOGRAPHY

Krieger, D. *Therapeutic Touch.* Englewood Cliffs, NJ: Prentice Hall, 1979.

Margenau, H. *Physics and Philosophy.* Boston: Ridel Publishing Company, 1978, p. 373.

Reprints of "Fields and Their Clinical Implications" are printed in three booklets: the first contains Parts I and II, the second Part III, and the third Parts IV and V. Send $1 for each booklet or $2.50 for the set of three to Theosophical Research Institute, P.O. Box 270, Wheaton, IL 60189. Bulk quantities are available from the Theosophical Publishing House at the above address.

18

High-order Emergence of the Self During Therapeutic Touch

DOLORES KRIEGER, Ph.D., R.N.

Two novel but diverse modes of human expression have entered Western culture over the past two decades. Both have served to mark a radical departure in the way man perceives his place in the universe and his relationship with other people. The first derives its meaning from the highly technical information age, an age which has only begun to pick up momentum. Nevertheless, it is already sweeping before its onrush the long accepted signs and signals of traditional and conservative cultural mores and rapidly translating them in terms of its own mother tongue, the *basics* and *logics* of computer language. The second mode, a quite dissimilar expression of our time, has come out of a uniquely individual networking of people in quest of personal growth experiences that would help them to actualize their potential as human beings. This expression finds its major interpretation through body-related language, particularly that of touch.

   The parallel development of these two major movements has given us a new descriptor of our age: high tech/high touch. Naisbitt, who first described this phenomenon, notes that as our society becomes more involved in the impersonal environment of high technology based enterprises, there arises a strongly felt need for compensatory high touch experiences. Naisbitt says, "The more high technology around us, the more the need for human touch . . . High tech/high touch. The principle symbolizes the need for balance between our physical and spiritual reality."[1]

Much of the impetus of the human potential movement arose out of a need for healing of oneself. However, once this healing has taken place many persons have gone on to learn how to heal someone else. Once healed (from the Old English, *haelen,* to make whole) these individuals realize that other people also have this potential for wholeness and therefore can be touched in a healing way.

Many healthy people are aware of an energy overflow, an excess of energy beyond their immediate physical needs, and those who are compassionate want to share this sense of well being with those who are ill. How this is accomplished in the infrequent instances when significant healing does occur is not well understood. People who have had some success in helping others say that something takes place unconsciously within themselves which they have difficulty verbalizing, and this in some way transmits an energy of a healing nature to the ill person.

Enough instances of healings under controlled circumstances have occurred in the recent past to lend credence to the assertion that there is a potential for healing that can be tapped, and that there are reliable teaching strategies by which a person can learn to play the role of healer.[2][3][4][5][6][7][8][9]

A type of healing called Therapeutic Touch, as developed by Dora Kunz and myself, is derived from, but not the same as, the laying-on of hands. Over the past ten years I have taught Therapeutic Touch to almost eight thousand persons who are professionals in the health field. Most of this teaching has been done in universities, hospitals or under the auspices of professional organizations. Because of the nature of these formal institutions, there has been ample opportunity to follow these students' experiences in a systemized fashion through responses to various questionnaires and personal interviews with them. Their reports make one aware that involvement in a highly personalized interaction such as Therapeutic Touch significantly helps the person playing the role of healer to strive beyond her own present limitation of ego while in the interest of helping another. If this is so, Therapeutic Touch may be one type of learned behavior that an open society with a strong interest in the balanced maturation of its members may want to encourage.

A few random samples from the above-noted questionnaires and interviews will indicate this movement toward transcendence of personal ego orientation. It will be noted that quite frequently this act of healing another, bolstered by a strong sense of compassion and clearly focused by intentionality, concomitantly brings the self into contact with one's own higher levels of being. Over a period of time the self, now no longer bound solely to the ego, identifies with higher-order psychodynamic and conceptual structures which have a greater complexity, display a high degree of integration and organization and are more unified. As this differentiation is internalized by the self, the functions of the emerging higher-order structure can be used consciously to reorient one's perceptions of and responses to interactions with the environment and with the other.[10]

As will be noted in the following sample statements, the student healers show a deep-level perseverance in their attempt to integrate unconscious contents by struggling to translate verbally what are essentially non-verbal states of consciousness experienced during the healing act. Authorities in both Jungian analysis and religions, such as Hinduism, which are structured to elicit a deep understanding of the ego, state that as there is ". . . a withdrawal of the center of psychic gravity centered around the ego . . . (there follows) the creation of a new psychic condition that is not ego-centric but excentric, meaning that the center of consciousness is in a state of flux."[11] It is this active process of reorienting the specific contents on which the ego relies that is called in Jungian terms the *symbolic life* or *individuation process.* It is a psychodynamic operation regulated by the self that strives towards integration, order, wholeness and self-transformation. Evidence of such high-order emergence can be demonstrated by significant shifts in perception and sense of identity, in emotional state and evaluative and cognitive processes, in temporal and spatial orientation and in how one gets meaning from experience.

A core phase of Therapeutic Touch, which appears to be at the heart of this high-order emergence of the deep structures of self, is an act of centering, which begins the healing process. Centering is a sustained act of interiority in which the healer turns her attention within, towards the innermost reaches of her consciousness of self. In the very act itself she enters into a qualitatively different state of consciousness and of quietude. She maintains this centered state throughout the other stages of Therapeutic Touch as she attempts to assess the healee's problem and then go on to help or to heal that condition. Thus, this centered state of consciousness is maintained throughout the healing experience.

The boundaries of centering are "permeable," says Carrington, and therefore the spectrum of experience can range from a deep spiritual awareness to an oceanic feeling of pleasant relaxation.[12] The inner experience depends on the individual herself and what she has invested in the act. In the situation we are discussing, the healing act, one can assume that this is undertaken with a considerable measure of compassion and altruism; however, whatever the motivation is, it can be said that in the act of centering one does become aware of an all-pervading sense of relationship as one opens to the finer energies of self.

Over time this cultivation of mindfulness can enter significantly into the individual's life style, for centering introduces a meditative quality into the background of one's activities of daily living. Slowly one begins to realize that that state "belongs" to oneself, that one is "really" part of that Reality. Even those who only have brief intimations of this say that when they are in this state they feel "good," "whole," "directed," and it becomes their baseline style, one they readily revert to when the opportunity presents itself.

In the above-noted sample, several questions were answered about significant shifts in consciousness. The examples will be limited, but representative of the sample as a whole.

Because the ego is actively involved in survival and

interactions in the outer world, one of the first questions asked was: How do you sense the external environment (during and after the practice of Therapeutic Touch), i.e., is there any change in the way you perceive things and people around you. Representative answers were:

A. During Therapeutic Touch the external environment seems to grow less important. At work I tend to have my mind on several activities at once, but when I'm doing Therapeutic Touch I lose some degree of contact with these external stimuli. I have a greater sense of self after centering and my attention is focused in upon my interaction with the patient. Other people about the room appear to be more distant and often I won't hear someone calling me until the second or third time. Furniture, equipment and other inanimate objects seem to remain stable, but I do tune out some of the sounds of the cardiac monitors and the respirators. It is as if I place an artificial stillness upon the external environment—I filter out the sound and the movement—to facilitate my concentration upon the therapeutic interaction with the patient.

B. I am less reactive to the external environment—there may be sounds, I hear them but I do not respond to these stimuli. They are unimportant. The energy field of the healee and my own field constitute the focus of my awareness.

C. I go into a sense of oneness with God, the universe and the healee. As long as I stay in that space I'm not much aware of what else is going on around me.

D. I feel like I am the one peaceful thing in the environment. Other things may be noisy, or other people may act as though their nerves are jangled, but during Therapeutic Touch I am a thing of peace.

E. I seem to notice things with more than the usual senses of touch, hearing, seeing, etc. and I am deeply aware of the person that I am working on in a way I can't easily explain.

F. Yes. I again have a richer sense, or sense a richer color and texture to nature around me, and I am more aware of my fellow men and of my own needs. I have more of a sense of unity or oneness with others and with nature.

G. The external environment seems removed, quiet, "in tune."

H. I tend to look into people or things; I try to understand their inner character and relate to that in a manner I had never conceived of before.

I. While I am doing Therapeutic Touch other things and people tend to be "distant." Even if I allow them to intrude into my perception, I still perceive them as somewhat distant. If I allow the sense of distance to return, to see distance as I normally perceive it, I am then in my normal state of awareness and not doing Therapeutic Touch.

When those in the sample were asked what roles they perceived themselves as enacting, or to describe their sense of identity during Therapeutic Touch, most frequently their statements indicated a deeply seated diffidence about their own involvement.

A. When I am healing I feel as though I am a conduit sending appropriate energies for healing or peace or love. The source of these energies does not seem to originate within me, but rather I seem to tap into it.

B. When I am doing Therapeutic Touch, I identify as a healer of universal mind-energy, an extension for a universal force of which I, myself, am only a small facet but, nevertheless, a connecting link for healing power and a loving power or consciousness.

C. I am an instrument of my God, the creative source of all energy. I only clear myself for the flow and allow the healing energy to do its work. The healee seems to take it and use it as is needed and desired.

D. I identify as a caring, aware, responsible helper to the patient. The patients themselves do the healing. In addition, for myself there is a definite growth process involved in each experience. Therapeutic Touch has taught me that I can help myself (no more excuses!). I feel that there is more potential than I can or will actualize; I feel an added depth and dimensionality to my identity.

Assuming that healing was a behavior enacted under the compelling influence of compassion, the subjects of the sample were therefore asked whether they had noted any changes in their emotions:

A. I think that the practice of Therapeutic Touch causes me to be calmer and, therefore, I suppose I do react differently. But I do not underreact; It's more like having my emotions and ideas in focus and, consequently, being more integrated.

B. I react in an entirely different way than usual. More compassionate and concerned. Alert. Ideas integrate easily.

C. I tend to react less in a stimulus-response manner than I did before. I try to deal with my emotions more; I consider this an important part of my becoming more aware of myself.

D. Yes. I react in an entirely different way than usual, and I am aware that I like this changed emotional response, but it is quite difficult to find the appropriate descriptors. Maybe I will be able to verbalize it better once the surprise wears off.

E. Increased sensitivity to situations that can't be explained. Many telepathic instances. High sensitivity to friends' problems, particularly where pain is involved, and this is coupled with a strong, insistent feeling that I may be able to help.

Questioned on significant changes in evaluative and cognitive processes, many indicated a more focused attention, an increase in intuitive processing, a concern with the moment, and incisive action.

A. I don't think so during the healing process per se. However, I definitely experience cognitive changes throughout my life situations, perhaps because I have been meditating regularly as well as practicing Therapeutic Touch.

B. Sometimes I now get impressions that arrive in my head fully formed as thoughts about patients' conditions at that moment. They come seemingly from nowhere—that is, apropos of nothing that I am involved in at that moment—and these incidents have always been confirmed by the patient when I checked them. I regularly check these impressions, if it seems O.K. to ask. At that moment they seem so far-out to my rational mind.

C. I am now acutely aware of what my attention is involved with. Thought processes seem less automatic and more consciously directed.

D. The rate of my evaluative and cognitive processing has increased; I seem to take in more information. The logic of my evaluations is not always discernible (and they [evaluations] surprise me when they turn out to be right!). The quality of my thought processes has taken on a renewed sensitivity.

E. If I can integrate the experiences [of my Therapeutic Touch practice], the logic of my evaluations comes from a very different framework than my usual mode of thinking.

F. There has been a high rate of telepathic information that now significantly influences my evaluative processing and perhaps my cognitive processing as well.

G. I now believe what I feel and act on it.

Peper and Ancoli, on the basis of encephalographic

analyses, have called Therapeutic Touch a "healing meditation."[13] It is of interest, therefore, that the responses to questions about changes in time-sense while doing Therapeutic Touch show close similarity to those reported in classical studies on meditation.[14]

A. During Therapeutic Touch my sense of time seems to slow down. Actually, I lose specific perception of time while engrossed in the healing process.
B. Time seems irrelevant; generally, I do not think of time going by.
C. The present seems expanded and time slows down.
D. Time is not a factor; that is, linear time. I am usually a hasty person, but while I am doing Therapeutic Touch both the rate of my physical actions and my perceptions slow down noticeably.
E. Time is "different."
F. Time seems to become timeless; i.e., I am not aware of time passing although I am aware of the here-and-now events, of the experience between the patient and myself. If anything, I suppose time slows down.
G. It seems of no importance or relevance. I simply lose track of time, there is so much else I want to attend to.
H. Time slows down; however, in a way it is really more fluid than slow. The present, the new, is what I am acutely aware of.

As noted above, it is not known how the healer actually heals; most healers feel that some sort of an "inside maneuver" occurs within them. Whatever that may be, the question remains: how do they get meaning from the experience?

A. I listen. Meaning on one level occurs deep within, sometimes not in a conscious way, but nevertheless clearly, coherently and usually correctly. On another level I am consciously bringing to the problem at hand my previous experience and education to integrate and make coherent the information I perceive with or through my hands in reference to patterns of energy flow.
B. I try to be sensitive to what is happening to me, through me, the reaction in the patient and the interaction between us.
C. I am aware of an inner dialogue in my head, so to speak, which is concerned with the intentionality to heal that is involved, and I sensitize myself to that and "listen" very carefully to its cues.

In recent years I have often reflected upon the responses to questionnaires and interviews such as those discussed above. I have been impressed by significant similarities between the healing act and the creative act. A full analysis of this assumption would require another article; however, perhaps the reader can follow the main outlines such a statement might take by a brief review of Marie Dellas and Eugene Gauer's well known profile of the truly creative individual.

Dellas and Gauer state that the quest of the creative individual is directed inward, in a manner that is permissive of the symbolic expression of repressed needs and desires. Creative persons are unhampered by formal boundaries of logic; they open themselves to the consideration of many different thoughts, allowing themselves wide variety of experiences, and they thus make significant contact with the dynamisms of the unconscious. A mark of their creativity is that they are able to integrate all this with the conscious mind and bring forth new patterns of expression. They have an openness to experiencing emotion and bring to these experiences a sensitively attuned awareness. They permit the self to indicate to the consciousness what are intuitive responses to problems. They seek opportunities to heighten their perceptual awareness, they have the ability to accept ambiguity; they actively seek out new frontiers, and they are not bound by pre-formed ideas.[15]

Our Western scientific methodologies would insist that the assumption of close correlation between the healing act and the creative act be demonstrated to be beyond chance expectations. This could be done by conforming to a formal research design, i.e., by having known creative persons answer the same questions as those given to the sample of healers, and then computing a statistical analysis of the comparison of answers. Perhaps this will be undertaken at another time. However, for now I offer my impression of the apparent close fit of the critical characteristics of the creative act and the healing act, both based in a high-order emergence of the self.

Mature societies in the past have recognized, honored and emulated their creative members. Perhaps in the future society will recognize that a similar inner experience awaits those who espouse what to me is one of the most humane of all human acts, the helping or healing of others.

REFERENCES

1. John Naisbitt. *Megatrends* (New York: Warner Books, 1984), pp. 51 and 52.

2. Harry Edwards. *A Guide to Spirit Healing* (London: Spiritualist Press, 1955.)

3. Dolores Krieger. *Therapeutic Touch: How to Use Your Hands to Help or to Heal* (Englewood Cliffs: Prentice-Hall, Inc., 1979).

4. Lawrence LeShan. *The Medium, the Mystic and the Scientist* (New York: Ballantine Books, 1975.)

5. Fr. Francis McNutt. *Healing* (New York: Bantam Books, 1976.)

6. Tokujiro Numikoshi. *Shiatsu* (San Francisco: Japan Publications, 1972.)

7. Stephan Palos. *The Chinese Art of Healing* (New York: Herder and Herder, 1971.)

8. Yogi Ramacharaka. *Psychic Healing* (Chicago: Yogi Publication Society, 1905.)

9. Gordon Turner. *An Outline of Spiritual Healing* (New York: Warner Books, 1972.)

10. Ken Wilber. *The Atman Project* (Wheaton: Theosophical Publishing House, 1980.)

11. Stanley Marlan. Depth Consciousness. In *Metaphors of Consciousness*, ed. Valle and Eckartsberg (New York: Plenum Press, 1981), p. 238.

12. Patricia Carrington. *Freedom in Meditation* (New York: Anchor Books, 1978), p. 8.

13. Erik Peper and Sonia Ancoli. The Two Endpoints of an EEG Continuum of Meditation: Alpha/Theta and Fast Beta. In *Therapeutic Touch* (op cit.).

14. Michael Murphy and Stephen Donovan. A Bibliography of Meditation Theory: 1931-1983. *J. Transpers. Psychol.* 15:2:181-228.

15. Marie Dellas and Eugene I. Gauer. Identification of Creativity: The Individual. *Psychol. Bull.* 1970, 73:55-73.

19

Therapeutic Touch as Meditation

JANET MACRAE, Ph.D., R.N.

Therapeutic touch is a method of facilitating healing which has been derived from the ancient practice of the laying-on of hands. It is currently being used in many hospitals and health centers across the country as an adjunct to traditional methods of treatment. Evidence supports the view that this technique is a natural human potential which can be actualized under the appropriate circumstances (Krieger, 1979). An individual who would like to learn Therapeutic Touch should be relatively healthy, should have a sincere interest in helping other people, and should obtain adequate instruction from an experienced practitioner. To gain expertise in the technique, regular practice and self-discipline are essential.

Comparing my experiences as a practitioner with those of my colleagues and students, I feel that the Therapeutic Touch process evokes a certain quality of being that can best be described as meditative. It is becoming obvious that Therapeutic Touch is not only a technique for helping to alleviate suffering but is also a vehicle or means of self-transformation. In this paper, therefore, I would like to explore some of the characteristics of meditation and relate these to Therapeutic Touch. As meditation is integral to yoga, I will also look at Therapeutic Touch within the context of the yoga sutras of

Patanjali. Although this discussion will focus on the specific technique of Therapeutic Touch, many of the ideas are universal and thus would apply to any situation in which one person reaches out to help another.

THERAPEUTIC TOUCH
AS A MEDITATIVE TECHNIQUE

The practice of Therapeutic Touch is based on the fundamental principle of unity or dynamic wholeness (Weber, 1979). This means that, within every human being, body, mind and spirit are completely interrelated; it also means that there is an interrelationship among human beings and all other organisms in the environment. Kunz and Peper (1982), describing an energetic model of human well-being, write that every individual can be viewed both as a distinct entity and also as a system of energy fields.

> These fields (like those known to science) permeate space. Each individual is a localization (concentration) of energy within these universal fields. Moreover, these individual local fields interact with one another, being part of one whole, dynamic, and interdependent system. (pp. 395-6)

Within this framework, illness is seen as disharmony and/or blockage of energy flow both within the individual and between the individual and the environment. During the process of Therapeutic Touch the practitioner, with a clear, focused intent, channels life energy through himself or herself to the patient. He or she also helps the patient to assimilate the energy by releasing congestion and balancing disharmonious rhythms. Thus the practitioner, through regular practice, must develop a sensitivity to the subtle energy which surrounds and interpenetrates the physical body. Borelli (1981) has written that this sensitivity to very subtle stimuli is a central characteristic of both Therapeutic Touch and meditation.

Therapeutic Touch was first described as being a meditation by Peper and Ancoli (1977). In their pilot study, Dr. Dolores Krieger, an experienced practitioner, practiced Therapeutic Touch while electroencephalographic (EEG), electromyographic (EMG), and electrooculographic (EOG) measurements were taken (see also Krieger, Peper and Ancoli, 1979). According to the researchers, the most significant finding was an unusual amount of rapid, synchronous beta EEG activity. They interpreted this pattern to be indicative of the state of focused attentiveness which is characteristic of meditation. They supported this interpretation by mentioning research done by Das and Gastaut (1955) and Banquet (1973) in which synchronous beta patterns were found in experienced meditators. Krieger reported that, when the measurements were being taken, she was effortlessly focused on the healing process without any extraneous thoughts or images.

Based on the findings of Peper and Ancoli's pilot study, one could view the Therapeutic Touch technique as a form of concentrative meditation. Through this type of meditative exercise the individual learns to still the mind by holding his or her attention on one specific object or process, such as a mantra or the rhythm of the breath. In the case of Therapeutic Touch, the focus of the meditation would be the patient or the process of helping the patient. As noisy and scattered mental processes become quieter and more one-pointed, the individual is able to connect with deeper, more subtle aspects of being from which arise peace, creativity and compassion (White, 1974; Naranjo and Ornstein, 1971). It is significant that the very qualities which meditation evokes from within the practitioner are those which are necessary for facilitating healing.

Many western writers, such as Goleman (1977), divide the vast array of meditative techniques into two broad categories: concentrative and insight. Although Therapeutic Touch can be seen as a form of concentrative meditation, as discussed above, I feel that the technique is also a form of insight meditation. In this type of exercise, the individual observes, in a non-attached manner, all the thoughts, emotions, and physical sensations which come into awareness. He or she thus learns to disentangle or disidentify himself or herself from these processes, and to perceive and act from a deeper perspective. During Therapeutic Touch the practitioner is totally focused and involved in the process of helping the patient and yet, paradoxically, is not personally identified with the patient or with the outcome of the treatment. It feels, as Krieger (1979) has described, "as though one has stepped behind oneself" (p. 72). This quality of non-attachment is characteristic of both meditation and Therapeutic Touch and will be discussed later in greater depth.

THERAPEUTIC TOUCH
AS A MEDITATIVE EXPERIENCE

Therapeutic Touch can thus be seen as a synthesis of concentrative and insight techniques. The essence of meditation, however, is not the particular technique we use, but the quality of being which the technique helps us to unfold. As Naranjo (1971) has emphasized, this quality of being is not something that we create, or add to ourselves; it is there already as our own deepest reality.

> . . . meditation is concerned with the development of a presence, a modality of being, which may be expressed or developed in whatever situation the individual may be involved.
> This presence or mode of being transforms whatever it touches. (p. 8)

In the case of Therapeutic Touch, this meditative presence would transform both the patient and the practitioner.

A meditative action, such as Therapeutic Touch, is performed in a completely focused manner. Most of the time in daily life we physically do one thing and mentally do another; for example, we have all had the experience of washing dishes and talking to someone at the same time. In meditation, however, this type of fragmentation decreases and one acts as a whole.

If we examine the Therapeutic Touch process we can see that, on every level, the practitioner is focused on the process of helping the patient. Physically, we have the gesture of extending our hands in an attempt to alleviate suffering. In a sense, this is an archetypal, or universal human gesture, which has been used in all cultures throughout the ages.

Emotionally, the practitioner reaches out to the patient in peace and compassion. Mentally, he or she makes the clear focused intent to help or to heal. Spiritually, the practitioner becomes attuned to the universal healing power and channels this energy to the patient. Thus the practitioner functions all together, "in one piece" (Kunz, 1978). The hands are extremely useful in directing the energy, but it is the holistic action of the practitioner which facilitates the healing process.

In a very thorough review of the electroencephalographic studies of meditators, Earl (1981) concluded that "perhaps the most distinguishing EEG characteristic of meditation is unusually high intra- and interhemispheric synchronization" (p. 162). This was found in the pilot study by Krieger, Peper and Ancoli which was previously discussed. The verb *synchronize,* by dictionary definition, means "to move or occur at the same time or rate." In meditation, one could say that all aspects of the individual are synchronized, or moving together in harmony. This physiological data, therefore, is consistent with the idea of meditative action being performed in a focused and integrated manner.

Another characteristic of meditative action is the quality of non-attachment. The act is done for the sake of itself rather than for a specific result or reward. We find this concept in all the great meditative traditions. For example, in the *Bhagavad Gita,* the famous Hindu poem, Krishna tells Arjuna the warrior:

> Do thine allotted task!
> Work is more excellent than idleness;
> The body's life proceeds not, lacking work.
> There is a task of holiness to do
> Unlike world-binding toil, which bindeth not
> The faithful soul; such earthly duty do
> Free from desire, and thou shalt well perform
> Thy heavenly purpose.
>
> (Arnold, p. 25)

Krishna's advice seems very appropriate for the practice of Therapeutic Touch. Lao Tsu, the Chinese sage, has also emphasized the quality of non-attachment. In his words:

Creating, yet not possessing,
Working, yet not taking credit.
Work is done, then forgotten.
Therefore it lasts forever.
(*Tao Te Ching,* verse two)

In my own practice, I have observed that the most effective treatments are those in which the practitioner does not think about the effect but is completely involved in the treatment process itself. Kunz and Peper (1983) have written that concern about results increases the practitioner's anxiety level which then constricts the energy flow making the treatment less effective.

From one point of view, "desireless action" is always difficult to attain because we human beings tend to judge our actions (and ourselves) by the type of results we obtain. Thus a concern about results permeates most of what we do in life, and it is hard to break this habit. From another point of view, however, desireless action during Therapeutic Touch is not difficult at all. The reason is that the healing process itself is interesting and full of wonder. Many beginning students have said to me that Therapeutic Touch opens up for them a whole new dimension of being. Philosophical concepts, such as dynamic wholeness, so beautifully described by Weber (1979), now become an experiential reality, and the sense of deeply participating in the healing process soon becomes its own reward.

This sense of participating with the whole of oneself in a universal process brings with it a feeling of meaning or inner purpose. It is interesting that the quality of "meaning" emerged as a central characteristic of the meditative experience in a phenomenological study conducted by Osis, Bokert and Carlson (1973). This experience of meaningful participation in the healing process is particularly important for health professionals in our modern, technologically oriented health-care system. As lack of meaning and purpose, boredom and frustration are symptoms of "burnout" (Brallier, 1982), health professionals could benefit by learning to care for patients in a meditative manner.

For Therapeutic Touch practitioners, one major obstacle to non-attachment is focusing too much on the personality of the patient. When we do this, we tend to have more compassion for people we personally like or identify with and less for those we dislike. Kunz (1979) has emphasized that this situation is a hindrance to healing and that our compassion must extend equally to all.

Quinn (1981), analyzing behavioral patterns of professional nurses, identified two primary modes of coping with patients. Using the Sympathetic Mode, the nurse, personally identifying with a particular patient, pours herself forth and becomes drained; using the Defensive Mode, the nurse, to avoid becoming drained, withdraws and avoids the patient. Quinn (1982) then notes that some nurses utilize one mode in particular, but most seem to unconsciously vacillate between the two.

Within the context of meditation, the Sympathetic Mode and the Defensive Mode would constitute a pair of opposites which arise together from a lack of wholeness or integrity. We feel insecure by ourselves, so we over-identify with others; then we feel violated, so we push them away. During Therapeutic Touch, however, the practitioner reaches deeper levels of being and integration in the process of opening the self as a channel for the universal life energy. And with this unitive experience emerges a greater degree of personal integrity or "inner certainty" (Sellon, 1983). Paradoxically, it is the sense of being rooted in "the common life of all which lives" (*Bhagavad Gita,* Book V), that allows true individuality to unfold (Bohm and Weber, p. 35). And with this growing integrity, the Sympathetic Mode and the Defensive Mode decrease together and compassion and healing flow more equally to all.

The experience of the unity of all things and the experience of self-identity are both necessary for facilitating healing (Kunz and Peper, 1983) and both develop through the meditative process. Here again, we see how the practice of Therapeutic Touch, as meditation, itself evokes from within the practitioner those qualities which are necessary for

Therapeutic Touch. Means and ends are thus inextricably intertwined; indeed, in all the great meditative traditions, it is said that the path and the goal are one.

One could say, then, that in the broad sense Therapeutic Touch practitioners or healers are also patients, because they make themselves whole through the meditative process. And the patients are also healers because they heal themselves with the help of the practitioners; and by participating in this process of interaction they help the practitioners' inner nature to unfold. Thus there is no sharp dividing line between practitioner and patient; during Therapeutic Touch both individuals benefit from the same healing energy. Shakespeare, in *The Merchant of Venice*, expressed this idea most beautifully:

> The quality of mercy is not strain'd,
> It droppeth as the gentle rain from heaven
> Upon the place beneath. It is twice bless'd:
> It blesseth him that gives and him that takes.

Thus as our integrity becomes strengthened through the meditative process, we can let go of rigid roles and attachments and become more fully present to the other person. When we can forget about ourselves the treatment flows spontaneously; it feels as though it accomplishes itself, occurring through us—not from or by us. This spontaneity, however, emerges out of discipline and persistent practice. As described by Weber (1979):

> The healing centeredness is a mysterious combination of high energy and absolute calm. It is both active and passive, movement and stillness, purposiveness without purpose, effortless effort. In short, the act of healing is meditation in motion. (p. 75)

It is interesting that Dr. Isabella Mears, in her translation of *Tao Te Ching*, writes that Lao Tsu did not teach "nonstriving" as is commonly thought, but rather "striving through the power of the Inner Life." (pp. 5-6) As the Inner Life is a universal principle, this translation is consistent with healing as meditation described above.

Sellon (1983) has emphasized that meditation is a creative process of self-transformation which is never twice the same. This is particularly evident in Therapeutic Touch because the focus of the meditation is an energy system in constant flux. The patient's energies change continually during the treatment and also from one treatment to another. The practitioner must be aware of these changes and respond freshly from moment to moment. One can see, then, that the practice of Therapeutic Touch both requires and evokes the receptive and spontaneous state of being which is characteristic of meditation.

When the treatment is spontaneously flowing, time becomes irrelevant; it dissolves or disappears. In fact, one cue that indicates the treatment is drawing to a close is that the spontaneity lessens and once again becomes conscious of the passing of time. This "finished feeling" can be compared to the feeling one has after an absorbing and meaningful conversation in which all has been said, or resolved, for the moment. Another analogy would be a work of art which one more stroke would make stale or overstrained.

In a sense one could view Therapeutic Touch as a form of "dynamic sculpture," evoking the wholeness, open and flowing rhythm, and balance or harmony which underlie all existence. Particularly appropriate is the ancient idea that the statue already exists in the stone and that the sculptor does not create the statue but frees it. Similarly, in meditation, the idea is to allow one's own inner nature, which is there already and perfectly whole, to express itself freely. During the Therapeutic Touch process the practitioner evokes this intrinsic wholeness within the patient—calls it forth or helps to free it—so that disturbed energy patterns can be reordered.

Therapeutic Touch is thus a creative, spontaneous act in which linear time seems to disappear. This experience of "timelessness," or complete involvement in the present moment, is integral to meditation. Goldstein (1976), discussing the experience of insight meditation, wrote:

> When we can settle back into the moment, realizing that past and future are simply thoughts in the present, then we free ourselves from the bondage of "time." (p. 31)

In a research study with the Time Metaphor Test, a significant difference was found between meditating and non-meditating subjects (Macrae, 1982). Describing their experience of time during meditation, subjects tended to choose non-linear, expansive metaphors, such as "a quiet, motionless ocean." Non-meditators, performing a simple relaxation exercise, tended to choose linear time metaphors such as "a speeding train." It is interesting that not one of the forty-five meditators chose "a tedious song" which might indicate boredom, and only two chose "the Rock of Gibraltar" which might indicate heaviness. In addition, almost half the sample chose the metaphor "budding leaves" which has the qualities of freshness, hopefulness and growth.

In addition to changes in time-sense the meditative experience is associated with changes in space-sense, in particular with what we would call our self-boundary. In phenomenological studies by Osis, Bokert and Carlson (1973) and Kohr (1977) subjects reported that their self-boundaries expanded or became more diffuse; they experienced this as a feeling of unity with their meditation group, a sense of "merging" with others and/or a non-personal experience of connectedness with the environment. In another study by Kornfield (1979), many subjects wrote that their bodies became light and expansive, and some subjects felt that their bodies disappeared.

During Therapeutic Touch, the practitioner reaches out in a feeling of compassion for the patient. With experience, he or she begins to feel himself or herself as a flowing pattern of energy which interpenetrates the energies of the patient. This might also be described as a feeling of inwardly connecting with, or empathizing with, the particular individual. And yet, at the same time, the practitioner also feels deeply harmonized with the universal flow of life, or, as Naranjo (1971) has written, "attuned to a law greater than himself" (p. 21). Thus Therapeutic Touch, as meditation in general, is both deeply personal and deeply impersonal.

THERAPEUTIC TOUCH AS YOGA

In the Hindu tradition, meditation is an integral aspect of a comprehensive system of self-transformation which is called

Ashtanga (eight limbed) Yoga. This system was codified by Patanjali over one thousand years ago. Literally, the word *yoga* means "to yoke" or "to join." I feel, though, that yoga could also mean "to heal" or "to make whole." On the physical level, we say that a cut or a wound has healed when the separated skin comes together again or joins. The healing process of yoga, however, is multidimensional and thus more complicated than physical healing. The practice of yoga heals the split between the personality and the deeper aspects of being, or between the particular individual and the universal source of life. Yoga heals the fundamental wound, so to speak, from which arises alienation, insecurity, and all human suffering. It is interesting that the word *heal* comes from the Anglo-Saxon word *haelan* which means "to make whole." Thus one could look at the practice of yoga as the facilitation of wholeness in the fullest sense of the word.

We have discussed how Therapeutic Touch, a method of facilitating healing or wholeness, is a form of meditation; if meditation is integral to yoga, then so also must be Therapeutic Touch. Indeed, Krieger (1979) has called this technique a "yoga of healing." There are many varieties of yoga; Therapeutic Touch could be viewed as a form of bhakti yoga because it is an act of love, or as a form of karma yoga because it is an act of service. I feel, however, that it is more appropriate to look at Therapeutic Touch within the context of the most comprehensive yogic system, that of Patanjali mentioned above. We can then find aspects of the eight limbs of this system within the one act of Therapeutic Touch. For the purpose of this paper, I will refer to *The Science of Yoga* by I.K. Taimni which contains a clear translation of the yoga sutras and a very thorough commentary.

Most of us have difficulty experiencing a sense of deep wholeness and peace because of all sorts of physical, emotional and mental disturbances and distractions. Patanjali's yoga is a holistic program of eliminating these disturbances so that the individual can feel connected to the spiritual ground of being in which all things are unified. The practice of Yama and Niyama, the first two limbs, reduces the anxiety that arises from unethical behavior. Asana and Pranayama reduce physical tension and create a rhythmic, undisturbed flow of vital energy. Pratyahara reduces distractions coming from the environment. Dharana (concentration) reduces the disturbance from internal thoughts, images, and feelings. Dhyana (contemplation or meditation) is the experience of unbroken "flow" which arises when disturbances have been quieted; some of the qualities of this experience have already been explored with respect to Therapeutic Touch. Samadhi, the eighth limb, is a very advanced phase of meditation in which the individual's self-awareness or sense of separateness is completely transcended.

In the fourteenth sutra, Patanjali says that yoga should be continued for a long time, without interruption and with reverent devotion. I feel that Therapeutic Touch should also be practiced in this manner. Krieger (1979), comparing Therapeutic Touch to yoga, writes that the expert practice of this technique "demands concentration and a deep sense of commitment to lifting a little the veil of suffering of living beings. It is an effort so constant that it can be a way of life." (p. 71)

Yama and Niyama together form an ethical foundation for the practice of yoga. Yama means abstinence or self-restraint; Patanjali says it requires abstension from violence, lying, stealing, incontinence, and possessiveness or acquisitiveness. Niyama refers to observances: the cultivation of love, contentment, purity, self-discipline and the study of universal truths.

During the process of Therapeutic Touch, I feel that the practitioner is acting in accordance with Yama and Niyama. As Therapeutic Touch is an act of non-possessive love and compassion, the practitioner must obviously abstain from any kind of violence. In fact, most practitioners perform a preparatory centering exercise to help get rid of any irritability or anxiety which might adversely affect the patient. The practitioner's intent to help or to heal has no ulterior motive or desire for personal gain; he or she must be content with the results, whatever these might be. The practice of Therapeutic Touch demands self-discipline and self-examination (Krieger, 1979) and it also demands a constant effort to understand the universal laws of healing and to work in accordance with them.

According to Patanjali, one's posture should be steady and comfortable. This is very important with respect to Therapeutic Touch for several reasons. If the practitioner is physically tense or uncomfortable his or her attention is likely to be drawn towards this personal discomfort, thus fragmenting the focused nature of the meditative healing act. Since energy systems are interpenetrating, the practitioner could easily transmit this sense of discomfort to the patient. Also, as mentioned earlier, anxiety and tension constrict the flow of vital energy thus impeding the healing process. One can see that adequate rest and relaxation are important for anyone practicing a technique such as Therapeutic Touch.

In yoga psychology, mind and body are seen as being completely interrelated. A physical posture is a reflection or an embodiment of a mental state (Swami Rama, Swami Ajaya, and Ballentine, 1976). Thus a tense, constricted posture is associated with a constricted state of being while a relaxed, open posture is associated with an open state of being. Hatha yoga is based on the idea that an individual can create a desired state of being by practicing the appropriate positions (asanas) and hand gestures (mudras). Within this context, the Therapeutic Touch practitioner's open, outstretched arms and hands would evoke qualities such as love and generosity which are essential for healing.

The fourth limb of this system of yoga is pranayama, which literally means "regulation of prana." Prana is described as the vital energy which maintains health and integrity. Within a healthy person the flow of prana is rhythmic and balanced, and there is a continuous interchange with the environment; when a person is ill the flow is dysrhythmic and/or blocked (Kunz and Peper, 1982). In the science of yoga, there is a very close relationship between breathing patterns and the flow of prana. Shallow, dysrhythmic breathing indicates an irregular flow of prana and therefore some sort of disturbance in the health of the individual. Through practicing various breathing exercises, the student of yoga rebalances the disturbances in his or her pranic flow, thus enhancing health and development.

The regulation of prana or vital energy is central to

Therapeutic Touch. The practitioner must not only regulate the flow within himself or herself, but must (a) intentionally channel this energy to the patient, and (b) help the patient repattern his or her energy flow in the direction of dynamic balance. A change in the patient's breathing pattern is a sign that the patient is responding to the treatment. Many practitioners have commented that their own breathing becomes deeper, more regular, and sometimes harmonizes with that of the patient.

Pratyahara, the fifth limb, is the withdrawal of the mind from impacts from the sense organs. It is the ability to consciously "tune out" distractions from the environment. This ability is essential for Therapeutic Touch because, as discussed before, the practitioner must be focused on the healing process. If he or she is continually being distracted, the treatment is not going to be very good. I have noticed that, for most people, the ability to "tune out" noise and other environmental distractions improves fairly quickly with regular practice. Although the technique is called Therapeutic Touch, contact with the patient's clothes and skin can often be a distraction. For this reason, practitioners most often work a short distance from the surface of the patient's body.

According to Taimni (1961) the last three limbs of Ashtanga Yoga, concentration, contemplation or meditation, and samadhi, form a continuum. Concentration is the act of holding the mind within a limited area; when distracting thoughts and images appear, the mind is brought back to the area of concentration. Concentration turns into contemplation or meditation when distractions disappear and there is an uninterrupted flow of the mind toward the area of concentration; in the case of Therapeutic Touch this, of course, would be the patient or the process of helping the patient. Samadhi is the most advanced phase of meditation in which the sense of a separate self is transcended. The transcendence of self during a moving meditation has been vividly described by Herrigel in *Zen in the Art of Archery:*

> ... the contest consists in the archer aiming at himself—and yet not at himself, in hitting himself—and yet not himself, and thus becoming simultaneously the aimer and the aim, the hitter and the hit. (p. 20)

This description of subject and object becoming one reality is consistent with descriptions of samadhi in the science of yoga.

During Therapeutic Touch, the beginning practitioner must develop the ability to concentrate solely on the process of helping the patient. With regular practice, internal and external distractions decrease and the action turns more and more into a meditative process, the qualities of which we explored previously. At the present time I can only speculate as to whether or not the practice of Therapeutic Touch would lead to samadhi. Most practitioners would agree that gaining expertise in Therapeutic Touch is a lifetime process. If concentration, meditation and samadhi do indeed form a continuum, then a state consistent with samadhi might be possible after many years of dedicated practice.

On the other hand, the practice of Therapeutic Touch is based on the idea of an energy transfer, which implies at least some degree of separation between practitioner and patient. Kunz and Peper (1983) have emphasized that the healing process is modulated by the practitioner's inner self-confidence or sense of self-identity. It is possible that some consciousness of one's identity as a distinct individual is necessary to focus the energy for a specific purpose; if this is the case, then the Therapeutic Touch process would not be compatible with a state such as samadhi, in which there is no awareness of separation between subject and object. To fully address this issue, however, we will have to record and analyze the patterns of experience of practitioners as the years go by. For Therapeutic Touch, in our culture, is relatively new and we have much to learn from the process. Thus far, it has been a wonderful journey into a little-known aspect of our human potential, full of interest, surprise and fulfillment.

BIBLIOGRAPHY

Arnold, Edwin (Trans.). *The Song Celestial.* Wheaton, IL: The Theosophical Publishing House, 1975.

Bohm, David and Renée Weber. Of matter and meaning: The super-implicate order. *ReVision*, 1983, 6, 34-44. (Box 316, Cambridge, MA 02138)

Borelli, Marianne and Patricia Heidt (Eds.). *Therapeutic Touch: A Book of Readings.* New York: Springer Publishing Company, 1982. (200 Park Avenue South, New York, NY 10003)

Brallier, Lynn. *Successfully Managing Stress.* Los Altos: National Nursing Review, 1982. (342 State Street, Los Altos, CA 94022)

Earl, Jonathan. Cerebral laterality and meditation: A review of the literature. *Journal of Transpersonal Psychology,* 1981, 13, pp. 155-73. (P.O. Box 4437, Stanford, CA 94305)

Feng, Gia-Fu and Jane English (Trans). *Tao Te Ching.* New York: Random House, 1972.

Goldstein, Joseph. *The Experience of Insight.* Santa Cruz: Unity Press, 1976.

Goleman, Daniel. *The Varieties of the Meditative Experience.* New York: E.P. Dutton, 1977.

Herrigel, Eugen, *Zen in the Art of Archery.* New York: Random House, 1971.

Kohr, Richard. Dimensionality in meditative experience: a replication. *Journal of Transpersonal Psychology,* 1977, 9, 193-203.

Kornfield, Jack. Intensive insight meditation: A phenomenological study. *Journal of Transpersonal Psychology,* 1979, 11, 41-8.

Krieger, Dolores. *The Therapeutic Touch: How to Use Your Hands to Help or to Heal.* Englewood Cliffs, NJ: Prentice-Hall, Inc., 1979.

Krieger, Dolores, Erik Peper, and Sonia Ancoli. Therapeutic Touch: Searching for evidence of Physiological Change. *American Journal of Nursing,* 79, 660-2.

Kunz, Dora. Healers' Workshop, Craryville, New York, 1978.

Kunz, Dora and Erik Peper. Fields and Their Clinical Implications: Parts I and II. *American Theosophist, 70,* 395-401 and 72, 3-21. (reprints available through the Theosophical Research Institute, P.O.Box 270, Wheaton, IL 60189)

Macrae, Janet. *A comparison between meditating subjects and non-meditating subjects on time experience and human field motion.* Unpublished doctoral dissertation, New York University, 1982.

Mears, Isabella (Trans.) *Tao Te Ching.* Wheaton, IL: Theosophical Publishing House, 1971.

Naranjo, Claudio and Robert Ornstein. *On the Psychology of Meditation.* New York: The Viking Press, 1971.

Osis, K., E. Bokert, and M.L. Carlson. Dimensions of the meditative experience. *Journal of Transpersonal Psychology,* 1973, 5, 109-35.

Peper, Erik and Sonia Ancoli. The Two Endpoints of an EEG Continuum of Meditation. Paper presented at the Biofeedback Society of America Conference at Orlando, Florida, March, 1977. (reprints available through: E. Peper, 2236 Derby Street, Berkeley, CA 94705)

Quinn, Janet. Client care and nurse involvement in a holistic framework. In Dolores Krieger's *Foundations for Holistic Health Nursing Practices.* Philadelphia: J.B. Lippincott, 1981.

Quinn, Janet. Therapeutic Touch workshop, New York University, 1982.

Sellon, Emily. Meditation and the process of self-transformation. Public lecture, New York Theosophical Society, 1983.

Swami Rama, Swami Ajaya, and Ballentine, Rudolph. *Yoga and Psychotherapy: the Evolution of Consciousness.* Honesdale, PA: Himalayan Institute, 1976.

Taimni, I.K. *The Science of Yoga.* Adyar, Madras, India: The Theosophical Publishing House, 1961.

Weber, Renée. Philosophical foundations and frameworks for healing. *ReVision,* 1979, 2, 66-77. Box 316, Cambridge, MA 02138) Also in *The American Theosophist,* 1979, *67,* 338-349 (Box 270, Wheaton, IL 60189) and Borelli and Heidt.

White, John (Ed.). *What is Meditation?* Garden City, NY: Anchor Books/Doubleday, 1974.

20

Compassion, Rootedness and Detachment: Their Role in Healing

A Conversation with DORA KUNZ,
Conducted by RENÉE WEBER

Dora Kunz was born in the Orient in Java, the Dutch East Indies, and grew up there influenced by Eastern philosophical traditions, amidst an intellectual and spiritually oriented Dutch family. She began to meditate from the age of five and has been interested in various forms of meditation all her life. "My mother," she laughs, "did not care what her children ate or whether they ate, as long as they did not skip meditation." Very early in her childhood she became aware that she had the innate ability to perceive fields of energy around all living things, i.e., that she is clairvoyant, something that she seems willing to discuss reluctantly and only rarely. For many decades she applied this ability to medical contexts, working with doctors in paranormal diagnosis and in counseling patients. (Some of her work on epilepsy and other disorders is written up by neurologist Shafica Karagulla, M.D., in Breakthrough to Creativity, *where Kunz appears under a pseudonym.)*

For the past twelve years Kunz has worked with a widening group of health professionals. Together with Dolores Krieger, Professor of Nursing at New York University, she developed Therapeutic Touch, an application of healing techniques designed especially for health professionals and the settings in which they work. Since the early 1970s Kunz and Krieger have held annual Healers' Workshops that are so much in demand that they are filled months in advance, with long waiting lists, and have become limited to health professionals. Those attending are nurses and professors of nursing, doctors, therapists, psychologists, rehabilitation specialists, and allied professionals. Kunz also lectures and gives workshops on

289

meditation and healing at places ranging from New York University to Interface.

She has always felt close to nature, especially to trees and forests. Decades ago she helped found the retreat centers amidst nature in which the Healers' Workshops are now held. What strikes one instantly is her down-to-earth style and common-sense approach to problems. In no way does she fit the stereotype of rarefied abstractedness and solemnity that cliches might mistakenly believe correlates with her work. What comes across—besides the sense of joy and laughter so infectious that one gets invariably swept in—is a grounded and practical person capable of establishing immediate rapport with those who seek her out. Her non-judgmental outlook and sensible suggestions make people feel understood, that somehow she has grasped the core of their problem. Personal qualities that never fail to arouse comment are Kunz's stamina and energy. She has travelled and lived all over the world, East and West, and currently lives near Chicago. She has been President of the Theosophical Society in America for the last nine years, Chairman of its Publishing House, and Editor-in-Chief of its magazine, The American Theosophist.

Weber: What is healing? How would you describe or define it?

Kunz: Healing is a process in which an individual in physical or emotional pain can be helped through another person, whom we can call the healer; or—in self-healing—by a willingness of the person who is suffering to change his way of thinking and feeling.

Weber: What is illness and how does healing intervene and restore health?

Kunz: Illness is disharmony in the organizing patterns of the body. This may take place at different levels. It involves not only the physical damage to the organism but if we think of man as an integrated system, it affects feeling, thinking and other levels. From my point of view, there is also a spiritual component in each person.

Weber: Is *all* illness due to disharmony?

Kunz: No. One cannot make that kind of an absolute statement. There are accidents, trauma, broken bones, for example. I have also found that low energy states at subtler levels of our being can make one more vulnerable to physical illness and these often precede the onset of disease long before it manifests physically. I think that all diseases have a psychosomatic component.

Weber: What about illness in very small children, infants?

Kunz: There is often a genetic component to this and, as I have been brought up in the Eastern tradition, I feel that diseases may be induced by remote past experiences. I accept, at least for myself, the doctrine of karma. That actually can be a cause of disease, particularly as a baby can have no present contributing part in it.

Weber: In other words the baby is too young to make disturbed emotional patterns that early, so the contributing causes might lie elsewhere?

Kunz: It might be the genetic part of his inheritance, but the cause might also lie in past incarnations.

Weber: You are saying that it does have a bearing on illness even though it is difficult to make it a one-to-one causal relationship. You're avoiding any simplistic correlation, but from the Eastern point of view karma somehow plays a role. This would be like the seeds that are stored up, as Patanjali argues in the *Yoga Sutras* and as other Eastern systems and theosophical philosophy claim.

Kunz: Yes.

Weber: In your experience with health professionals you are reputed to be as careful and empirical in your approach as is possible in these sorts of investigations. Do you think that there is *in principle* any way to study these matters empirically, the question for example of how karma plays a role in illness?

Kunz: I can't answer that, but if you accept karma, there *is* an element of determinism. The two go together. Karma is a hypothesis, but if one accepts the hypothesis, determinism must enter the picture to some extent. At the same time, there are other forces which may alter the outcome. The intervention of a healer may also be part of that person's karma.

Weber: Isn't it also true that karma bears on autonomy just as it bears on determinism? Karma holds that *how* I regard what happens to me and what I *do* about it lies to a large degree within my power.

Kunz: I think it has a bearing on it. My point of view is to look at the illness realistically, but also to realize that we are dealing with a human potential. When we accept the *fact* of the illness many other dimensions may become activated, and these could bring in the spiritual power of healing and thus even eliminate the disease.

Weber: When we accept what has happened, our energy isn't used up in fighting or denying it?

Kunz: It isn't used up in negating it, but instead of that, one may become aware of how one can draw on other energies to change the physical symptoms.

Weber: You've said that illness involves many levels of our consciousness and in your writing you call these levels "fields." Can you explain what they are and how they are related to well-being and disease?

Kunz: The fields are all around us. Each person is associated with various fields: physical, vital, emotional, mental, intuitional etc. and radiates these energies. This implies that we constantly interact with one another both in our feelings and thinking. Most people are completely unaware of this constant energy exchange except where there is a close relationship. In that case, what the person feels will be registered by the one to whom the feeling is directed, whether it is a positive feeling or a disturbing feeling. This is especially apparent in family life.

Weber: You're saying that all of us influence one another through these energy fields. To you they are real, but most people are simply not aware of them.

Kunz: While we are all somewhat aware of how we react to other people's feelings, it is not necessarily a conscious awareness. For example, people's moods are catching, whether they are negative or positive. Healing involves the conscious and focused interaction of these energy fields within a person and also between the healer and the patient.

Weber: We are talking about all sorts of healing. Therapeutic touch, for example, has been well known in the last decade, but surely healing didn't just begin then. Can you say something about its pervasiveness in world culture?

Kunz: Different methods of healing in different cultures

and religions have been with us for thousands of years. It appears new because the recent emphasis has been so much on medical technology. But alternative healing methods have been a common practice and still are a common practice in the United States and in many other countries, even where there are different systems of medicine. How the different healers (and I have close contact with many well-known healers) describe their method or what method they employ depends very much on the source of their religious training and upbringing, in other words on their background and conditioning. They may use different words or different methods, but basically there is a common denominator in healing, from whatever source it comes.

Weber: In spite of the different cultural backgrounds and symbol-systems of many healers, they have certain features in common. What are these?

Kunz: From my observation, there are several common denominators which seem essential. First, the healer has to have a conviction or faith that there is a power which is greater than himself, on which he can draw. Secondly, he of course must have a genuine compassion and the desire to help others. Thirdly, to be truly effective, he has to leave his own ego or sense of self-importance out of the healing process.

Weber: It's set aside for the time being?

Kunz: Yes. Between the healer and the sick person there often develops a close, empathic relationship. If the healer feels that he is personally involved in the patient's pain, he will feel anxiety, and anxiety, at whatever subtle level, is an energy that will be conveyed to the patient along with the healing energy.

Weber: So there is a rationale for the healer's having to set aside even his anxiety about the outcome of the healing.

Kunz: This will interfere and in some cases I have even observed that people who identify with other people's disease process may feel the pain in their own body. This is really not good for the healer, because it weakens his own energy.

Weber: You said that the healer has to have faith in a healing power; can that power be described in any way?

Kunz: To me, this healing power exists and is real. I feel it has three characteristics: order, wholeness, and compassion.

Weber: It is part of nature?

Kunz: It's part of nature and it's universal. Therefore, it does not matter who calls upon it nor by what name. It is not for any race nor any particular religion. I think this is important.

Weber: In the *Bhagavad Gita,* Krishna says, "By whatever name you call me, it is I who will answer you." Is there a similarity?

Kunz: Yes.

Weber: How do order and compassion relate to healing?

Kunz: If we could think of disease as disorder, then the healing power is a force which can restore order to the person's fields, because physically the body always tends toward order. The body is compensating constantly for the failures in different organs. Where there is physical disease, there is also a disturbance in the emotional and thinking processes. They go together. Thus if a healer has an effect, this healing energy has to affect the person at all levels. The healer, through this fresh energy, can hasten the body's own recuperative power. Being low in energy, as I said earlier, is often the precursor of disease.

Weber: The healing force and its energies somehow speed up the innate tendencies toward order in the body. Now what is the specific role of the healer in this?

Kunz: The role of the healer is just to be an instrument; by his compassion and by his focusing to allow this healing force to flow through him to the patient.

Weber: Why is that instrument necessary?

Kunz: It is not necessary if the person himself has the strength to open himself up to the healing power, and is willing, at the same time, to become aware of his emotional and thought patterns which help to keep him in the state of illness, and to change them.

Weber: So self healing, the direct harmonization of the ill person with the healing power, is possible.

Kunz: Yes, but it requires one's awareness of his disordered patterns and a willingness and ability to let go of them.

Weber: That sounds difficult.

Kunz: It is very difficult. I have worked with a great many people who are ill and they often feel that they *are* their patterns so that it's more comfortable not to make an effort to change them.

Weber: Is this related to the person's self-image?

Kunz: A person's self-image—what he (often unconsciously) thinks of himself—is a very important factor in healing. If he thinks of himself as constantly failing and rarely able to achieve his goals fully, this makes for a negative self-image which is very difficult to change. Most of us are completely unaware of how we really picture ourselves. We may feel patterns of depression recur without connecting them to the lack of self-confidence in ourselves that we repeatedly are building up within us.

Weber: Does a constant negative self-image affect our health adversely?

Kunz: Yes.

Weber: Suppose a person becomes conscious of these negative patterns, how can he change them?

Kunz: It is a very tedious process. One has to become aware of how one develops the beginning of this self-doubt every day and say to oneself: "I have enough desire to be willing to stop it the moment it starts and at that first moment of awareness to open myself to the positive energy which I can draw upon, which is also *me* because I am part of the universe and thus part of this healing power." By becoming aware of the pattern the moment it begins, we nip it in the bud and change it by drawing upon the will. That *de-energizes* the disturbed pattern and allows a new energy to enter in that may attenuate it. Self-image and health are connected because the different levels of consciousness are interconnected at all times.

Weber: That applies to self-healing. But suppose a person cannot do it, what then is the role of the healer?

Kunz: The role of the healer is to focus on the person's potential for wholeness, which I feel is present in every individual.

Weber: What do you mean by the potential for wholeness?

Kunz: From my point of view, there is a point of consciousness within everyone which has the seed of wholeness. By wholeness I mean the potential to realize integration within oneself, and to actively *direct* the forces of one's life, not to *react* only to the problems or the negative parts of one's self. In each person's makeup there may be many negative patterns but there is also strength, creativity and insight; a person need only be willing to draw on them, and these forces I consider the potential for wholeness.

Weber: Most human beings therefore scarcely tap the great reservoir of strength and potential creativity which you are calling wholeness. Do you actually *perceive* these to be part of our makeup, as you observe the fields in your diagnostic work with patients?

Kunz: It is part of our human constitution. People who are born with great handicaps in life surmount them through something within themselves and reach that other level. Practically every person if he can move through a crisis in his life and surmount it, feels at that moment a sense of inner calmness, a sense of direction.

Weber: Why don't most of us draw more on that calmness and strength in daily life? Why does it seem to be latent and passive instead of active in most people?

Kunz: Our whole attention in daily life is given to the minute details of living, particularly in our present society where we seem to depend on entertainment and stimulation from outside. We really are not aware of our own potential. Most people are involved with what catches their immediate interest or with the search for pleasure, not with the search for creativity and self-renewal.

Weber: That distinction and our lopsided priority in favor of pleasure rather than creativity has been picked up by many philosophers: Plato, Spinoza, even pessimists like Kierkegaard and Nietzsche. You're relating that to health, to healing, to wholeness and to active creativity as a factor in well-being.

Kunz: Yes.

Weber: Do people who become aware of these potentialities in themselves—people who are very interested in healing—do they at the same time strengthen that side of themselves?

Kunz: I think they strengthen that side of themselves, but of course that does not mean that they turn into perfect human beings. They still may feel distraught and distracted by periods of lack of self-confidence or by other problems. It is hard for us to realize that everything is in flux, and most people have moments of feeling down, moments of lowered energy; but if they accept this period of fallowness as temporary they will regain the sense of being active. I have worked with many different healers and what is remarkable is that during the healing process, the healers can continue without a loss of energy because all their attention is focused on an outward movement—helping others, and during this process they forget completely about themselves.

Weber: To function in that outgoing way renews one's energy, whereas to be self-absorbed and always revolving around the self drains one. Have the great healers that you've known been centered?

Kunz: Centered and altruistic.

Weber: How are centeredness and wholeness related?

Kunz: In teaching Therapeutic Touch, (which Dr. Dolores Krieger of New York University and I developed mainly for the health professions), we stress how essential it is for the potential healer to know something about centering. Centering is a practice which must be done daily. If one is a nurse, for instance, this form of meditation is not only practiced in solitude at home but right in the emergencies which come up during a busy hospital day.

Weber: The person must therefore be capable of achieving centering at any time and to achieve it quickly.

Kunz: Yes. Centering is a focusing within. It is helpful to focus one's energies in the heart region. The first step is to be aware of any anxiety we might feel at the time and to try to dissociate from it for the moment. Shifting the focus to this center of quiet within is important in the healing process. Most healers experience it in one form or another, though often it is second nature to them and they can shift into it without much effort, without prodding from the conscious mind. When we train nurses, however, we teach them to do centering consciously.

Weber: What about the role of the hands and of touch in healing?

Kunz: There are many modalities of healing but Therapeutic Touch is one that seems eminently suitable for nurses. Therapeutic Touch entails that the nurse or healer, after centering, visualizes himself as an instrument for healing. The use of the hands makes it more effective, but it is not essential. The energy fields of the healer are focused through his hands and reach the energy fields of the patient and this helps speed up the innate healing power within the patient himself.

Weber: You have worked mostly with health professionals: nurses, doctors and therapists. Do you think they seem better able to learn healing because of their general commitment to helping patients, or can most well-intentioned people learn to heal?

Kunz: It is easier to teach health professionals because this is part of their daily work, and therefore they are probably more aware of the needs of people than is the average person. I think everybody *could* learn it if they can learn ego-detachment.

Weber: This coheres with all the wisdom traditions: self-transformation, non-attachment, compassion, and spiritual integration. Learning to become a healer seems related to all that. But you are emphasizing that letting go of the ego is an indispensable step.

Kunz: Yes. The non-professional, of course, has the same opportunity but very often laymen also are more emotionally involved with the person and drawn into the problem because they may not have learned—as the professional *must* learn— to be an *observer* of what the disease pattern is. But this road is open to anyone who has the dedication and compassion.

We also have to come to grips with the fact that the outcome of many diseases is death. If one can accept this and help a person through compassion in any way to reduce pain and to die peacefully, that also is a kind of healing.

Weber: Being helped in the subtler fields to achieve a sense of well-being, even though the body cannot reverse its pathology, also matters.

Kunz: Yes, I believe that.

Weber: Of course from the point of view of orthodox medicine it would not be construed as an instance of healing. They would consider it a failure.

Kunz: Yes, they would.

Weber: Your view is that the more detached one can be from the *outcome,* the less pulled into the patient's pathology, the more useful one will be as a healer. But of course you are not equating detachment with indifference.

Kunz: No.

Weber: Can one *learn* compassion, or is it either there or not there within oneself?

Kunz: Some people are very inward turned and do not relate to others. One develops compassion only if one is willing as a first step to use one's energies to help another. If one is really indifferent to what others feel, then clearly it is not possible to develop compassion.

Weber: Let us assume that the intent to help is there. Does the *intent* to be more compassionate increase it?

Kunz: Yes, very definitely.

Weber: The word *intent* has come up repeatedly. What is its role in healing?

Kunz: Intent is focusing one's mind. One wants to project one's energy towards a specific person or point of disturbance. It is focusing the healer's mind which is important, because habitually our mind is scattered, not focused. Centering quiets both the mind and emotions and thereby helps develop the power of focusing and intent.

Weber: That allows the energy to be amplified and more effective?

Kunz: That's right.

Weber: Are intent and will the same thing?

Kunz: Intent is a more momentary effort; will is an ongoing and long-range process of self-transformation. Will is using an energy which is innate in everyone. If for example, one works at overcoming a habit the will must be a sustaining energy which breaks the habit and draws on energy at the level of intuition or beyond. This is an ongoing process of development.

Weber: "Will" as you use it is supra-personal. You're distinguishing between will as a universal power and what we call "will-power," which is more like *forced* effort.

Kunz: Yes.

Weber: How would you define intuition?

Kunz: It is being able to sense the unity of diverse patterns. In order to have insight, the power of intuition is necessary.

Weber: In your healing workshops you often emphasize two terms that you say are interconnected: *rootedness* and *detachment.* What are they and how do they relate to each other and to healing?

Kunz: Rootedness is a strong sense of this center of wholeness within oneself. Even if someone does not have it at all times, there is an underlying certainty of it within himself.

Weber: In some people this takes on symbolism, such as the notion of God.

Kunz: It is an experience and a conviction that there is within oneself a power that gives off a center of calm. In some people, like Mother Teresa, it expresses itself as a tremendous driving power of confidence in God and in herself.

Weber: How does confidence in oneself relate to letting go of one's ego? Why don't they conflict?

Kunz: The sense of rootedness and confidence is not an ego-sense; it's a sense of certainty, and a clear decision that one wishes to *direct* one's energy and not be at the beck and call of one's momentary changing moods. And let me say this: Detachment is not the opposite of rootedness. It is a conviction that each patient is first of all a human being with a point of wholeness within, which is unaffected by the pain and frailty. The healer has to have a sense of wholeness within *himself* so that he can reach that in the patient, whatever that person's suffering and no matter how great his pain. One can convey it to another only if one experiences the wholeness within oneself.

Weber: Somebody like Mother Teresa has self-confidence and we distinguish that from ego. The person has an awareness of wholeness at some dimension of herself, and therefore also in the other, in everyone. That dimension is not swept under by the pain and localized suffering. Therefore the healer tries to resonate from that level of herself with the same level in the other person, to transcend the pain or pathology of the moment. When Mother Teresa says "I see Christ in everyone, even in the filthiest person lying in the gutter in Calcutta," she is conveying the same idea in her own language and symbol-system. That's the confidence that great healers have, which is not the same as magnifying one's ego, right?

Kunz: That's right.

Weber: This description would also fit great spiritual figures like Buddha and others.

Kunz: Yes.

Weber: They were able to help others to experience that dimension because they had access to it in themselves.

Kunz: Of course.

Weber: That points to the notion that the more integrated a human being is, the greater his potential for being a good healer.

Kunz: Being a good healer *at the moment.*

Weber: You stress time and the moment a great deal.

Kunz: I'm stressing "at the moment" in order to make people aware that in our present civilization very few people can function at that level of wholeness all the time.

Weber: You're saying that to claim the contrary is not realistic, because in fact it is so rare.

Kunz: Yes.

Weber: It is helpful for us to realize this so that people don't become overwhelmed and discouraged if they can only do it some of the time.

Kunz: Yes.

Weber: You have a unique metaphor for healing that has moved many people, and that's the metaphor of the tree. You relate it to healing, the healer, and to the patient.

Kunz: All my life I have had a strong identification with nature and a great many of our workshops take place with the trees surrounding us. To me a tree is an excellent metaphor because it is rooted in the earth, which is a symbol of physical reality. In order to live, it is always growing upwards towards the sun, which is the symbol of the spiritual part in man. And yet the tree is often buffeted by the wind, by storms, and thus this really is a symbol of our daily life with its problems. The tree, in order to live, has to reach toward the sun continually. Therefore I think trees are a wonderful symbol for every one of us and particularly for somebody who wants to be a healer.

Weber: In an interview with David Bohm, I asked about the consciousness of trees and even rocks. Bohm says that everything is alive and conscious to some degree. Do you agree?

Kunz: Yes.

Weber: The tree stretches toward the light and at the same time it is rooted. If one were to put it anthropomorphically, one might almost think of the tree as having a certain kind of detachment. Is there anything to that, from your perspective?

Kunz: From my point of view, a kind of "acceptance" is part of the very slight consciousness of the tree. It is built into it, not in the human sense of course. It's as if the tree feels rooted in and in harmony with its niche, its environment—as if it accepts that it belongs to this place.

Weber: Perhaps at this point we should clarify that when you say "from my point of view" you mean something rather specific. You're not using idle language. Can you talk a little about your special point of view as a "sensitive" or clairvoyant?

Kunz: For years I have counselled many people with all forms of sickness. I was born with a sensitivity enabling me to see and observe the patterns of people's emotional reactions and to relate these to the diseases of the physical body.

Weber: In other words you actually *perceive* these fields that you described before?

Kunz: Yes. Also, I have developed a sensitivity to what other people are feeling. Between observation and sensitivity and working with other healers, we developed Therapeutic Touch. When I talk about "my point of view" I'm referring to my many, many years of experience in dealing with various human problems, even the most degrading and difficult, such as heroin addiction.

Weber: Is sensitivity a combination of perceiving it as the patient might experience it, together with empathy and compassion? Or is sensitivity something more than that?

Kunz: Sensitivity is a very close empathy, and an understanding of what the other person is feeling, without being in any way identified with that feeling. It's an observation without identification.

Weber: You know it as if you *were* the patient, but you do not get pulled in personally.

Kunz: I know how that patient feels emotionally, and I know how the patient feels physically.

Weber: And yet you do not translate this into feelings in your own body or emotions.

Kunz: It does not affect how I personally feel at any time.

Weber: One feels compassion and yet is detached; therefore one is able to help more. If one translates the patient's disturbances into one's own body and feelings, one gets swept in. In that case one leaves his own standpoint and goes over to the standpoint of the patient. Then one cannot at that moment help the patient. Therefore you never get *personally* identified?

Kunz: Not in any way whatever.

Weber: Yet, for many years, you've worked with doctors, doing paranormal diagnosis, using these abilities you were born with.

Kunz: Yes.

Weber: So you've observed and correlated these various fields with one another and built up a vocabulary over the years, a system of correspondences between a person's patterns of thoughts and emotions, and their physical illness. Is that a correct way of putting it?

Kunz: Yes. Let me say this. I feel that a great healer (or any healer, depending upon how open he is to this healing force) affects people because he draws on that healing power at a higher level, the level of intuition and even beyond that. At that level a person experiences the feeling of being unified within himself, with mankind and nature, and thus he loses the sense of separateness. If the healing power is drawn from that level and goes through the different levels of our feeling and thinking, its power is very much stronger than that of our emotions and our physical body.

Weber: If we were to use the metaphor of quantity: it takes a small "quantity" of the healing power that originates at the intuitive level to reverse or repair damage at other levels. A little bit of that power is so vast that it can reverse the damage at lower levels, even at the physical level. At the intuitive level, we cannot become disordered. It is always whole and thus an aspect of us *is* whole. That is what you earlier called our human potential.

Kunz: Yes. When a person (as I've seen it happen) is healed instantly from a disease, it not only affects the physical body, but a transformation happens at all levels. His point of view about himself and his capacity for giving are changed.

Weber: Is that rare?

Kunz: It is very rare. An instantaneous healing is rare, and such a complete transformation of the personality following it is very rare.

Weber: Do you have any theory that accounts for why it happens when it does happen?

Kunz: I'd have to use the word *synchronicity,* which includes a person's readiness for such a transformation, their openness to really change. The healing power goes through at *all levels* instantaneously. Whether it's from a spiritual source, from any source, the only explanation possible is in terms of synchronicity. It is interesting that in the records kept at Lourdes, most of the successful patients have been very close to death, and most of the patients I have observed in an instantaneous recovery have also been close to death. By that time they have almost let go of their patterns. They don't have the energy to hang onto them at that point, and I think this makes healing possible. At least, it may be one factor in these complete and rare instantaneous recoveries.

Weber: That seems to bring it back to detachment, a kind of letting go. Do you see any significance in the fact that today not just religious people but down-to-earth health professionals are actively trying to contact this intuitive level in order to help heal others?

Kunz: I think we are going through a transition period in the whole world. The world is much more closely related than ever before, and thus there is a greater collective awareness of the problems and of one another's anxiety. This has given rise to a greater search for meaning. In the last decade, especially, we find an intensified search for new meaning and values at all levels of society.

Weber: In Therapeutic Touch the patient is in the healer's presence. What about sending this energy to someone who is not physically present, or sending healing intent to a war-torn and violent world?

Kunz: I believe in field theory: that all thought affects others. Distance would not make a very great difference.

Weber: Thoughts and feelings, in other words, find their mark and leave their effects across distances?

Kunz: Yes.

Weber: So time and space are not obstacles?

Kunz: No. Not to this healing energy.

Weber: Then this has potential for healing in the broadest sense of the word, not just healing a specific illness but perhaps as an effort towards world peace?

Kunz: Yes.

Weber: One thing is not quite clear: when you spoke of habit patterns the examples you gave were negative. Are they usually negative and destructive to our health or are there also positive and creative patterns?

Kunz: Patterns like Mother Teresa's—her desire to give and her all-pervading compassion—are positive energies that are consciously built up, and they are just as important as the potentially negative ones. There are people who have no education, but they are by nature very loving and giving. These are positive, healthy patterns in which our energies go outward, and they actually enhance our own well-being. Altruism is a powerful means of self-renewal and of recharging us with fresh energies.